PIRACY TODAY

OTHER BOOKS BY JOHN C. PAYNE

The Fisherman's Electrical Manual

The Great Cruising Cookbook: an International Galley Guide

Marine Electrical and Electronics Bible, Third Edition

Motorboat Electrical and Electronics Manual

Understanding Boat AC Power Systems

Understanding Boat Batteries and Battery Charging

Understanding Boat Corrosion, Lightning Protection
and Interference

Understanding Boat Communications

Understanding Boat Diesel Engines

Understanding Boat Electronics

Understanding Boat Plumbing and Water Systems

Understanding Boat Wiring

Published by Sheridan House

Visit John C. Payne's Websites at:

www.yacht-sailboat.com
www.offshore-oil-rig-jobs.com
www.fishingandboats.com

PIRACY TODAY

Fighting Villainy on the High Seas

JOHN C. PAYNE

SHERIDAN HOUSE

This edition first published 2010 by
Sheridan House Inc.
145 Palisade Street
Dobbs Ferry, NY 10522
www.sheridanhouse.com

Library of Congress Cataloging in Publication Data

Payne, John C.
Piracy today : fighting villainy on the high seas / John C. Payne.
    p. cm.
  Includes bibliographical references and index.
  ISBN 978-1-57409-291-2
    1. Piracy. 2. Piracy—Aden, Gulf of. 3. Piracy—Malacca, Strait of.
4. Hijacking of ships—Prevention. 5. Hijacking of yachts—Prevention.
6. Shipping—Security measures. I. Title.
G535.P39 2010
364.16'4—dc22   2009050621

ISBN 978-1-57409-291-2

Printed in the United States of America

Edited by David W. Shaw

*For mariners whom pirates have murdered,
wounded, or held hostage, and for the families
of those still languishing in captivity*

Contents

PART 1

The Resurgence of Piracy

1

With Seeming Impunity

Modern piracy has nothing in common with the pirates you see in the movies or read about in novels. There's no walking the plank, no Long John Silver. There are no Jolly Rogers hoisted anymore apart from the owners of pleasure yachts who do it for fun. Robert Louis Stevenson's *Treasure Island* makes piracy seem exciting and fun. The celebrated maritime author Joseph Conrad once referred to pirates as colorful vagabonds of the sea. Others called them the scourge and pestilence of the sea, a more realistic description.

It is somewhat ironic that one of the original pirates of the Caribbean, Captain William Kidd, had his 300-year old former wrecked ship discovered in 2007 off Hispaniola, the island which includes Haiti and the Dominican Republic. He abandoned his ship to return to New York in an attempt to clear his name, having maintained that he was a privateer who captured pirates. His eventual fate was to be arrested and imprisoned there, taken back to London, tried and then hanged and his body placed in a suspended iron cage to rot for a couple of years (or gibbeted, as they called it) for all to see and to act as a deterrent to all those who would descend into piracy.

Pirates are perceived as romanticized folk heroes, affable swashbuckling adventurers. The very successful and entertaining *Pirates of the Caribbean* movies, and many other films over the years, have helped foster this image. However, the reality is very different. Piracy has been an ongoing and serious problem in Asia, Africa and South America for a long time, and active efforts have and are being made to contain the problem. With piracy so much in the news lately, it's easy to think it has resurfaced, and to a large extent this is true. However, piracy has always been present on the high seas. It never went away. It has just grown and spread in recent years to the point where the world is finally sitting up and taking notice.

Pirates have been a problem since the days of ancient Rome, and even earlier than that, along the shores of Turkey before the Roman Empire came into prominence. Piracy boomed in the sixteenth century when English privateers were renowned for their attacks on Spanish shipping. During this same period, pirates continually attacked and looted ships in North African waters.

In the eighteenth century, the Indian Ocean island of Madagascar was a prime destination for pirates. It was a major hangout, quite similar in some respects to the pirate den that thrived during the late eighteenth century in the port of Nassau, on the Bahamian island of New Providence. From the sixteenth century through the nineteenth century, the Barbary Coast was controlled by the Islamic states that fell under the powerful and extensive Ottoman Empire, and wealthy backers sponsored the Barbary pirates and received a handsome 10 percent take of the loot. The reign of the Barbary pirates ended with the intervention of the United States during the Barbary Wars in the early 1800s.

Pirates were active in the Far East as well. The most dominant was Zheng Zhilong, a seventeenth-century Chinese pirate leader who lived during the Ming and Ching dynasties. Another noteworthy figure was an infamous female pirate known as Cheng I Sao. She was a former prostitute who married a pirate and with her husband organized a confederation of pirates numbering some fifty thousand men. At one point,

Cheng I Sao and company almost defeated the Imperial Chinese Navy, quite an undertaking, to say the least.

Most Asian pirates were eventually driven to ground, and they had all but disappeared by the early seventeenth century, though some did remain active. As was the case elsewhere, when pirates interfered too much with trade, caused enough losses in ships, and inflicted a sufficient number of casualties, nations took action to stop them. Ultimately, the powerful navies that patrolled Asian waters under the Tokugawa Shogunate, and in China under the Ching dynasty, systematically slaughtered the pirates, mostly ridding the high seas of the scourge.

Yet, in certain locations, piracy persisted. Now it is back in force, but much different from what it once was. In the twenty-first century, piracy is a ferocious and big money business. For some of us, it is a bit hard to believe that gangs of pirates are able to attack large merchant vessels in the busiest shipping lanes in the world. But they are doing it, often and without mercy to the hapless crews who are frequently held hostage for large ransoms. Modern pirates are disrupting international trade on some of the most crucial maritime sea routes and oceans on Earth with apparent impunity. They are adversely impacting trade, and creating quite a stir in international politics.

Piracy in the twenty-first century has flourished in part because merchant ships have become more technologically advanced, and, consequently, crews have become smaller. The world's largest container ships, which carry between eleven thousand and fourteen thousand containers, are fully automated. A crew of only a dozen or so merchant mariners is all that's needed to operate these vessels, and with such a small crew it only takes an equally small number of heavily armed pirates to snatch a ship. Years ago, much smaller merchant vessels required a crew of forty-five hands. Such a large crew would pose a major logistical problem for pirates determined to seize a ship and hold the mariners hostage.

Piracy is also helped by the vagaries of jurisdiction, sometimes confused and tumultuous international diplomatic relations, and divisive international political issues, all which work in its favor. Pirates and their sponsors know how difficult it is for nations to stop them, and they use the situation to maximum advantage. Modern piracy falls into a few different categories. There are opportunistic pirates who attack and rob ships for cash, valuable materials, and the personal effects of the crew. There are pirates who set the crew adrift in lifeboats and hijack the ship. They repaint, rename, and re-register it, and sell it and the cargo.

Still others change the ship's identity with forged documentation, then charter the ship and load the cargo, only to disappear with the cargo, which is then sold. These pirates are most prevalent in Asia. A final category of pirates has surged to prominence in the last decade. These are the ones you read about most often. They attack and take a ship and crew, holding both for ransom. Primarily this occurs within the Gulf of Aden. However, there have also been many ransom incidents in the Malacca Straits and South China Sea.

The pirates of the past and the pirates of the twenty-first century do share some similarities. Pirates need somewhere to prey upon shipping. In the sixteenth century the Caribbean was an ideal spot. Spanish galleons laden with gold and silver from the New World were easy pickings. Today, pirates favor the Gulf of Aden and the Straits of Malacca, ripe with ships carrying an unlimited variety of easily disposable cargoes.

Pirates also want a safe haven. They've got a good one in the Malacca Straits, with more than seventeen thousand islands that make great hiding places and with a population willing to protect and shelter them. In the Gulf of Aden, the lawless and anarchic Somalia provides a similarly welcome haven for pirates. Like the pirates of the past, today's buccaneers have plenty of firepower, as opposed to virtually defenseless merchant mariners.

Misinformed journalists in media reports continue to portray the pirates as amateurish thugs, often trivializing them in articles and making references to the romanticized swashbucklers seen in the movies. But today's pirates are not amateurs. They are professionals out to make big money, and they have no regard for human life unless it can turn a profit through a ransom payment. The pirates are very efficient at attacking in small boats and then capturing large, unprotected high-value ships with equally high-value cargoes.

Just a few pirates are able to hold the ship, its cargo, and the unfortunate crews for large ransoms, usually amounting to millions of dollars. And the problem is made worse because they almost always get the money, generally without harm to the hostages or themselves. That is if all goes according to plan. When it doesn't, people die. As the saying goes, success breeds success. In 2005, the typical ransom averaged between $100,000 and $200,000. By 2009 the average ransom had soared to more than $2 million.

Obviously, then, piracy today is lucrative. That's why it's on an upward spiral. For example, the United Nations reported that Somali pirates collected roughly $150 million in ransom payments in 2008. Total losses in ransoms, ships, and cargoes as a result of piracy are estimated at around $15 billion.

The piracy problem persists and grows despite the presence of large, modern navies from powerful nations that routinely patrol pirate-infested waters. At times, the navies seem powerless to stop the attacks, though their presence does seem to deter attacks in some cases. Often, the navies are unable to rescue captured vessels and crews. They are also politically and judicially shackled as to the prosecution and punishment of any pirates they do capture, which further enhances the environment for piracy to flourish.

Some experts in the shipping industry believe that piracy will usually go unpunished, regardless whether they report an incident or not. Unfortunately, they are correct. Some industry

7

experts also say that only 10 percent of all piracy incidents are actually reported, a sad but largely true statistic. In addition, they believe certain national governments or agencies are involved in piracy and support it, or at least look the other way. True again. Theories that spies working for pirates have infiltrated shipping companies, port and customs authorities, and other entities abound. This may or may not be true.

Why owners of merchant ships are reluctant to report piracy incidents is understandable, even if it encourages the pirates to increase the number of attacks to garner more and more profit. If an attack occurs and is unsuccessful, it's typically ignored and unreported because a piracy report generates negative media coverage and increases insurance premiums. If a piracy attack occurs and is successful, shipowners often keep quiet about it and negotiate directly with the pirates without involving government officials. Reporting an incident can cost a lot of money in daily operating expenses for a ship idled during an investigation and for delayed delivery of valuable cargoes.

Daily operating costs average $10,000 for smaller ships and up to $100,000 for larger craft. These larger ships can carry cargoes valued up to $100 million. Insuring ships, crews, and cargoes is expensive, and so are ships sitting in port when they should be at sea. Filing reports and instigating investigations causes time-consuming delays. Investigating authorities are often incompetent individuals correctly assuming that there will be no positive outcome to the investigation in most instances, so the perception in the industry is that reporting piracy amounts to a waste of time and money. The reality is that the costs and losses incurred when reporting an unsuccessful or even a successful pirate attack are typically higher than the cost of the attack itself.

Most of us have a basic idea of what piracy is, but in the legal arena it has some very specific definitions. While it makes for a bit of dry reading, it's well worth keeping in mind the legal terms when you think about piracy. After all, piracy is as much a crime today as it was in the days of Edward Teach, otherwise known as Blackbeard, who ended up having his severed head dangling from the bowsprit of a British naval ship after he was killed in battle.

Piracy and armed robbery are clearly explained in the following definitions, as applied to incidents at sea. Many argue that robbery of vessels at anchor or at a dock is not piracy, and perhaps rightfully so. For our purposes the term pirate applies to all ships attacked while under way, either on the high seas or in territorial waters. The term robbery will be used for incidents that occur while a ship or yacht is anchored or tied up at a pier. Politically motivated attacks, such as terrorist acts, are not executed for material gain and are also not classified as piracy in its truest sense.

The gist of Article 101 in the 1982 United Nations Convention on the Law of the Sea defines piracy as consisting of any of the following acts: any illegal acts of violence or detention, or any act of depredation, committed for private ends by the crew or the passengers of a private ship or a private aircraft, and directed on the high seas against another ship or aircraft, or against persons or property on board such ship or aircraft. The language also includes a ship, aircraft, persons, or property in a place outside the jurisdiction of any state, and any act of voluntary participation in the operation of a ship or of an aircraft with knowledge of facts making it a pirate ship or aircraft. Any act inciting or intentionally facilitating an act described above also counts.

Armed robbery against ships, which is defined in the Code of Practice for the Investigation of the Crimes of Piracy and Armed Robbery Against Ships (resolution A.922 (22), Annex, paragraph 2.2), is a little less complicated and reads as follows:

"Armed robbery against ships means any unlawful act of violence or detention or any act of depredation, or threat thereof, other than an act of piracy, directed against a ship or against persons or property on board such ship, within a State's jurisdiction over such offences."

As previously mentioned, pirates generally are not captured or punished, making the above legal definitions somewhat moot in many cases. However, laws are on the books that provide for punishing acts of piracy, though they differ from nation to nation in severity and effectiveness. They are also difficult for some national governments or agencies to enforce. Somalia is a hotbed of piracy, as evidenced in the news on a regular basis, and throughout this book the piracy problem there will serve as an excellent example of piracy today worldwide. Let's take a look at what happens to pirates who are caught in Somalia.

Centuries ago pirates were punished with extraordinary brutality. In 75 B.C, Cilician pirates from southern Turkey kidnapped Julius Caesar while he was on a voyage across the Aegean Sea. He was held for ransom at the Dodecanese islet of Pharmacusa. The pirates initially demanded a ransom of twenty talents, not a very large sum of money. Somewhat miffed, Caesar insisted that the pirates increase the ransom to fifty talents, a sum more in keeping with his position. On payment and his release, he raised a fleet of ships, hunted the pirates down, and crucified them all.

Nobody cared much when pirates were hung, beheaded, or otherwise brutalized, and that is not surprising. Pirates were and are a menace. In London, the central location for capital punishment was known as Execution Dock. The name arose in the nineteenth century when British naval vessels brought many pirates there for execution. The British were superb pirate hunters (and pirates, too!). In the United Kingdom, the death penalty for piracy on the high seas remained on the statute books until 1998.

Modern pirates know that unless things go seriously wrong and they get killed during the execution of an attack, or they encounter a naval vessel, they will either get the money or will get captured and then released because no one knows what to do with them. Punishment is actually the lesser of the risk than attacking a ship or running from a naval vessel. Instead of arrest and imposing the death penalty, the United Kingdom, for example, has told its naval forces not to detain pirates. The fear is that detention might breach the human rights of the pirates, or that the pirates may even claim political asylum.

The British Foreign Office reasoned that any pirates subsequently returned to Somalia after detention could have their human rights violated, based on certain Islamic laws. It said the pirates might be beheaded for murder or have a hand cut off as the penalty for theft. Apparently, this was unacceptable punishment in the view of the Foreign Office. This line of reasoning was and still is highly objectionable to some people in the United Kingdom, who believe that the Somali pirates should get what they deserve under the laws of their own country. One politician, a member of parliament, was reported as saying that the pirates commit horrendous offenses and that the convention on human rights quite rightly doesn't cover the high seas. He went on to say that the action was a pathetic indictment of what the legal system in the United Kingdom had come to.

While the pirates in Somalia and elsewhere do act with relative impunity, some of them get caught, tried, and convicted. The number is small at this time, but perhaps it will grow as more nations begin to take the worldwide piracy problem more seriously. As the piracy problem off Somalia ramped up, the Russian Navy took decisive action. In the spring of 2009, it had twenty-nine pirates in custody aboard its naval vessels operating in the area. France held fifteen, and sent eleven of them for trial ashore in Kenya. France was and still is serious about combating pirates. By mid-2009 it had detained seventy-one pirates and killed four. Three Somali pirates detained in the French city of Rennes faced a judicial investigation following their capture after a hostage rescue. The United States was holding one pirate in the spring of 2009 after the famous *Maersk Alabama* incident, which will be highlighted later. The pirate was awaiting trial in New York at this writing. Three pirates were shot and killed in the same incident.

In all, the U.S. Navy sent 101 alleged Somali pirates to Kenya for trial. Seventeen of them were detained after failing to seize the Egyptian cargo vessel *Amira* in May 2009, after putting up some initial resistance to U.S. Navy forces and marines from the South Korean Navy. To date, ten of these pirates have been convicted and have received prison sentences of only seven years each, a fairly short term given the nature of the crime. At the time of this writing, holding cells in Mombasa, Kenya, were running short. Additional suspects were to be transferred and held in the coastal town of Malindi, about eighty miles north of Mombasa.

The Somali police are also trying to clamp down on the piracy problem. On one occasion a senior police commander in Puntland led a raid on a pirate base near the port of Boosaaso, where they arrested five alleged pirates as they prepared to head to sea to perpetrate more mischief. The pirates were armed with AK-47 rifles and a rocket-propelled grenade launcher. They were arraigned in a local court on piracy charges. One significant factor in the renewed vigor in chasing pirates is that the Somali government is now paying salaries to their employees, including the police, when in the past they weren't due to the continued economic plight of the nation.

In another case, a Mombasa court found ten Somali men guilty of piracy after a long trial. The destroyer USS *Winston S. Churchill* captured them following the hijacking of an Indian dhow, *Safinat Biscarat*, and its crew of sixteen off the coast of Somaliland. The pirates were trying to use the dhow as a mother ship to attack other vessels. The U.S. destroyer confronted the dhow, chased it, and fired warning shots. The pirates surrendered. The judge in Mombasa described the men as dangerous criminals and dismissed their claims that they were simple fishermen who had been rescued by the Indian vessel after their own boat experienced mechanical problems. A piracy conviction carries a possible life sentence in Kenya.

In July 2009, twenty-two alleged Somali pirates were brought before a court in Aden to face piracy or attempted piracy charges for acts committed within the Gulf of Aden. Russian and Indian naval vessels had captured the men in late 2008 and early 2009. One group were said to be involved in the seizure of a Yemeni fishing dhow and the kidnapping of twelve Yemeni fishermen, who were held as hostages. The pirates then used the dhow as a mother ship from which to launch an attack on an Ethiopian merchant vessel. The Russians captured ten of the men after they attacked an Iranian fishing boat off Socotra Island. All of the accused pleaded not guilty under the Yemeni Counter Abduction Law. The sentences, if they are found guilty, range from five to ten years in prison. The pirates claimed that they were all fishermen and that the charges were trumped up fabrications at the hands of nefarious Western forces.

Essentially, pirates are waterborne gangs, and it's common for the gangs to fight one another over any number of issues such as territory, base locations, and, of course, money. In a noteworthy case, two gunmen killed one of the most notorious pirates in Somalia, Bi'ir Abdi, along with another pirate, while he was driving the streets of Garoowe, the capital of Puntland. The gunmen were captured shortly thereafter and kept in protective custody to guard against a retaliatory attack. The killings stemmed from a dispute over money.

Pirates seizing fishing vessels for use either as mother ships or as attack boats is a common pattern throughout the world, and especially in Somalia. These actions have upon occasion generated a violent response among the Somali people. In fact, regional leaders in northern Puntland went so far as to organize a militia of fishermen to hunt down known pirates and bring them to justice.

Any captured pirates in Somalia are now more likely to face the death penalty under recently reinforced measures announced by the Somali government. In April 2009, Somali militiamen captured twelve heavily armed pirates in two boats and turned them in to Somali officials for prosecution, an indication of efforts to stamp out the piracy problem using any means possible. This is a hopeful development, but it's akin to a sandcastle in a rising tide. The rapid growth of piracy in Somalia and elsewhere is simply too big a problem for militias to handle. It will take a concerted effort on many levels—social, economic, political, and military—to make any progress in the war against villainy on the high seas.

2

Unanticipated Consequences

When you think of illegal fishing, you don't necessarily think of pirates, but fishing illegally is often and appropriately called piracy. Essentially, it amounts to stealing a resource instead of a cargo. For example, Somali pirates often say the Asian and European fish pirates in their waters are part of the catalyst behind the current crisis. To a certain extent, their assertion is correct. Finding a solution to illegal fishing will go a long way toward reducing the number of pirate attacks against merchant vessels in Somali waters and elsewhere.

Let's take a look back at the origin of the current piracy crisis in Somalia and how fish pirates played a part in setting the stage for the growth of piracy against merchant vessels. The same cycle is occurring elsewhere in the world, too. An examination of fish piracy worldwide is also important because the act of stealing a valued natural resource is absolutely piracy all on its own, and it has far reaching consequences for rich and poor countries alike. Indeed, it is a little known subject and often ignored in international politics, as is piracy against merchant ships and its rapid upswing in recent years. The increased incidence in attacks and the escalation of casualties are only now coming fully to the attention of the general public through news reports of high-profile incidents.

In Somalia, the prelude to today's trouble with piracy began in 1992 when the Barre regime was ousted and both the Somali Navy and the Police Coast Guard were effectively disbanded. Somalia suffered a severe drought in 1974 and in 1986. As a result, a large number of Somali nomads lost their livestock due to a lack of water and fodder. The nomads were resettled in the many towns and villages along the Somali coast. Many of these villages expanded into significant fishing bases, with boats operating mostly within Somali territorial waters extending twelve nautical miles offshore.

As the Somali civil war ramped up in 1991, foreign trawlers started entering Somali waters to fish. No Somali naval forces were there to stop them. These trawlers actively competed with Somali fishermen for high-value pelagic fish and lobsters. The trawlers were there because Somali waters are one of the richest fisheries in the world. Confrontations escalated between Somali fishermen and foreign trawlers, until the situation exploded into violence. Somali fishermen were killed, boats were sunk, and nets were destroyed. Naturally, the Somali fishermen responded. They armed themselves with better weapons and began attacking the trawlers and seizing the catches. Italian, Korean, Ukrainian, Indian, Egyptian, and Yemeni fishing vessels were captured and released after payment of ransoms.

It didn't take long for the Somali warlords and corrupt government officials and the Puntland administration to capitalize on the situation. Shell companies were established in Europe and Saudi Arabia to facilitate the issuance of counterfeit fishing licenses for the payment of a fee, enabling the licensee to continue fishing under the pretence of legality. Selling counterfeit fishing licenses became a big business. Some licenses cost $30,000 for a four-month seasonal permit. The various deals netted tens of millions of dollars for the various factions involved in the scams. Many of these same entities were also directly or indirectly engaged in seizing ships and crews and demanding ransom payments.

Fish piracy in general is a multifaceted illegal enterprise, and it generates millions of dollars in profits for the pirates. Take laundering of illegal fish catches as an example. The practice is widespread throughout the world, impacting some of the poorest countries. It entails fish factory mother ships being used to handle transshipped illegally harvested fish mixed in with legally caught fish. The total catch is loaded into a refrigerated cargo ship at sea. The trawlers and the factory ships are refueled and resupplied at sea, so they rarely enter a port and are essentially untraceable and uncontrollable. Fish piracy depletes valuable resources at the expense of impoverished fishermen who will sometimes turn to piracy out of simple desperation.

Countries accused of Somali fish laundering include the Seychelles, Mauritius, and the Maldives. Other illegal fishing trawlers are reportedly from Spain, France, Italy, Greece, Russia, Ukraine, and the United Kingdom. Asian countries are involved, too, including Taiwan, South Korea, Japan, and India. Regional trawlers are from Egypt and Yemen. In spite of the current dangers Somali pirates pose today, the foreign trawlers keep coming. And the Somali pirates keep capturing them and holding the vessels and crews for ransoms, which almost always get paid. The vicious cycle seems to have no end in sight.

The history of illegal fishing by driftnet vessels is a long one. The reported illegal activities include underreporting the catches, keeping dual fishing logs (one true and one false), the deliberate misreporting of vessel names, registration numbers and vessel locations, the disconnection or destruction of transponders to avoid detection, and illegal fishing in many Exclusive Economic Zones (EEZ). Although by no means the sole offenders, Taiwanese fishing crews have had their vessels impounded by Argentina, Australia, Indonesia, Malaysia, the Philippines, South Africa, and Vietnam for alleged illegal fishing and other infractions.

The illegal use of squid driftnet vessels to illegally harvest salmon in the North Pacific is yet another form of fish piracy, though it isn't fostering the birth of pirate clans that attack merchant vessels as well as fishing boats. Nevertheless, the practice is in clear violation of international agreements and international law. The illegal transshipment of fish at sea or the processing of fish catches into fish meal to make the catch unidentifiable is another variation of fish piracy, as is re-flagging vessels to avoid conformance to treaty obligations. The list of infractions worldwide is lengthy.

As previously mentioned, the Somali fishermen are a good example of the ills of pirate fishing. They are indeed double victims in the current crisis. Pirates seize their boats and use them to attack merchant ships, as well as hold them hostage for ransoms. And foreign trawlers unfairly compete for a depleted natural resource, namely the fish. Somali fishermen have complained bitterly to the United Nations and the international community in general about illegal foreign fishing and its impacts. The response has been muted, if not nonexistent. The fishermen described the use of indiscriminate and prohibited fishing practices that included the use of driftnets and explosives. They have protested against the destruction of endangered species such as whales, sea turtles, and sharks, along with the wanton destruction of reefs and fish habitats.

The United Nations Food and Agriculture Organization (FAO) reported that there were an estimated seven hundred foreign-owned fishing vessels actively engaged in unlicensed fishing in Somali coastal waters in 2005. The FAO also stated that it was virtually impossible to monitor fishery production in general, or the condition of the exploited fishery resources. It said there was a suspicion that illegal dumping of industrial and nuclear waste was happening off the Somali coast. Somali fishermen described it as both economic and ecological terrorism. They correctly surmised, as have a number of fisheries experts in Europe, that the fishing industry off Somalia would be totally destroyed in a relatively short period. Given the circumstances, it is unsurprising that some fishermen turn to piracy, further exacerbating the escalation of violence in Somali waters.

In the Pacific Ocean, Greenpeace has been involved in a joint surveillance and enforcement operation to monitor pirate fishing. The case of the Korean pirate-fishing vessel *Dong Won 117* is typical. The Dongwan fleet operates with apparent impunity and almost tacit support of the South Korean government, which seems to do little in the way of regulating and controlling this and other fishing fleets. At this writing, *Dong Won 117* had been at sea for a year or more. It had not been reported to the relevant authorities and was effectively a ghost-fishing vessel. Its movements, its catch, and its catch quantity were unknown. When Greenpeace and Kiribati officers caught up with *Dong Won 117*, they ordered fishing to cease.

In June 2007, Greenpeace activists chained the propeller of the Russian pirate fish cargo ship *Murminskiy* to the docks in the Dutch port of Eemshaven in an attempt to prevent the ship from continuing illegal pirate fishing which is rapidly depleting fish stocks in the Barents Sea. The move came after the relevant authorities refused to either blacklist or penalize the ship, even though it was clearly documented by the Norwegian Coast Guard as illegally transshipping fish to a refrigerated cargo vessel known as *Sinbad*. *Sinbad* operated without a flag and under the unregistered name *Marlin*, and while this ship was blacklisted, *Murminskiy* was not. Greenpeace has also accused governments of inaction in dealing with the fish pirates who use illegal fishing vessels, and who underreport catches.

According to reports from the United Nations, 74 percent of

global fish stocks are either depleted or fully exploited. Pirate fishing is playing a big part in the declining fish stocks worldwide, so it's not a small problem. And in cases such as Somalia, it has far reaching consequences that are leading to violence on an increasingly widespread basis. Fish piracy is also a major issue in the Pacific and Indian Oceans, and along the West African coast, where piracy against merchant vessels is on the rise. Greenpeace performed an extensive survey of pirate fishing fleets with its vessel *Esperanza*, and in a recent report the organization stated that off the Guinea-Conakry coast about 50 percent of the ninety-two fishing boats operating in the area were illegal.

In the South Pacific, Fiji cited the illegal transshipment of fish as a major problem. The fact is that fishing vessels in violation of the law can only be impounded if they are fitted with satellite monitoring transponders showing they were not in the location they were required to be in. Most are not so equipped. Roughly 75 percent of the world's catch of four million tons of tuna was taken in the region by about one thousand fishing vessels, many of them illegal.

Russia frequently has problems with pirate fishing vessels encroaching on its territorial waters, and it responds with force. A case in point involved Asian fishing vessels pirating crabs and fish around Sakhalin Island and adjacent areas. The incidents with vessels from China, Japan, Cambodia, and Taiwan caught in Russian waters frequently hit the news. Russian border guards often use firearms during the detention of vessels, and that gets the attention of story-hungry reporters. Russia banned live crab exports in 2007, but there is still a lot of pirated Russian crab reaching Japan and South Korea. I know this to be true as I recently spent a couple of years on a ship project in South Korea. I was a frequent customer at my favorite crab restaurant which had tanks of fresh, live and no doubt pirated Russian crab.

You may not have considered fish when thinking about piracy today, but clearly the theft of one of the world's most important natural resources, a resource that is under intense pressure, has much to do with the root causes of piracy against merchant vessels as well as yachts. Fish piracy itself is a leading contributor to the pressure on fish stocks. You may not realize it, but the fish on your dinner table may well be pirated. If it is, you unwittingly played a part in fish piracy, which is estimated to generate an annual gross of about $9 billion. And if that fish on your plate is pirated, you have also played an indirect part in the growth of piracy against merchant ships and yachts, albeit a very, very small part.

Naturally, it would be simplistic to attribute too much of the piracy problem to pirate fishing, though it is indeed a critical part of the equation. Social, political, and economic unrest represents still another piece of the piracy puzzle that will be addressed in more detail when specific regions are examined. For our purposes here, a look at the ebb and flow and ultimate upward swing in piracy will prove revelatory in terms of the evolution of a disturbing trend, no less disturbing because innocent people are getting killed as the problem worsens.

The main tracking source for piracy attacks is the International Maritime Bureau, which was formed in 1992 as a subsidiary of Commercial Crime Services, a division of the International Chamber of Commerce. The IMB is headquartered in Essex, England, and operates the Piracy Reporting Center from Kuala Lumpur, in Malaysia. The IMB publishes a weekly summary of pirate attacks worldwide. The group receives funding from twenty-one organizations, which comprise shipowners and insurance companies. The center leads a coordinated response to attacks, issuing warnings to mariners about problem regions. Reports are based on information passed on from shipowners whose crews and vessels have been attacked.

An in-depth analysis of these reports going back to 2001

shows the extent of the problem and how it is increasing, particularly in Somali waters and in the Gulf of Aden. In 2001, pirates were most active in the South China Sea, Indian Ocean, West Africa, the Malacca Straits, South America, and in East Africa. The majority of attacks occurred within port areas or while the ship was lying at anchor, which, as you may recall, doesn't even really fall into the realm of piracy in its truest sense. The incidents are more accurately described as armed robbery of vessels. Nevertheless, the piracy, or armed robberies, had consequences beyond the monetary. Eight crewmembers are known to have been murdered in the process of the robberies, and one ship's entire crew went missing. One ship was hijacked.

Hijackings increased in 2002, involving twelve ships. Eight ships disappeared and pirates are considered the most likely cause. Six crew were killed, fifty were wounded, and thirty-eight went missing. Thirty-eight were thrown overboard and rescued.

In 2003, there were forty-one acts of piracy in the South China Sea. Eight piracy incidents occurred in South American waters, six in the Caribbean Sea, two in the Pacific Ocean, twelve in the Indian Ocean, twelve in West Africa, eight in the Malacca Straits, and one in East Africa. While these numbers illustrate a marked increase, the majority of attacks fall under the definition of armed robberies in ports or while the ships were at anchor. As to casualties, only one crewmember was killed and four were wounded. Still, it was no picnic for the mariners. Crews were assaulted and in one case an entire crew was forced into lifeboats and set adrift. One hapless mariner was actually marooned on an island. Two merchant vessels went missing.

In 2004, piracy and armed robberies continued to increase, with 113 incidents occurring in the South China Sea, 46 in South America, 46 in the Caribbean and South America, 41 in the Indian Ocean, 57 in West Africa, and 13 in East Africa. The increase was quite pronounced in the Malacca Straits, with a jump from eight incidents in 2003 to sixty incidents in 2004. The number of casualties skyrocketed. Thirty crew and passengers were murdered and eighty-seven were wounded. Hostage situations also increased. Roughly 140 people were held hostage, and, sadly, 43 of them simply disappeared and were presumably killed. Nine ships were hijacked and three were sunk.

The incidence of piracy and armed robberies inexplicably decreased in 2005 by as much as 50 percent in many regions. Incidents in the South China Sea dropped from 113 in 2004 to 97 in 2005, and in the Malacca Straits there were only 20 reported incidents. West African incidents dropped to 23 and in the Caribbean and South America there were 26 incidents. However, the decrease wasn't worldwide. East African incidents nearly quadrupled to 49 and in the Indian Ocean incidents edged up to 51.

While the overall numbers seem encouraging at first glance, a disturbing aspect embedded in many incident reports is an almost universal increase in violence. And yet, fewer people were actually killed. In 2005, 152 merchant mariners were either assaulted or injured, while 652 were taken hostage or kidnapped. Eleven of these people were never seen again and were presumably killed. Sixteen ships were hijacked, marking an increase over 2004.

Obviously, shipowners began raising the alarm about the trend of piracy on the high seas and armed robberies in ports throughout the world. Although some regions saw decreases in piracy, in part due to beefed up naval patrols, such as in the South China Sea, the violence was on the rise. Little action other than enhanced patrols in some areas was taken. In 2006, thirteen merchant mariners were killed, and 112 were wounded. One hundred eighty were held hostage or kidnapped, and thirty-seven were never seen again and presumably killed. Ten ships were hijacked.

Piracy and armed robbery incidents increased by 17 percent worldwide in 2007. Twenty merchant mariners were killed and three who were kidnapped were never seen again and presumably killed. One hundred fifty-three were wounded and 194 were held hostage or kidnapped. Sixteen ships were hijacked. The statistics for 2008 show six murders and thirty-eight mariners who were kidnapped and presumably killed. Forty-two mariners were wounded.

The numbers for 2008 reveal a change in pirate tactics, a shift to hostage taking and hijacking for ransom. Eight hundred eighty-nine merchant mariners were held hostage or kidnapped and fifty-one ships were hijacked. The pirates evidently learned that a dead hostage and a sunken ship were not as profitable as a live hostage and a largely undamaged ship. Violence is certainly still common in many pirate incidents, but like most criminals, pirates want to get away unscathed. Piracy against merchant ships today is all about money.

Starting in 2008 and continuing through 2009 and beyond, piracy attacks in Somali waters and in the Gulf of Aden increased dramatically, greatly boosting the total number of attacks reported worldwide. In 2008, there were a total of 263 attacks worldwide, and 111 of them occurred in Somali waters and in the Gulf of Aden. The rise is directly connected to the continued political unrest in Somalia and adjacent nations, the depletion of the once thriving Somali fishery, and the vast sums of seemingly easy money available in the form of ransoms for captured merchant ships and crews. A group of impoverished fishermen armed with AK-47s and rocket-propelled grenades can become rich overnight, and the money streams into the local economy, raising the standard of living for those associated with the pirates.

In the first six months of 2009, there were 240 piracy incidents of all types worldwide, and 130 of them occurred in Somali waters and the Gulf of Aden. Globally, seventy-eight vessels were boarded, seventy-five were fired on, and thirty-one ships were hijacked. Five hundred sixty-one merchant mariners were taken hostage, six were killed, nineteen were wounded, and seven were kidnapped. Eight mariners were missing after encounters with pirates and presumably were killed. Although Somali waters and the Gulf of Aden are rife with piracy, pirates continue to pose a threat to life and property throughout the world. Here's a breakdown of the most dangerous places for merchant ships and yachts.

Gulf of Aden and the Red Sea

Pirate attacks, hijackings, and armed robbery against merchant vessels and yachts in this region continue to make news, and no doubt will for the foreseeable future. It may seem unbelievable and odd, but pirates have even attacked warships from the United States, France, and Germany. In many cases, pirates are armed with AK-47s and rocket-propelled grenades, and use fast skiffs with powerful outboard engines. They attack alone or in wolf packs, and they use mother ships to carry them far offshore into major shipping lanes.

Southeast Asia

Straits of Malacca

The Straits of Malacca were once a hotbed of piracy, but there has been a significant drop in incidents as a result of concerted efforts by Singapore, Malaysia, Indonesia, and Thailand. Starting in July 2005, these countries increased naval patrols in the Straits. The rate of attacks began to drop, indicating that the piracy problem in other regions can be addressed and reduced if action is taken. In May 2009, patrols were decreased because the problem seemed to be under control. However, ship captains are still being advised to maintain strict antipiracy surveillance when transiting the Straits. Small oil tankers are still common targets in this area.

Singapore Straits
Pirates and robbers have been launching attacks on the many ships at anchor in the Singapore Straits and there have been a number of incidents where ships have been attacked while under way. Tugs towing barges are a common target.

Indonesia
This region almost made the top of the list for piracy attacks in 2007. Balongan, Balikpapan, and Belawan were and remain the highest risk areas, and incidents have been reported throughout Indonesian waters. As is the case elsewhere, many shipowners whose vessels have been attacked in this region do not report the incidents. Thus, the incidence of attacks is likely higher than records indicate. Tugs towing barges are a common target, as are small oil tankers.

Bangladesh
Compared to other regions and nations, piracy has been relatively rare in the waters of Bangladesh. Between January 2006 and May 2009 there were sixty-two reported incidents. The pirates target ships anchored in rivers. Most attacks appear to be based in the port of Chittagong anchorages and in the port approaches. While the frequency of attacks has declined, the area is still considered risky. Attacks take place at night when robbers come aboard, usually armed with knives, and often when a vessel is still moving into the anchorage. The main targets are ship's stores and equipment. When confronted, the pirates usually depart quickly without violence.

The Philippines
The Philippines has always had a reputation for piracy and the main focus of pirate activity is Manila, where pirates are targeting ships at anchor, often with violence. Attacks against ships and yachts have often occurred around Mindanao.

Thailand

Common targets are tugs towing barges and ships at anchor. Yachts are also targeted.

South China Sea

The South China Sea has long had a reputation for piracy, and attacks on ships under way are still occurring. There have been a number of reported attacks in Vietnamese waters. In 2006, Vietnamese authorities implemented some successful counter-piracy measures. In one incident, a pirate gang armed with AK-47 weapons attacked and boarded fishing vessels off the southern Kien Giang province. The pirates attempted to take the fishermen into Cambodian waters before being intercepted by a Vietnamese patrol boat. Several of the pirates escaped. However, four were captured along with firearms and ammunition.

West Africa

Nigeria

The area around Lagos and Bonny Island remain one of the world's leading piracy hot spots. The pirates often use excessive violence and launch attacks on vessels under way, and board and rob ships at anchor. In many cases, they kidnap the crews and hold them for ransom. Many of these attacks are politically motivated, edging them into the dark realm of terrorism. Since August 2007 fifty attacks have been reported in Nigerian waters. Twenty-five of these incidents were off the capital of Lagos and twenty-five were in the Bonny River area.

No Nigerian waters are considered safe from pirate attacks. Within the first three months of 2009, seven acts of piracy were reported, and there is anecdotal evidence to suggest that at least another thirteen unreported attacks also occurred. Virtually all the incidents have taken place against oil tankers and oil field service and support vessels.

Cameroon

There have been several incidents and they are now on the increase. Caution is advised for all ships in the area. Many attacks also have a political motivation.

East Africa

Tanzania

The port and anchorage off Dar es Salaam remains the main piracy hot spot in Tanzania. Attacks on anchored ships and those at the dock occur on a regular basis.

South and Central America

Brazil

The port of Santos remains the most dangerous in Brazil. While attacks have decreased, they have not disappeared. The attacks are also generally violent with deaths and serious injuries being commonplace. The use of firearms at the outset of an attack is the norm.

Peru

In 2009, piracy attacks in Peru nearly doubled, though the numbers are low, with a total of seven successful attacks reported. Four attacks were reported in Peru in the last quarter of 2008.

Venezuela

Piracy has been common in Venezuela's ports and in its territorial waters. Yachts are frequent targets and usually the attacks involve violence and murder. Sailors are also wounded.

The Mediterranean and Europe

Piracy in the Mediterranean dates back centuries. Today, it's less common and attacks are generally limited to yachts in the

Greek islands. There are isolated incidents elsewhere. Serbia is a hot spot. Between 2008 and 2009 as many as thirty-eight Bulgarian and Ukrainian ships have been robbed at the Serbian port of Smederevo. Heavily armed pirates attacked and stole entire cargoes while the ships were docked on the Danube River. In some cases, merchant mariners have been wounded.

Not since the time of the Vikings and the Slavic pirates in the Baltic in the twelfth century and the piracy that threatened shipping into the fourteenth century has there been any piracy in Northern Europe. In fact the first person known to have been hung, drawn and quartered, was the Englishman William Maurice in 1241 under the rule of Henry III for piracy.

3

Cause and Effect

Most of us have had to deal with an insurance company at some point, and sometimes the process can be frustrating and difficult. Interpreting insurance policies and making successful claims for damage or the total destruction of a home is often a headache, and it is even more vexing for an incident involving a boat. Marine insurance is particularly complicated and murky.

The pirate attacks off Somalia and in Nigerian waters have posed some interesting challenges within the maritime insurance market, and the attacks have greatly increased the cost of insurance for ships traveling in high-risk regions. Some shipping reports say that premiums have risen by a factor of ten. In a recent statement, leading insurer Lloyd's of London said that the cost of insuring a vessel passing through the Gulf of Aden had risen from $500 in 2008 to roughly $20,000 per vessel for each voyage.

Large commercial ships carry three types of insurance. The hull or marine insurance covers the physical risk to the ship, such as running aground, or being damaged in heavy weather, among other things. The second insurance coverage is for protection and indemnity (P&I) to address any issues related to the crew. P&I insurance is obtained through P&I Clubs. War risk insurance covers acts of war, terrorism, and insurgency, and usually covers piracy and hijackings. Many insurers will levy a surcharge on a shipping company when the insured ship transits an area classified as high risk, like the Gulf of Aden. Insurers are introducing new insurance products that cover losses arising out of piracy, including ransom payments and cargo delays. Imagine the losses if an entire cargo of perishable food went bad because a ship was captured or delayed due to piracy, and you'll get an idea of why these new insurance products are needed.

Today, many insurers are classifying piracy as a war risk, not a general risk, because war risk premiums can be raised for entire regions. Given the large number of ships pirates are capturing and the large payouts in ransoms, there are other pressures emerging on insurers and shipping companies. For about four centuries there has been a debate between insurers and shipping companies as to which party is responsible for paying to secure the release of hostages taken by pirates. At this time, marine insurance underwriters cover crew ransoms under the cargo and vessel risk policies. There are some who contend that crew insurance underwriters should also carry some of the risk for the ransoms. Similarly, there are debates regarding the splitting of ransoms between life and property coverage.

Some of the world's leading insurers have been lobbying P&I Clubs to remove war risk exclusions within coverage conditions so that shipowners have improved coverage certainty in the case of any pirate attack. At the present time, coverage is uncertain in many cases, based on the vague and ambiguous language in some policies. The P&I war exclusion is open to interpretation by insurers, and as pirates always use military weapons it casts the issue of coverage into a gray area. It is all about risk and exposure and money.

Some in the industry have suggested that since P&I Clubs have all the expertise in handling liability claims, then it would be best if primary P&I war risk was moved to hull coverage. Insurers are grappling with many questions. For example, is piracy covered by the P&I Club rules? When is piracy not covered by the P&I Club rules? How exactly is piracy defined and how is it distinguishable from terrorism? What is the definition of "weapons of war" and are ransom payments recoverable?

As the issue of arming merchant vessels continues to arise and the use of armed security guards is also considered, then further insurance questions will no doubt crop up. Should a shipowner employ armed guards or not? Is the insurance coverage prejudiced by the use of armed guards or the use of security company contractors? With the calls by some naval and political authorities to arm ships, the insurance dimension comes into play because arming ships can either limit or aggravate liability. If ship insurers could prove that a piracy incident involved the unlawful use of weapons at sea by the shippers (the crew acting as agents or representatives of the shippers), then the insurer would probably not have to pay for any damage or loss to the ship or its cargo.

Many Indian shipping companies are purchasing kidnap and ransom policies for virtually every voyage. It is estimated that the premium for coverage of about $2 million in ransom would cost as much as $150,000. Nearly every general insurer offers kidnap and ransom coverage, and internationally American International Group (AIG) is one of the leading insurers. Lloyd's of London underwriters introduced a new coverage to plug gaps in its standard policies. Any loss of earnings by charterers and cargo owners during any pirate detention period is covered. When a ship is taken, the ship charterer usually has to foot the cost of paying for the extra time, usually two months or more, without any income to show for that period. The cargo owners also face the risk of contract cancellations due to the delays, and this is amplified with seasonal cargoes.

For ship captains, changing course or choosing another

route to avoid a piracy area can be a trap for the shipping company and expose it to insurance claims on the part of charterers related to delays and increased fuel consumption. When a captain does choose to deviate from a standard route to avoid piracy areas, it is necessary to contact the insurers and cargo owners first. The same applies when planning to use armed or unarmed guards on a ship as protection against pirates.

With the dramatic escalation in piracy off Somalia and in the Gulf of Aden, and the insurance issues related to it, some shipowners and ship charterers are avoiding the area completely. Instead of steaming for the Suez Canal, they are sending ships on the much longer route around the Cape of Good Hope. Naturally, this is a costly undertaking. For example, an oil tanker on a voyage from Saudi Arabia to the United States would add around 2,500 nautical miles to the voyage at an annual increase in fuel costs of about $3.5 million. Money is also lost because the voyage takes more time on the longer route, meaning the ship could have made more paying voyages if it had taken the shorter way.

On the other hand, the reduction in available tanker capacity created by ships going around the Cape of Good Hope is a godsend for many shipowners. The current global financial downturn has put the shipping industry in a crisis situation, with an oversupply of ships laid up looking for cargoes. This has resulted in increasing freight rates, which have plummeted to barely breakeven levels. Those that have decided to go around the Cape of Good Hope to avoid higher insurance premiums and the piracy capture risks are also contributing indirectly to the present high Suez Canal charges, as fewer ships go through. Ships are also slowing down to save on fuel expenses in an attempt to turn a profit in what today is a very tough business, with or without adding pirates to the mix.

In recent incidents, naval forces from France and the United States have killed pirates in the process of foiling attacks. The situation is viewed as an escalating war, and that is leading insurers to raise premiums even more because the risk of violence and death to ship crews seems even higher. Shipowners will have to carry increased coverage and over a larger geographical area as pirates increase their range of operations. In problem areas like Somali waters, where enhanced naval patrols are reducing the number of successful attacks, experts grimly predict that any attacks that are successful will require payments of larger ransoms.

While insurers and shipowners are bearing a significant financial burden due to piracy, the crews face even greater risks. The trauma of being shot at, the prospect of injury or death, and the possibility of capture puts phenomenal stress on crews transiting waters where pirates are active. Politicians and other authorities don't really understand the psychological effects of a pirate attack. Imagine that your home is invaded, or that you are held at gunpoint in a hostage situation during a bank robbery. Now try to imagine the hostage situation lasting from one to ten months, the typical time period captured crews are held, and all the while enduring the threat of death and hoping the shipowner or insurance company will pay a fat ransom for your release. That would be stressful, right?

Piracy has always been an occupational hazard for merchant mariners, but the recent significant increase in pirate attacks and the prospect of long hostage confinements is hardly inviting. Some mariners are quitting the sea because of this problem. Others have no choice but to keep working, like many Filipino and Indian sailors, who make up the majority of most crews. Calls on governments to take action have been raised all over the world, and in most cases nothing has been done, though that is slowly changing.

The Philippines are the single greatest provider of merchant seafarers in the world. More than 300,000 Filipinos are working on ships. I have sailed with several crews and have many Filipino friends and I know that no other group is under greater stress worldwide. They are naturally outraged at the ongoing piracy problem, and they should have a powerful voice. If mariners from the Philippines refused to sail through problem areas like Somali waters the world's trade would come to a grinding halt. That's not likely to happen, though, because the Filipino sailors need their jobs.

Between 2006 through early 2009 more than two hundred Filipino merchant mariners were captured with their ships and held hostage in Somalia or offshore. In some cases, sailors were killed or wounded. Others were only released on payment of ransoms, which were handled privately. The Philippine government did not intervene on behalf of the mariners, adhering to a strict policy of not negotiating with pirates or paying ransoms in all hijacking and kidnapping cases.

In September 2008, the Philippine Department of Foreign Affairs did pay lip service to the problem. It instructed the many Philippines-based crew placement agencies to implement some basic safeguards in the event that pirates captured a ship with a Filipino crew. A spokesman was reported to have said that ships should not veer away from identified safe shipping lanes in African waters, and all vessels should proceed in a convoy when passing through the narrow gap in the Gulf of Aden. That's sound advice, but the captains were already doing it. And, believe it or not, the agency also suggested that Filipino sailors might want to take some basic language courses and learn the words for no, yes, eat and water so they could communicate with their Somali captors. In general and much to the dismay of the seafarers, the government appeared to be avoiding any commitment to participate in any proactive measures against the pirates.

The large number of Filipino sailors captured in Somali waters is a relatively new phenomenon. Of the more than two hundred captured to date, only eighty or so had been detained as of September 2008. At that time, the president of the United

Filipino Seafarers Union proposed that mariners be given high-powered weapons to deter pirates. However, international law prohibits carrying guns on commercial vessels. The proposal wasn't ever going to be a viable option, but it illustrates the level of frustration among Filipino sailors. The president of the union pointed out that the law against firearms on commercial vessels didn't seem to apply to everyone, adding that some crews on American commercial vessels were armed.

The lack of concern and inaction by shipowners and governments regarding the plight of crews and the suffering endured under extended pirate captures was encapsulated in a letter signed by eighteen Filipino seafarers held hostage after pirates captured the oil tanker *Chemstar Venus*. In all, there were twenty-three crew aboard. Most were Filipinos, while five were from South Korea. The open letter outlined the deep disappointment of the crew in the failure of their employer to secure their release and bring them safely home to their families. Although the Somali pirates and the shipping company were in negotiations, virtually nothing had moved forward. The company remained intransigent in ransom negotiations, and, as a result, the attitude of the pirates hardened.

The eighteen Filipino sailors described their conditions as risky and they said that illness was starting to afflict most of them. They said that they were experiencing diarrhea, coughs and colds, skin diseases, and psychological problems. One of them suffered a mild stroke and his condition was causing concern. They also stated that food supplies were nearly exhausted and they only had one meal every two days. The drinking water was gone, they had used up all the medicine on the ship, and the fuel oil bunkers were practically empty.

Even more frustrating was that the crew had signed fax messages describing the awful conditions and sent them to the shipping company. No messages from the company were received back, which further annoyed the pirates. Unknown to the crew, their families were not receiving accurate information about them from the shipowners. At one stage, false hope arose on the part of the families when they were told their loved ones would be released and were coming home. Obviously, when the crew (and the pirates) learned of this, more messages were sent contradicting the rosy assertions from the shipping company and requesting that negotiations for their release should be made with all haste. The shipowners appeared to act as if the sorry situation would just resolve itself.

Finally, the crew appealed to the Philippine government to take whatever legal action or execute whatever enforcement procedures were required to pressure the company to make fast decisions and resolve the impasse. It was pointed out that these mariners were part of an important group within the Philippines and that they were among the many sailors contributing to the economy at home.

As previously mentioned, the Philippine government did not respond effectively. It's a bit puzzling, even with strict policies against negotiating with pirates and paying ransom, that citizens of the Philippines and mariners in obvious distress would be ignored like that. The apparent appreciation of these men and women is plastered on a billboard at the Manila airport, expressing the thanks of a grateful nation to its citizen mariners for their important contributions to the national economy. As a further injustice, Filipino sailors are placed within the lowest category of nationals, Category E, which is the lowest priority that will be given protection by the multinational naval coalition forces.

After the steadily increasing anger at home rose to fever pitch, Philippine President Gloria Macapagal-Arroyo approved a proposal that would ban the deployment of all Filipino sailors to Somalia and other waters considered as high-risk zones. In response, Philippines-based shipowners and crew placement agencies cried foul, saying that such a ban would hurt their businesses and put thousands of Filipino sailors out of a job. The assertion was somewhat empty. In the current economic downturn, shipowners are scrambling for crews and can't find enough sailors to fully staff their ships. Any job losses would have been temporary.

Ultimately, the proposed ban was never implemented. A compromise was reached, stipulating that Filipino mariners would only serve in ships using the patrolled corridors in Somali waters or only serve in ships steaming well away from the Somali coast. In yet another odd statement at about this time, one politician went so far as to nearly blame the victims, stating that maybe Filipino sailors should keep a better lookout for pirates and that might help mitigate the situation. There were also calls for the Philippines to actively support the policing effort in Somali waters.

A union leader called for an increase in the level of security in Somali waters and in the Gulf of Aden, stating that the United Nations should be asked for increased naval patrols and helicopter surveillance. Rather naively he said he thought with enhanced security piracy in these waters would be stamped out in six months. One Philippine senator also called on the Arroyo government to establish a crisis team and station it in the Somali region to coordinate efforts aimed at protecting ships. The same senator also stated that sailors should receive increased hazard pay when operating in high-risk waters, and that they and their families needed better insurance coverage.

Joining the hue and cry was one of the world's largest shipping companies and a large employer of mariners. The company issued statements saying that the Philippines government should cooperate with its foreign counterparts regarding new maritime international security measures. It suggested that the government should work closely with overseas government agencies on enhancing security.

In July 2009, the Philippine government announced that a

naval officer had been selected to deploy to Manama, Bahrain, to act as naval attaché and a liaison with the multinational forces. His appointment and role was ostensibly to help monitor the condition of and to coordinate assistance for forty-four Filipino sailors being held hostage at that time. In late July 2009, Gloria Macapagal-Arroyo approved a $20,000 contribution to a United Nations trust fund to assist the Somali Transitional Federal Government in its fight against piracy. The amount of the donation reveals the low priority piracy was receiving in the Philippine government (and others around the world). In August 2009, a memorandum of cooperation was signed between the Philippines and the United States, calling on both nations to enhance vessel security and also for mariners to conduct antipiracy drills.

As previously mentioned, Indian sailors are also a large contingent aboard ships around the world. They, too, number high on casualty and hostage lists in piracy incidents, particularly in Somali waters. The following incident illustrates their situation. In September 2008, an Indian ship owned by Mercator Lines Limited was on passage to Kuwait. The ship was stopped and anchored for two days off the coast in poor weather conditions because the crew refused to sail the ship any farther without protection during the transit through those pirate-infested waters. After long negotiations between the shipowner and the crew, along with their union, the vessel weighed anchor and continued the voyage.

In the case of Indian sailors, the General Secretary of the National Union of Seafarers of India warned that unless security was improved in Somali waters and the Gulf of Aden, NUSI would advise its members to boycott vessels bound for those waters. It also stated that a boycott would have a considerable economic impact on India's economy. While the debate continued, more seafarers were held hostage after the Indian vessel *Stolt Valor* was hijacked. The Indian Defense Ministry ruled out any direct intervention by Indian warships to rescue them. In an effort to diffuse the situation, and with pirate attacks occurring well away from patrolled areas, various shipowners, unions, and crew placement agencies agreed to extend the boundaries of designated high-risk piracy zones where merchant mariners would receive double pay, along with death and disability compensation.

In the United Kingdom, the main union for merchant mariners, Nautilus U.K., also started lobbying for decisive action. When the Foreign Secretary called for the international community not to negotiate with pirates holding ships and sailors as hostages, Nautilus U.K. strenuously objected. The union contended that failure to protect ships from piracy meant that companies had no choice but to negotiate so that mariners were not hurt, the ships remained undamaged, and that no environmental disasters resulted from pirate attacks. While the Foreign Secretary was correct in stating that ransom payments encouraged further hostage taking, the official statements seemed to ignore the fact that shipping companies and unions were pleading for attack prevention, and seemingly getting little action, until recently.

Nautilus U.K. was also lobbying the British government to take the lead in launching a major reassessment of the International Ship and Port Facilities Security Code. The objective of the reassessment was to create a code that better reflected the new maritime realities, such as smaller crews operating larger, automated ships, the onboard security equipment carried, and the role of onboard security officers. At this writing, the code remained unchanged.

A British ship security survey administered by Nautilus U.K. found that more than 66 percent of respondents felt that larger crews were an effective way to increase protection against piracy. Roughly 30 percent favored naval protection, and about 25 percent wanted armed guards on board. The reality is that the maritime shipping industry is unable to find enough merchant mariners to serve as crew for all the ships in the world's fleets, especially given the current economic pressure on the industry. Increasing the size of crews is unlikely, even if it is a good idea.

If a greater number of crew on a given ship might serve as a way to protect against piracy, than it stands to reason that arming merchant ships and sailors, or having shipowners hire private security forces trained in the use of military weapons and tactics, would also be a good idea. However, as noted previously, only 25 percent of the respondents to the Nautilus U.K. survey said they favored firearms or armed guards aboard. In addition, current international law prohibits the carrying of heavy weapons on commercial ships, and then there is the issue of insurers to consider. If weapons or armed guards aboard might allow an insurer to duck paying a claim, the cost of arming a ship could be exceptionally high in the event of a pirate attack that voided a claim. The debate about arming merchant ships and employing security forces is robust and multifaceted, and it continues in earnest.

Most major shipping companies maintain a policy of not arming crews and also not allowing armed security forces aboard merchant vessels. The argument is that weapons on board has the real potential for escalating the violence and further puts the crew at risk. It also raises many multi-jurisdictional legal issues, both in the carriage of these weapons and in the event of death and injury to those on board or those being shot at or killed. If merchant ships were to carry heavy weapons, automatic rifles and rocket-propelled grenades, to name just a few options, it would be the first time since World War II that this type of vessel voyaged on the high seas ready for armed conflict, and then it was in response to the German U-boat campaign that saw literally dozens of ships sunk each week. The merchant marine is an inherently peaceful occupation, and descending into war is counter to that peaceful pursuit of commerce.

Those lobbying for arming merchant ships or hiring armed security guards are typically naval officers and civilian naval officials. Militarizing ships designed to carry freight and that are operated by sailors with no military training at first blush seems like an easy fix to the piracy problem. In reality, doing so would probably cause more deaths, both to the sailors and to the pirates, and simply escalate the problem. It would likely encourage pirates to shoot and kill more readily.

Some security contractors are pushing shipowners to hire them to guard ships and crews transiting pirate prone waters, and some are trying it, though not many at present. Yet, the security companies are using these few instances to make it appear that shipowners are clamoring for their services. Where there is money to be made in a seemingly new and lucrative market, it's little wonder that companies want a piece of the action. One Asian shipowner was reported to be employing a British security company to guard some vessels when transiting the Gulf of Aden. These security people were evidently to be used to deploy and operate defensive sonic devices, and details of such devices are clouded in secrecy. As one rather cynical seafarer friend of mine said: "Beware of pirates wearing industrial-style ear defenders!"

The International Maritime Bureau has stated that while a shipowner has the option of hiring armed guards to serve aboard merchant ships, the organization cautions against it. The reasoning is that armed defenders will escalate the situation with both armed attackers and defenders having to use lethal force, along with all the political and legal implications that entails. A second major reason for caution is that firing automatic rifles and rocket-propelled grenades on a gas, oil, or chemical tanker is pretty dumb. The consequences of an explosion or spill could be catastrophic. The Spanish government has authorized Spanish-flagged vessels to employ private security guards when sailing off the Somali coast, but only with authorization from the Interior Ministry. The Netherlands government doesn't allow armed personnel aboard merchant vessels, and neither does Norway.

Escalation of violence may result from arming merchant ships, but there are many other possible consequences and issues. For example, when do you start shooting? This is a major concern for yacht owners, too, if they are carrying guns aboard. There is no clear answer to the question, and in the heat of the moment, it's easy to see how potentially lethal mistakes could be made. The legal issues are also considerable, such as those associated with carrying firearms. Many countries have strict laws regulating firearms on foreign vessels entering territorial waters or ports, and the headaches in sorting through those regulations are myriad.

There are also questions as to which laws would be applied when a firearm is used, depending on where the ship was when the incident occurred. If it happened in international waters, then the laws of the nation where the ship is flagged would apply, or the laws of the nation of the person who fired the weapon would apply. As you can see, the legalities get complicated.

Ships are generally accorded the right of innocent passage, so is that situation changed when they carry firearms? That's a very good question indeed, and nobody has a definitive answer because the answer differs depending on the laws of particular nations. One question being asked is that if the pirates are shooting at the bridge of a merchant ship with rocket-propelled grenades and automatic weapons without actually aiming at people, does that preclude an armed response? Intuitively, you'd think not, but in reality it is a good question. The answers remain unclear.

There are other issues to consider as well. How about a seized vessel being used for piracy while the unfortunate crew is still aboard, and then gets caught in a cross fire when a warship intervenes in the new attack? This actually happened to the hapless crew of a captured Thai trawler pirates used to launch new attacks when an Indian naval vessel intervened. All but one of the crew was killed during the shootout with the pirates.

The tanker owner group INTERTANKO has come out against the use of firearms on merchant ships, as have most other ship operators and owners. It firmly believes such practices will escalate the violence of pirate attacks and armed robberies with a resulting increased loss of life. It also states that crews should not be armed and cites a lack of training as a reason why. It says that crews should not be required to defend themselves and the ship, with good reason. In any other workplace this sort of thing would never be allowed. Does the responsibility for protecting the cashbox in a fast food restaurant during an armed robbery fall to the person slinging the burgers? Of course it doesn't, nor should it should fall to sailors.

Shipowners and other organizations in the merchant marine also advise that when private security services are used aboard ships, the personnel should be unarmed and that they should only serve as advisers. These entities caution ship operators and owners against engaging private security firms that provide armed escorts and guards. The lack of any quality control process, liability issues, command and control with respect to use of lethal force, as well as insurance related issues are simply too problematic. As previously mentioned, people in the shipping industry are acutely aware of the potential disaster from a firefight on a ship carrying explosive or hazardous materials, and they want to avoid such liabilities.

Today, there are some ship protection measures on the market, that include a system from Secure-Ship that is a non-lethal electric fence for installation around the deck perimeter. The electric fence has a 9,000-volt pulse to shock would-be boarders. Basically, it is a beefed-up cattle fence. When the boarder receives the shock, it is supposed to deter him from continuing, but it's also likely to really annoy him, too! The fence can be hooked into audible alarms and lights. There are also automated tracking systems for ships such as the ShipLoc satellite tracking system. It allows a company or operator to monitor the precise location of its ships. This system enables the crew to activate an automatic alarm that transmits a message to the shipowner and authorities if an attack is occurring. The message is sent over a secure signal, so it can't be detected by anyone aboard the distressed ship or by any nearby ships. It's very similar to a silent alarm in a bank.

One security contract company is working to provide protection and recovery services for shipowners and crews. It has formed a group of ex-British marines known as the Rapid Rescue Antipirate Force. The company reasons that when a high-value ship with its high-value cargo is attacked, the crew is often set adrift or killed, and the ship is repainted, renamed, and sold along with its cargo. This was indeed a common practice in cases of past Asian piracy incidents. However, that is not the practice in Somalia and elsewhere in East Africa. The company claims it was successful in thwarting just such an incident in Malaysia, but an interdiction in a hostage situation in or around Somali waters could easily end up getting the hostages killed.

Another company based in Granot, Israel, is teaching merchant mariners how to think like pirates. Security operatives are also often anonymously embedded on ships, in particular on passenger vessels. The reasoning behind embedding is similar to the air marshal concept. If pirates know there are defenders aboard but cannot identify them, it makes it harder to figure out the odds. They won't know how many defenders are aboard. The idea sounds great in theory, but in practice it is very difficult to implement, not least in getting the word out to pirates. An Israeli security team was aboard the *Melody* when it was attacked. When the pirates attempted to board, the captain instructed the Israeli security guards to retrieve their pistols from the ship's safe and return fire.

Israeli security guards are in very high demand because they are renowned for their military training and experience and have a somewhat fearsome reputation. The Israeli Foreign Ministry has stated in the past that the Israeli government is not involved in fighting piracy. It has also stated that companies involved in combating piracy against merchant vessels are private enterprises contracting security guards for private shipping firms. It is estimated that there are thousands of Israeli security guards employed within maritime security worldwide.

The issues associated with piracy today are obviously complex. When pirates attack merchant ships, it has a ripple effect, prompting responses and reactions in the industry and across the broader political spectrum. It impacts individual mariners and groups of mariners like the Filipinos. It forces navies to get involved, and it forces insurers and shippers to look anew at laws and practices governing maritime commerce that date back centuries. The root causes of piracy are equally complicated, and they differ somewhat from region to region, but in one aspect the causes share common ground: Poverty and greed are key drivers. Outside of a utopia, the solutions to the problem appear difficult to orchestrate, though people are trying to do just that as the problem takes on even grimmer proportions in spite of some deterrent effect from naval patrols in troubled areas.

4

The Naval War on Piracy

A naval war on piracy is under way in Somali waters and in the Gulf of Aden. One leading maritime security analyst publicly warned that the U.S. Navy and its international allies should be careful not to conduct it like the war on terror and the war on drugs, which at times appears to be ineffective. The analyst correctly surmised that piracy will never be completely eliminated, and that's proven by more than one thousand years of continuing piracy. Some of his comments, however, were probably somewhat startling to many and asserted that piracy can be managed and defended against to a level where it becomes another basic cost within international commerce. Indeed, the shipping industry has taken this view of piracy for many years.

One of the more sobering sentiments is that the international trading system could probably withstand considerably more attacks and hijackings over and above that experienced in late 2008 and 2009 off the Somali coast. When piracy is reduced to hard cash values, the actual cost of piracy is estimated at around $16 billion annually, if not more. That figure may appear to be large, but it is actually small when compared to the $7.8 trillion international trade generates every year.

While the monetary value of attacks is sustainable, the risk to life and limb on the part of ship crews is not. Also, the political pressures that piracy triggers worldwide may not and do not in many cases reflect the commercial reality. For example, banks don't generally consider the costs of piracy as something that can be ignored, whereas many shipowners do look the other way because it costs them less in a long run. With no law and order offshore and in nations where piracy thrives, and if pirates can strike with impunity and little fear of capture and prosecution, the acts of violence will of course continue. The root causes of the piracy problem, as is often stated, lie ashore in troubled countries and regions. Those root causes do not appear likely to change any time soon.

The war on piracy is increasing as numerous navies steam for Somali waters and the Gulf of Aden. The number of successful pirate attacks in these waters did decrease in early 2009, in part because naval vessels have become more effective at thwarting the attacks in progress. That is a good sign. As in past centuries, it demonstrates that naval power can have a positive impact on reducing acts of piracy if a concerted effort is made. To date, though, the degree of force has not been sufficient to eliminate the piracy problem.

In June 2008, the United Nations Security Council passed a resolution that permitted foreign warships to enter the territorial waters of Somalia. Yet, several commentators said there was a lack of political will with regard to committing effective naval forces to combat the pirates. The International Maritime Bureau was reported as saying that a significant reason behind the upsurge in hijackings was the inability of coalition warships to deter the pirates. It said that while coalition naval forces were doing the utmost to stop pirate attacks, the main focus remained squarely on ongoing Middle East military operations and antiterrorism patrols.

One report stated that if civilian aircraft were attacked using arms on a daily basis as ships are, most governments would respond very differently. In other words, governments would take far more decisive action. Although ships comprise the lifeblood of world economic activity, piracy against shipping is not as visible to the general public as an airline hijacking. It is a classic out of sight, out of mind scenario. Yet, ninety percent of the world's trade by volume is carried by sea. At any given time, there are an estimated 10 million shipping containers in transit on the world's oceans and inland waters.

Another report said that it was inconceivable that governments were unable to secure Somali waters and the Gulf of Aden, which are among the world's most strategically important waterways. One major criticism is that the naval forces operating within the area are unable to take an active role because they are limited by their respective rules of engagement. International laws are very complex with respect to acting against pirates, and navies can only act if pirates are caught in the actual act of boarding and seizing a ship, and that window is generally only twenty minutes. Otherwise, naval forces are really just like attack dogs chained to a fence.

The most problematic areas in Somali waters and the Gulf of Aden are patrolled by the multinational Combined Task Force 150, which includes elements of the U.S. Navy's 5th Fleet based in Manama, in Bahrain. Other countries with ships in the task force are France, the United Kingdom, Canada, Pakistan, Denmark, and Germany. Each nation contributes ships to the force by rotation. Command of the task force rotates from one country to the next on a predetermined basis. The task force primarily conducts maritime security operations in and around the Strait of Hormuz, Gulf of Aden, Gulf of Oman, Arabian Sea, Indian Ocean, and Red Sea.

Combined Task Force 150 was initially created in August 2008 in support of the International Maritime Organization's call for international assistance to discourage attacks on commercial vessels transiting the Gulf of Aden. The mission includes criminal activity prevention, counterterrorism, and the prevention of human and drug smuggling. These naval vessels have been instrumental in deterring many pirate attacks. However, the eight or nine naval ships on station at any given time cannot hope to effectively patrol such a large geographical area.

To provide more targeted protection with the limited resources available a Maritime Security Patrol Area was established in the Gulf of Aden. The patrols cover a relatively narrow corridor about 621 miles in length and about six miles wide. Ship and aircraft patrols are constant. The military strongly requests that all ships and yachts transit through this route to maximize protection. The Commander of the U.S. Navy's 5th Fleet was quoted as saying that the international shipping industry needs to take on more responsibility for protecting vessels and crews against pirate attacks given that there are not sufficient naval resources to provide round-the-clock protection. Whether shipowners and operators actually do take these steps or not, the added security in this hot zone is a welcome development.

In the past, international laws for dealing with captured pirates mandated a simple trial and summary execution on the scene. However, in recent decades these tough laws were repealed in the mistaken view that piracy was no longer an issue. No new laws were enacted to replace the old ones. This has naturally led to confusion when pirates are caught, creating a difficult situation for naval commanders. The greater number of naval vessels involved in thwarting piracy is leading to an increasing number of cases where command decisions must be made with less than ideal guidelines to follow. By the end of July 2009, twenty-one warships were patrolling Somali waters and the Gulf of Aden. Twelve were from the European Union, five were operating under the auspices of the North Atlantic Treaty Organization (NATO), and four hailed from the United States. The following summarizes the extent to which international naval power has been brought to bear on the piracy problem in Somali waters and in the Gulf of Aden. More than the above-mentioned nations are involved.

United States

The U.S. Navy has a long history when it comes to battling pirates. The two Barbary Wars in 1801 and 1815 on the coast of North Africa came about when the United States decided it would no longer make tribute payments to pirates, and when U.S. forces were victorious in 1815 these payments ceased. It is perhaps little known that the U.S. Marine Corps played a major part in these battles. The opening line from the famous *Marine Hymn* makes a direct reference to the fight against the Barbary pirates: "From the Halls of Montezuma to the shores of Tripoli." The Marines also got nicknamed Leathernecks during this period because their uniforms at that time had high leather collars to protect them from the swinging cutlasses of pirates.

On October 12, 2000, the U.S. destroyer *Cole* was attacked while in the Yemeni port of Aden. A boat laden with explosives was driven into the side of the ship and detonated. The resulting explosion killed seventeen sailors and wounded another thirty-two, and it blew a large hole in the ship's hull. While not an act of piracy in the strict sense of the word, the case does demonstrate that the U.S. Navy was involved in conflict in these waters at an early stage. Indeed, the U.S. Navy has been constantly involved in actions against pirates in the region over the years, and today it is central to the naval effort aimed at making shipping safer.

As many incident reports indicate, the U.S. Navy is making a valuable contribution to the antipiracy effort. American naval vessels are using advanced technology to cover the vast areas that require patrols. For example, it is deploying unmanned surveillance drones to look for suspected pirates and pirate mother ships. The drones are able to fly at altitudes of around 3,000 feet and transmit images with a sufficient level of detail to determine the national flag of a fishing boat. Video and photographs are streamed back to American naval vessels, and then relayed to other task force members as required. Some drones also have night vision capability.

In one drone-assisted interception, the U.S. Navy caught pirates armed with automatic weapons and a rocket-propelled grenade launcher. The drone was flying at night and it photographed a suspicious boat equipped with a boarding ladder. An American naval vessel scrambled helicopters to provide air cover and ongoing surveillance while a boat was deployed with a search and seizure team. The team boarded the suspicious boat and discovered the weapons, which obviously were not needed for fishing or any other legal activity. Nine pirates were detained, though before U.S. forces arrived they had tossed the incriminating boarding ladder overboard. With images from the drone clearly showing the ladder, throwing the boarding ladder overboard did no good for the pirates. The photographs were sufficient evidence of their intentions. This is just one example of how technology can aid in the fight against piracy.

North Atlantic Treaty Organization

In response to the piracy problem in Somali waters and the Gulf of Aden, NATO established the Combined Task Force 151. The primary mission objective was to escort and protect vessels carrying humanitarian aid from Mombasa, Kenya, to Mogadishu, Somalia, for the World Food Program. NATO has been doing this since 2007 when the task force was formed after the attack and seizure of several vessels carrying food.

The NATO Portuguese warship *Corte-Real* successfully prevented a pirate attack on a Norwegian-owned oil tanker. Nineteen pirates were pursued and after three hours were captured on their dhow. Portuguese Special Forces boarded the boat and found a cache of AK-47 rifles. A vessel search uncovered additional AK-47s, rocket-propelled grenades, and, more disturbingly, four sticks of dynamite. The dynamite was unusual. The pirates were disarmed and released because they had not attacked Portuguese ships or citizens.

Corte-Real was also involved in a rescue in June 2009. The crew came to the aid of fourteen Indian sailors a day after pirates attacked their ship, looted it, and fled. The Indian sailors said they had been beaten while in captivity, following the seizing of their dhow *Visvakalyan*. The pirates stole all the crew's possessions, including cash, radios, cell phones, and even gifts from family. They also took nearly every scrap of food and other provisions, leaving the crew with just three chickens to eat.

When the pirates were finished taking what they wanted, they reportedly fired their weapons into the air and mocked the Indian sailors. The Indians sailed their dhow toward the Yemeni island of Socotra to get help, and their situation grew dire. They were weak from lack of food. Fortunately, *Corte-Real* intercepted the dhow about twenty nautical miles off the pirate port of Hobyo. The crew gave them food and fuel, and reported that the Indian sailors may well have died of starvation if they had not received help.

France

The French have been proactive in interdicting and thwarting pirate attacks, and they have also been playing a lead role in taking the fight to the pirates. The French have a large naval base in Djibouti, making it easier for them to conduct operations. One incident involved the French frigate *Premier Maitre L'Her*, which thwarted an attack on the cargo ship *S. Venus*. Its crew intercepted two pirate skiffs with eight pirates as they attempted to board the cargo vessel, apprehending the pirates and handing them over to Somali authorities. In addition, the French crew seized weapons and ammunition.

European Union

France and Spain initiated the European Union maritime coordination unit in response to the piracy situation. This was called EU NAVFOR Somalia—Operation Atalanta. Since September 2008 French naval vessels have escorted European ships transiting the Gulf of Aden. In 2009, the task force consisted of twelve vessels. The Atalanta antipiracy naval mission has an annual estimated cost of $300 million. The Atalanta mission mandate was only temporary, slated to end in December 2009. At the time of this writing, the European Union was considering an extension.

The crew of an Italian frigate working on the Atalanta mission captured nine pirates after the pirates attacked two vessels. Following a distress message from a Greek-owned ship under attack by pirates firing rocket-propelled grenades, the Italian naval vessel *Maestrale* scrambled a helicopter. When the helicopter arrived on the scene, the pirates had already diverted to attack a Danish-owned vessel. The helicopter fired warning shots at the pirate skiff and a boarding party from the *Maestrale* arrested the suspects.

In mid-2009, the European Union had begun to extend the EU NAVFOR—Operation Atalanta and the associated Maritime Security Center Horn of Africa (MSCHOA). This mission was conducted in coordination with NATO, the Combined Maritime Forces (CMF), and other regional and participating navies. In the period since the internationally recommended transit corridor was established, there has been a significant reduction in successful piracy attacks. In August 2009, the Dutch naval vessel *Evertsen* sailed to join the European Union force and took command from the Spanish vessel *Numancia*.

Greece

Greece is one of the largest shipowners in the world, and yet it remained somewhat silent on the issue of piracy. It was by no means immune to attack, though. Between January 2005 and April 2009 Greek shipowners suffered the highest number of ships attacked by pirates. Most Greek ships are operated under flags of convenience and are staffed with foreign crews, mainly from the Philippines, but the captain is usually Greek. As a consequence, few Greek citizens were and are captured.

In September 2008, the Ministry of Mercantile Marine filed a request to the Ministries of National Defense and Foreign Affairs seeking the deployment of a Greek naval vessel to Somalia to join the multinational task force.

Russia

The Russian government deployed its first vessel, the frigate *Neustrashimy* (Fearless), from its Baltic Fleet at the end of October 2008. The deployment followed the pirate seizure of the Ukrainian vessel *Faina*, which was loaded with weapons and will be discussed in more detail later. The stated objective was the protection of Russian citizens and to ensure safe navigation. The frigate was equipped with antisubmarine and air defense missile systems, a 100-millimeter artillery gun, torpedo systems, and rocket-assisted bomb launchers. The frigate also carried a Kamov Ka-27 helicopter. By the time the frigate rotated out of active duty in the region it had escorted thirteen convoys, or a total of fifty-one ships, and it had been involved in several successful pirate interdiction incidents.

Neustrashimy was replaced on January 7, 2009, with the Russian Pacific Fleet destroyer *Admiral Panteleyev*. It arrived with a tugboat and two fuel tankers. The guided missile destroyer was a Udaloy-class vessel armed with antiship missiles, 30- and 100-millimeter cannons, and Kamov Ka-27 helicopters. The ship quickly saw action after its arrival when the crew prevented a pirate attack on a Dutch container ship. When *Admiral Panteleyev* departed in mid-June 2008 to return to its Pacific Fleet base in Vladivostok, it had escorted forty-one ships and seized a boat with twenty-nine pirates aboard, who were suspected of having attacked a Russian-crewed tanker as well as another vessel traveling in a convoy. The Russians then deployed the *Admiral Vinogradov*, followed by the Udaloy-class destroyer *Admiral Tributs*, with two helicopters, a tugboat, a tanker, and a unit of naval infantry.

China

In January 2009, three Chinese naval vessels joined the international naval task force in the Gulf of Aden. This was a significant event because it represented the first time since the fifteenth century that Chinese naval vessels had sailed so far from mainland China on a combat mission. The political decision to deploy the flotilla of two destroyers and a supply vessel was probably difficult for China to make. The flotilla comprised the destroyers *Wuhan* and *Haikou*, and the supply ship *Weishanhu*, and it included eight hundred sailors as well as seventy troops from China's Special Forces.

Of course, prior to the deployment various political analysts all studied the potential implications of this unprecedented move. China had been accused of inaction and its officials would have known that sending the ships would bring accusations of power projection and military expansionism. The deployment expanded the scope of the Chinese Navy from a coastal force to a blue water force, and that proved to be a touchy subject. The flotilla was successful, and China dispatched a second one comprised of the destroyer *Shenzhen*, the frigate *Huangshan*, and the supply ship *Weishanhu*. And then China sent a third flotilla, which included the guided missile frigates *Zhoushan* and *Xuzhou* and the supply vessel *Quiandaohu*. These ships were from the East China Sea Fleet.

The Chinese also made claims in the media that in addition to being protected by the Chinese Navy, its merchant ships were receiving protection by super pods of dolphins! Evidently, there is a video (no doubt it's on YouTube) showing a large number of dolphins, literally thousands of them, getting between a Chinese merchant ship and Somali pirates who were intent upon boarding. The pirates aborted the attack in the face of this overwhelming natural obstacle. Having twice in my own seafaring life had the privilege of being witness to one of these super pods of dolphins, I know that it is indeed awe inspiring.

India

When the Indian Navy deployed vessels to the Gulf of Aden, it soon became involved in many successful piracy prevention incidents. As previously noted, it also received bad press when an Indian naval vessel sank a Thai fishing vessel in November 2008 after the supposed fishing crew opened fire. It turned out that the Thai boat had been captured by pirates, who were using it as a mother ship. The crew was aboard and all but one were killed.

On May 31, 2008, the Indian stealth frigate *Talwar*, acting on a distress call, intervened in an attack by pirates on the Norwegian-owned merchant vessel *Maud* about 225 nautical miles east of the Yemeni port of Aden while it was traveling in an escorted convoy with two other vessels. Aboard *Maud* were an Indian captain and nine Indian sailors.

Eight pirates in a skiff attacked the merchant vessel. It started performing evasive maneuvers. *Talwar* and a Chetak helicopter with marine commandoes headed to the ship, and two pirates attempting a boarding on a ladder were observed. The helicopter crew fired warning shots from its 7.62-millimeter machine gun and the pirates fell into the water. A boarding party in rigid-hull inflatable boats apprehended the pirates without encountering resistance, searched the pirate skiff, and confiscated weapons and other equipment. The frigate resumed its protection of the convoy when other warships arrived. No news was given on what happened to the two pirates who went into the water. It is interesting to note that this may have been the first recorded instance where a pirate attack had been stopped while pirates were boarding a vessel.

Malaysia

The Royal Malaysian Navy was one of the first naval forces to react to the Somalia situation. Malaysia dispatched military support following the hijacking of *Bunga Melati Dua* and

Bunga Melati Lima on August 19, and August 29, 2009. Following the release of the two Malaysian ships, a month later the Malaysian naval vessel *Sri Inderasakti* remained deployed in the Gulf of Aden. It intercepted and stopped two pirate attacks, one of the most notable of which involved the well-publicized attack on the Chinese merchant ship *Zhen Hua 4*.

The Malaysian Navy supply ship *Sri Inderasakti* helped repel a pirate attack while on passage to the Suez Canal. Pirates in two skiffs attacked a nearby merchant vessel and the captain issued a distress call, which the crew on *Sri Inderasakti* received. In response, a Fennec helicopter was scrambled. The Malaysian naval helicopter successfully thwarted the hijacking attempt.

At the time of this writing, the Malaysia International Shipping Corporation seems to be the only shipping company adopting a proactive stance against pirates. It modified its 699 TEU container ship *Bunga Mas Lima* into a naval auxiliary vessel for use as an escort vessel. This work was performed in conjunction with the Royal Malaysian Navy and Malaysia's National Security Council in a direct response to the hijackings of MISC's ships *Bunga Melati Dua* and the *Bunga Melati 5* in the Gulf of Aden.

Under international law, an auxiliary naval vessel is classed as a ship other than a warship that is directly under military control, and therefore receives sovereign immunity. The MISC naval auxiliary's crew received training from the Malaysian Navy. The vessel carried regular Malaysian Navy officers and crew to perform security functions. Any pirates attempting to attack or hijack *Bunga Mas Lima* are in for a very big surprise!

Japan

Japan also deployed forces to Somali waters and the Gulf of Aden, and it was an unprecedented move. It marked the first time since World War II that Japanese armed forces were sent into a potential combat situation. Past peacekeeping missions in Iraq and Afghanistan as well as United Nations peacekeeping missions have been strictly in support and logistics. Under Japan's post-World War II pacifist constitution, the military can only use force for defense, or to protect Japanese nationals, ships, and cargoes.

About 2,000 Japanese ships transit the area each year, so that Japan has a strong commercial and strategic reason for defending its assets and interests. In March 2009, Japan deployed two destroyers to join with multinational forces already in place. In addition, Japan deployed two PC3 Orion maritime surveillance aircraft that will be based in Djibouti.

Just a month after the deployment of Japanese naval forces, the 4,650-ton destroyer *Sazanami* intervened in an attack against a Singaporean ship. The attack involved four pirate boats. This was its first action and a momentous one for Japan, even though no shots were fired. The second vessel deployed was the 4,550-ton *Samidare*.

Taiwan

The Taiwanese military responded to the hijacking of the Taiwanese fishing vessel *Win Far 161* near the Seychelles by announcing it had no plans to send warships to patrol the Indian Ocean. Many Taiwanese politicians demanded swift government action to rescue the crew and protect other fishing boats. As in most cases, the political debate soon ramped up, and it was stated that Taiwan's diplomatic situation and the distance between Taiwan and Eastern Africa were factors to consider. Taiwan is diplomatically isolated within the region and this is attributable to the diplomatic success of China. Taiwan and the Chinese mainland split during the civil war in 1949. Since then a battle has raged as Taiwan attempted to gain international recognition. The *Win Far 161* was the fifth Taiwanese fishing boat hijacked since 2005. The crew consisted of seventeen Filipinos, six Indonesians, five Chinese, and two Taiwanese.

South Korea

Like many governments, South Korea's was criticized for its apparent inaction in deploying naval vessels to protect South Koreans against pirate attacks. An estimated 460 South Korean merchant vessels transit the Gulf of Aden each year. Somali pirates have captured a number of South Korean cargo vessels and held the crews as hostages. In April 2009, the South Koreans deployed an Aegis destroyer and it commenced patrols. As was the case with some other nations, the deployment marked a groundbreaking event because it was the first overseas mission for its navy. The destroyer quickly saw action. Ironically, it rescued a North Korean vessel.

In April 2006, a South Korean tuna fishing boat with a crew of twenty-five was hijacked and were only released after four months and a ransom was paid. In 2007, Somali pirates seized two South Korean vessels and twenty-four sailors, which included four South Koreans. The crews were eventually released in November 2007 after spending six months in captivity. The *Dong Won*, with eight Korean merchant mariners aboard, was seized and released after 117 days. Other hijackings occurred in May and October 2007. In February 2008, South Korean merchant mariners were among twenty-three hostages released after months of captivity.

After the hijacking of the *Bright Ruby* and its crew of eight on September 10, 2008, the Korean government discussed the option of deploying naval vessels to Somali waters and the Gulf of Aden. The Ministry of Defense dismissed the idea. The usual political debate ensued and it was obviously a major first for the government to have to consider such a deployment. On March 4, 2009, the South Korean government announced that it would mobilize a destroyer the day after the historic decision by the parliament to make the first ever overseas combat naval deployment in the country's history.

The *Cheonghae* unit was formed and was named after an ancient Korean naval base initially established to combat pi-

60

rates. The unit comprised a 4,500-ton destroyer with 270 crew, a helicopter, and thirty troops from Special Forces. The deployment involved the destroyer *Munmu the Great* on March 13, 2009. It joined the Combined Task Force 151. This ship was replaced with the destroyer *Dae Jo-yeong* in July 2009. The Koreans stated that their long experience and expertise in dealing with North Korean boats attempting to infiltrate made their close combat experience perfect for dealing with pirates.

The South Korean destroyer *Dae Jo-yeong* soon made itself useful and assisted in the rescue of the Egyptian-flagged *Amira*, which came under attack around seventy-five nautical miles south of Al Mukalla, Yemen. A team of South Korean snipers boarded a helicopter that took off from *Munmu the Great* and flew over the suspected hijackers. As a result, more than twelve pirates were captured aboard a mother ship with the assistance of the U.S. guided missile cruiser *Gettysburg*. Several assault rifle rounds and one rocket-propelled grenade round struck the ship during the attack.

In addition, the pirates attempted boarding using ropes, but the attack was thwarted. The SH-60B helicopter assigned to the Helicopter Antisubmarine Squadron Light 46 located the suspected dhow mother ship with seventeen people aboard. A team from *Gettysburg* boarded the mother ship, along with members of the U.S. Coast Guard Legal Detachment 409. They took the pirates into custody after finding eight assault rifles, a rocket-propelled grenade launcher, and one rocket-propelled grenade.

United Kingdom

As previously noted, the government of the United Kingdom ordered the Royal Navy not to detain pirates, based in part on fears that the pirates might seek asylum. In addition to this, the Royal Navy was warned that confronting, arresting, and fighting pirates could violate human rights conventions, and it was told that its presence in the region was to act solely as a deterrent to piracy. Many naval personnel were outraged and shocked at the apparently passive role they were being asked to play.

The European Community Shipowners' Association demanded that direct action be taken against the pirates, like the French Navy had done. In one news report, a British naval officer was quoted as saying that as a nation the United Kingdom should hang its head in shame. The government response to the criticism indicated confusion. No one seemed to know which branch ordered the Royal Navy to take such a passive role. The Ministry of Defence (MoD) was reported as saying that its rules of engagement were an issue for the Foreign Office. The Foreign Office responded that it did not give the Ministry of Defence instructions on how to operate. The pirates were no doubt encouraged by this.

Then, on November 11, 2008, the frigate *Cumberland* intercepted a Yemeni-flagged dhow identified as one possibly involved in an attack on the *Powerful*, a Danish cargo ship. The frigate made an attempt to stop the dhow, but a firefight ensued. Royal Marines aboard two inflatable boats engaged the pirates, and two of the suspected Somali pirates were killed. Eight Somali nationals were detained on the frigate and then transferred to the Royal Navy auxiliary vessel *Wave Knight*, where they remained while the Foreign Office decided what action to take.

There were apparently seventeen men aboard the dhow, and eight of them were found to be Yemeni nationals who were the dhow crew, the remainder being alleged Somali pirates. One of the Yemeni sailors was found severely injured, apparently from an earlier incident with the pirates. He subsequently died. The United Kingdom did not appear to consider invoking powers contained within the Piracy Act of 1837 to bring the suspects back to Britain for trial. Sections of the act remain in force, and, following a recent Law Commission review, it was determined that some of its provisions were sufficient to define piracy as a specific criminal offense that was punishable with life imprisonment. Capital punishment for piracy was abolished in 1997.

The Royal Navy handed over the eight suspected pirates to Kenyan authorities for prosecution. It emerged in court that *Powerful* had been attacked twice on the same day. The captain of the ship testified at the trial held in Mombasa that eight of the alleged pirates had attacked in two skiffs, each with five pirates aboard (two of the pirates were killed in the firefight, as previously noted). After the arrival of a coalition helicopter, the attack ceased. Later in the day, the captain observed two dhows, one trailing three skiffs and the other towing one. One of the dhows chased the ship and five armed men tried to board using a ladder, but one fell into the sea. The attack was aborted and the pirates went to look for the man in the water.

On June 12, the Royal Navy frigate *Portland* intercepted and chased two suspicious skiffs. A Lynx helicopter provided air cover while Royal Marines boarded and arrested the ten people aboard the skiffs. The Royal Marines discovered and seized rocket-propelled grenades, automatic weapons, and ammunition. The pirates were disarmed, one skiff was destroyed, and the pirates were released.

Germany

Germany is one of the world's largest shipowners and operators. Like Japan, Germany is unable to engage in any active military operations overseas because it is prohibited from doing so under its pacifist post-World War II constitution. However, Germany reviewed the United Nations Security Council's resolution that called on all states to combat piracy, believing it might provide the basis for the deployment of German naval ships. Some German politicians supported the idea and sought Bundestag approval for a naval deployment.

An earlier resolution passed by the Bundestag stated that German armed forces could not be deployed to fight pirates, and some German officials argued that a German naval deployment was unnecessary, saying that since other nations, including France and the United States, were already contributing forces Germany did not need to. One German naval officer was quoted as saying that Germany did not want to play the role of the world's policeman. The sentiments in the major shipping port of Hamburg were much different. German companies were paying hefty ransoms to release German-owned ships and German crews.

One of the obstacles hindering the deployment of a German naval force to Somali waters and the Gulf of Aden is that such protective tasks are considered the responsibility of the federal German police, which cannot operate outside German territorial waters. German naval vessels can only provide emergency assistance if an attack is witnessed or if pirates attack German naval vessels. Some politicians stated that German warships operating in foreign waters under Operation Enduring Freedom, an internationally supported antiterror campaign, were essentially serving only as supporting elements, not in active combat roles. Thus, the naval involvement did not set a precedent for a deployment to actively pursue and engage pirates. It was also stated that in several incidents German naval forces observed attacks in progress and did nothing to stop them, even though they could have intervened in those instances.

Some German politicians are calling for a constitutional amendment to allow the deployment of naval forces to combat piracy. However, others counter that such a change is not required because the navy can be deployed against pirates under the Law of the Sea, which Germany ratified in 1994. The political battle over what to do about the piracy problem goes on, and probably will for the foreseeable future. In June 2009, it was announced that German-flagged merchant vessels would carry armed marine contingents for protection.

One major piracy incident involved the German vessel

Lehmann Timber, which was owned by a Lübeck-based company. The vessel was attacked and captured by pirates while on a passage to the Suez Canal. In Nigeria, another major piracy hot spot, the crew of a German ship owned by Duisburg-based Baco Liner was held hostage for three and a half weeks in 2007. Baco Liner responded. It began equipping its ships sailing in Nigerian waters with barbed wire to discourage boarders, and it hired between six and eight Nigerian naval guards for each ship to provide protection.

Australia

On May 23, 2009 Australian naval vessels thwarted Somali pirate attacks on two merchant vessels about 170 nautical miles off the Yemeni coast. The pirates were armed with automatic weapons and rocket-propelled grenades. The Australian frigates *Sydney* and *Ballarat* responded to a distress call from the crew of *Dubai Princess*. The ship's officers reported that they were under fire from pirates using rocket-propelled grenades and that the pirates were attempting to board. *Sydney* closed in on the vessel under attack and scrambled a Seahawk helicopter. In another incident, the warship intervened when the merchant vessel *Stella* was attacked in the same area.

Spain

Spain sent a P-3 Orion surveillance plane to patrol Somali waters and the Gulf of Aden from a base in Djibouti. The aircraft worked in conjunction with the European Union task force. In May 2009, Spain announced that it would send another P-3 Orion surveillance plane to Kenya to strengthen the protection of Spain's tuna fishing fleet during the fishing season off the coast of southern Somalia. Sending the second aircraft was in response to a piracy incident that involved the seizure of a Spanish fishing vessel. The crew was held hostage, but were eventually freed after a ransom of $1.2 million was paid.

Following a pirate attack on the merchant vessel *Melody*, the crew of a Spanish naval vessel apprehended nine suspected pirates.

Sweden

The Swedish Navy has been active, deploying two vessels to serve as part of the European Union task force. In one incident, the corvette *Malmö* intervened in an attack on the Greek merchant vessel *Antonis* off Somalia. Seven suspected pirates were detained. The naval ship fired cannons, machine guns, and utilized snipers with high-powered rifles to stop the attack. The pirates responded with a rocket-propelled grenade, but no one was injured. Swedish forces boarded one of the fishing vessels being used by the pirates while another pirate vessel escaped. The Swedes also seized weapons and a global positioning system. *Stockholm* was the other Swedish naval vessel deployed to the area.

Denmark

The Danish Navy launched an active antipiracy effort in response to pirate attacks in the region. Denmark took over the command of the multinational Combined Task Force 150 in September 2008. There have been many successful operations. In one incident, the Danish naval vessel *Absalon* answered a call for help from a Netherlands Antilles-registered cargo ship under attack by five pirates. *Absalon* scrambled an armed helicopter. The helicopter fired warning shots at the pirates and the Dutch merchant vessel fired emergency flares at the pirate boat, setting it ablaze. The pirates jumped overboard and were rescued by the naval vessel and detained. *Absalon* sunk the burning pirate boat so that it posed no further threat to navigation.

The rescued pirates remained aboard *Absalon*, until they were released nine days later because there were no legal grounds for prosecution under Danish law. None of the countries in the Gulf of Aden region were prepared to prosecute the pirates. Consideration was given to transferring them to Somalia, but it was not done because of fear of violating international human rights conventions that prohibit sending individuals to a nation where they might be executed for their crimes.

In another incident, *Absalon* seized two suspected pirate boats and ten alleged pirates. After boarding the boats, a large quantity of handguns, automatic rifles, and rocket-propelled grenade launchers were discovered. In addition, equipment for boarding merchant ships was found. This was the first instance where suspected pirates had been captured by a naval force.

In April 2009, *Absalon* returned to Copenhagen after a successful mission of eight months. During this period the ship's crew captured five Somali pirates, who were sent to the Netherlands for prosecution. The Danish Shipowners' Association, to which one the world's largest shipowners, Maersk, belongs, stated that it wanted the *Absalon* back in the Gulf of Aden to protect Dane-owned vessels. Five to six Danish ships transit the area every day, making protection essential.

Norway
Norway is one of the largest shipowners in the world, and controversy regarding the apparent lack of government intervention to protect Norwegian maritime assets continues to simmer. However, in August 2009, the new frigate *Fridtjof Nansen* was deployed for six months. Its arrival coincided with the end of the monsoon season, which is typically when piracy increases in the region.

Turkey
Turkey has ships on patrol in the Gulf of Aden as part of Combined Task Force 151. On July 24, 2009, after responding to a distress call, Turkish naval commandos intercepted a skiff

when pirates were about to launch an attack on a merchant ship. Five pirates were apprehended, with forces from the frigate *Gediz* and helicopter assistance from another Turkish vessel, *Gaziantep*. In May 2009, Turkey took over command of Combined Task Force 151.

Somalia

In June 2009, Somalia began training recruits to serve in the nation's first naval force to be formed in twenty years. Its main objective is to fight piracy.

Yemen

It probably isn't uppermost in people's minds, but the Yemeni government has been very active in countering piracy off the coast of Yemen. In September 2008, the Yemeni Coast Guard established an antipiracy unit. Coast guard officials were quoted as saying that this unit would have sixteen fast patrol boats purchased from Australia. Each patrol boat would carry sixty marines specifically trained to combat piracy. The vessels would also be equipped with artillery, radar, and advanced communications capabilities. The stated mission of these forces was to enhance the protection of ships and to stop Somali pirates in the Gulf of Aden and Bab al Mandab Strait.

In May 2009, Yemeni authorities referred twelve Somali pirates for criminal prosecution on charges that they hijacked four Yemeni ships in the Gulf of Aden earlier in the month. The action that led to the detention of the pirates involved members of the Yemeni Coast Guard as well as Yemeni marines, who killed four pirates during a firefight to free the Yemeni oil tanker *Qana* and three smaller Yemeni vessels which were hijacked about twenty nautical miles off the Yemeni coast. Four of the tanker crew were wounded and a fifth man went missing, but fishermen in the Arabian Sea found him.

In another incident, the Yemeni Navy answered a distress

call from a Philippines-flagged oil tanker when it was about fifteen nautical miles off the Red Sea port of Makha. Upon arrival at the scene, the Yemeni marines were advised that two pirate boats were trying to hijack the tanker. The crew said that two boats fired on the ship and four pirates managed to get aboard. The pirates stayed aboard for a period before going back to their boats, and they continued to shadow the tanker.

In July 2009, the Yemeni oil tanker *Yemen Oil 7* was on passage between Aden and Hodeidah when fourteen pirate skiffs closed in for an attack. Yemeni marines intervened and fought a fierce battle, eventually driving the pirate fleet out of Yemeni waters.

Saudi Arabia

On February 16, 2009 the Saudi naval frigate *Al-Riyadh* intervened to protect the Turkish cargo vessel *Yasa Seyhan*, after receiving a distress call. Three pirate skiffs were attacking the ship, but the attack was aborted.

Iran

In May 2009, Iran deployed two naval vessels to patrol the Gulf of Aden and to provide protection for its merchant vessels. Iran relies heavily on its oil tankers to deliver its oil exports, and it owns a large oil tanker fleet. Thus, it is not surprising that it acted to defend against pirate attacks. In December 2008, Iran announced that it would deploy a naval vessel and it was unclear whether the deployments of 2009 were additions to that earlier mobilization.

In January 2009, it was reported that a Hong-Kong registered cargo ship chartered by Iran was released after being hijacked the previous November. In October 2008, Tehran had reportedly paid a ransom to release an Iranian merchant ship hijacked off the Somali coast. In July 2009, Iran dispatched two additional warships to replace those on patrol.

Pirate attacks on naval vessels

The pirates are so intent on boarding vessels of any type that they often choose the wrong ship. It should be in a Piracy 101 Course that ships that are grey in color and especially those with guns are generally not viable targets. There have been a few episodes where pirates have launched attacks on such vessels. The following incidents demonstrate the extent to which pirates will go to acquire a target, even if it is one that can and will fight back.

On May 25, 2008, pirates attacked the German naval supply vessel *Spessart* while it was under way in the Gulf of Aden. They approached the vessel in a small boat and opened fire with automatic weapons. The German naval personnel immediately returned fire. The crew aboard *Spessart* notified other warships and aircraft in the vicinity and requested assistance. Several naval ships responded to the call, including a Greek and a Dutch frigate, a Spanish warship, and the U.S. amphibious assault ship *Boxer*. A Spanish aircraft was patrolling in the area, and two U.S. Marine Corps Cobra helicopters also joined in the pursuit of the pirates.

About five hours later, a contingent of Greek sailors reached the pirate skiff, boarded it, and seized the seven suspected pirates, along with their weapons, which included assault rifles and rocket-propelled grenades. The pirate suspects were disarmed and transferred for interrogation aboard the German frigate *Rheinland-Pfalz*. They were detained until a decision on whether they could or would be legally prosecuted was made. What this episode illustrates, besides incredible stupidity on the part of the pirates, is that well coordinated multinational naval capabilities in antipiracy operations can reap dividends.

In September 2008, a security team fired shots to warn off two small boats approaching the U.S. naval oil supply vessel *John Lenthall*. The shots were fired when other defensive measures failed, and the two dhow-type motor vessels continued their approach. The warning shots struck the water around fifty yards from the closest boat. The vessels turned away.

The U.S. Navy dry cargo and ammunition ship *Lewis and Clark* was attacked while steaming off the east coast of Somalia. Two pirate skiffs chased the naval vessel for an hour, apparently trying to board and hijack it. The ship's security team issued verbal warnings to the pirates, and the pirates responded by opening fire. No rounds hit the ship. The pirates aborted the attack when the vessel increased speed. The commander of Task Force 53 later said that increasing speed was what was advocated for merchant vessels seeking to escape attacking pirates. Most merchant vessels don't have such reserves of power, so making a run for it is not always possible.

Another instance when pirates attacked a naval vessel occurred on May 5, 2009. Eleven pirates foolishly attacked the French naval vessel *Nivose* thinking it was a merchant ship. Apparently, the pirates approached the ship at high speed with the sun in their eyes, so they could not tell it was a naval asset. French marines, supported by a helicopter firing warning shots, engaged and captured them.

A well-publicized incident involved the Indian stealth frigate *Tabar*. The warship had investigated a suspected mother ship towing two skiffs similar in description to one suspected of being behind several pirate attacks. The vessel was requested to stop for an inspection. The pirates responded, warning the frigate that they would blow up the Indian naval vessel if it approached. Pirates were observed on the upper deck carrying automatic weapons and rocket-propelled grenade launchers. Then in a singularly bizarre act of defiance the pirates fired on the frigate.

Obviously, the crew aboard *Tabar* retaliated. Rounds from the French ship evidently hit caches of ammunition in the pirate vessel, causing an explosion that sank the ship. The actual death toll is not known. The Indian Navy was later forced to defend this action, and the pirate vessel was later confirmed as a hijacked Thai fishing boat. The International Maritime Bureau said that pirates had captured *Ekawat Nava 5* earlier the same day and the crew was bound and aboard. One Cambodian crewmember was found alive after he spent six days adrift. The other fourteen crew aboard the vessel are missing and presumed dead.

In March 2006, there was also an incident where twenty-seven Somali militiamen, who said they were patrolling the Somali coast to stop illegal fishing vessels, faced down the U.S. Navy. The Somali militiamen claimed they were defending themselves after the U.S. naval ships *Cape St George* and *Gonzalez* stopped the 32-foot alleged pirate boat for an inspection. The boat was towing two skiffs. The Somali crew was armed with what appeared to be rocket-propelled grenade launchers. The crew opened fire on the naval vessels.

Naturally, the U.S. forces returned fire. One militiaman was killed and five others were wounded. Twelve were taken into custody. Upon boarding the vessel, automatic weapons and rocket-propelled grenades were discovered. This incident prompted other Somali pirates to announce that they would kill any hostages that were captured unless the detained men were released.

5

Cruise Ship Attacks

If pirates can receive millions of dollars in ransoms for under twenty crew aboard a merchant ship, imagine how much they could get if they captured a cruise ship. Obviously, the notion has crossed the minds of more than one group of pirates. It has also crossed the minds of security experts and executives of cruise ship companies. Although it happened in 1985, memories of the two-day standoff with four members of the Palestinian Liberation Front aboard *Achille Lauro* in the Mediterranean still remain fresh. During the incident Leon Klinghoffer, a wheelchair-bound American Jew, was shot dead and summarily tossed overboard. More than four hundred passengers were held at gunpoint while the terrorists bargained for the release of prisoners. Ultimately, the ship was allowed to dock in Egypt and the four terrorists were later captured.

Cruise ships may represent a potential bonanza for pirates, but they are not as easy to attack as merchant ships. A cruise liner can attain speeds well in excess of twenty knots, the crew is huge, and the sides of the hull rise from the sea like the walls of a cliff or fortress, making it hard for pirates to board. Nevertheless, pirates in Somali waters and in the Gulf of Aden, the world's most active pirate zone, have indeed attacked cruise ships, creating some very tense incidents.

In 2005, six heavily armed pirates in two boats attacked the cruise liner *Seabourne Spirit* about 186 nautical miles off the Somali coast. The pirate skiffs were apparently launched from a mother ship. As the cruise liner started evasive maneuvers, the pirates opened fire, slamming it with rounds from automatic rifles and a rocket-propelled grenade. The passengers were terrified, huddling under cover, and one member of the crew was slightly wounded. The ship managed to evade the pirates and escape, but it was a harrowing attack.

The same cruise ship tangled with pirates two years later, in November 2007. As pirates sped toward the liner, the officers on watch put through a distress call, fearing the worst. The closest naval asset, Britain's *Campbeltown*, was approximately 120 nautical miles away. The British crew responded, saying they would send help right away. They scrambled a Lynx combat helicopter, which was soon on the scene, but the pirates were gone when the chopper arrived. They quite likely left because they figured the liner would be too difficult a target to actually capture.

As piracy incidents continued to increase in 2008, the Japanese government reportedly considered issuing a rare security order to deploy a Japanese destroyer to escort two Japanese luxury liners, *Asuka II* of NYK Cruises Co. and *Nippon Maru* of Mitsui OSK Passenger Line Ltd. The ships were carrying nearly 1,600 passengers off the coast of Somalia and the deteriorating security situation proved worrisome. Ultimately, the Japanese government concluded that the protection of civilian cruise ships was not within the mission scope of the destroyer that was at that time operating in the Indian Ocean, and was part of the Japanese refueling mission for multinational antiterrorism forces. Japanese officials instead requested escort assistance from the United States and Britain, and the cruise ships transited safely through the area.

Another cruise ship attack occurred in the Gulf of Aden in 2009. The liner *Nautica*, with 684 passengers and 400 crew aboard, was bound for the port of Salalah, in Oman, when six to eight pirates in two skiffs equipped with twin outboard engines closed in. The ship's officers noted the suspicious movements of the boats, and the 30,277-ton liner took evasive action, speeding up and zigzagging, while the passengers were ordered to stay in their cabins. The skiffs did not give up. They revved up their outboards and pursued *Nautica*, opening fire at a range of less than 1,000 feet.

As with some piracy attacks, reports can get a bit fuzzy on the details. In the case of *Nautica*, some witnesses said pirates fired eight rounds at the vessel, and that none hit the ship, though one passenger claimed he heard rounds striking the hull. No person aboard was injured and no damage to the liner occurred. There were conflicting reports that coalition warships had stopped the attack. It was also reported that a French warship alerted by the Danish Navy scrambled a helicopter, which arrived on the scene and chased the pirates away.

The pirate threat was considered grave enough for cruise ship company officials to advise the passengers that a piracy risk existed while the liner was transiting the area. Passengers were also told that an acoustic device might be used to blast any attacking pirates with painfully loud sound waves, as loud as 150 decibels, considerably above the normal pain threshold of 120 decibels. A number of passengers reported that the crew had indeed sound-blasted the pirates while others reported hearing two loud booms. Whenever you have a shipload of witnesses, there is bound to be contradictory testimony, but clearly the liner did come under attack, creating a stressful situation for everyone involved.

When *Nautica* arrived in Oman, print and broadcast reporters swooped in. The incident hit the news in a big way, as passengers told their stories. Some passengers clearly didn't understand the danger, including a woman who actually went to a cabin balcony to observe the shooting. She described the pirate boats in detail, meaning if she could see them then she was in a potential line of fire. People do strange things in stressful situations, which is unnerving for the owners of cruise ships wishing to avoid deaths, injuries, and expensive lawsuits.

Another case of confusion and strange antics on the part of passengers occurred on the cruise ship *Athena*, owned by Classic International Cruises Australia. Evidently, after the liner encountered a large fleet of fishing boats a number of passengers promptly phoned home, saying that pirates had just attacked the ship. One passenger even called the Associated Press and reported a large coordinated pirate attack. The captain supposedly rebuked the passengers over the onboard public address system when he found out what was going on, saying that the claims were without substance and spreading misinformation created considerable alarm. The captain had merely used extreme caution while his ship passed through the fishing fleet because these fleets are often used to shelter pirate boats. Part of the trouble may have arisen because he asked the crew to tell the passengers to stay in their cabins until the liner was clear of the fishing fleet.

Still, in spite of the captain's assurances that no attack had taken place, some crew and passenger counterclaims ensued, insisting that an attack had really occurred. Some even said the captain admitted on the public address system that pirates actually did attack *Athena*. Other accounts indicated that fire hoses were used to help repel the attack, and yet no shots were reportedly fired at the ship.

As the German cruise liner *Astor* was steaming along in the Gulf of Aden in December 2008, the crew was completely unaware that two pirate boats were stalking the ship. However, the German frigate *Mecklenburg-Vorpommern* was nearby, noted the two suspicious boats closing with the liner, and intervened about three nautical miles from the cruise ship, which had 493 passengers and crew aboard. Warning shots from the frigate forced the pirates to abort any attack in the offing.

Although some cruise line companies are becoming wary of transits through the Gulf of Aden, Royal Caribbean Cruises has stated that it will continue sending ships there. Its vessel *Legend of the Seas* has reportedly passed through the area without incident, and the company assures its passengers that it will continually monitor and review the security situation.

On April 25, 2009, pirates attacked the Italian cruise liner *Melody*, with 991 passengers and 536 crew on board, about 600 nautical miles off the coast of Somalia and about 180 nautical miles from the small island nation of the Seychelles situated 1,000 miles off East Africa. These waters were and are classified as a safe or low-risk zone. The ship had just made a port call at Victoria, capital of the Seychelles, and the passengers were enjoying a late night classical music concert.

Under the cover of darkness, twelve pirates approached the cruise ship in a skiff and began blasting away with automatic weapons. They came alongside, and tried to board using a grappling hook on the lower deck. Courageous passengers repelled boarders using deck chairs, which they threw at the pirates. An armed Israeli security team was aboard, and they streamed on deck with weapons and fired on the pirates as they pulled away from the liner. A short battle ensued, with each force firing at the other. The decks of the liner had rapidly changed from a place to enjoy some classical music to a combat zone. Bullets slammed into the ship's lifeboats and hit three of the windows on the upper decks.

As the firefight continued, the captain ordered all speed and began zigzagging. The ship's lights were extinguished to make it a more difficult target. Obviously, the passengers were terrified of what might happen next. The ship escaped and no one was injured. The next day, an Italian warship with a helicopter escorted the ship until it cleared the area, much to the relief of the passengers and crew.

It seems counterintuitive to seek pirates out for thrills, but some entrepreneurs are doing just that. Some Russian cruise line companies have announced plans to offer pirate-hunting excursions in luxury private yachts off the Somali coast. The cruises will cost around $6,000 per day. The yachts will cruise slowly and close to the coast in the hope of enticing pirates to attack, essentially acting as juicy bait. If pirates do attack, the paying passengers will get to shoot them with rented AK-47 rifles and even rocket-propelled grenades! Former Special Forces soldiers will accompany them.

As should be clear by now, piracy can make people do crazy things. This venture most assuredly fits in that category. Some opponents of it rightly assert it's tantamount to paid murder, while others say the pirates are only going to get what they deserve, a mighty big and possibly lethal surprise. An unfortunate consequence of activities like these, as well as arming sailors or hiring armed security guards, is that pirates may get wind of it, shoot first and ask questions later. They do this now, of course, but the enterprise is generally about money, not outright slaughter.

PART 2

Hot Zones

6

Piracy in Somalia and the Gulf of Aden

Somalia is often in the news these days. Fighting continues between extremist groups and the Somali government on a virtually continuous basis in the capital of Mogadishu. Sadly, the violence isn't new. Somalia has been in a state of unrest for more than two centuries. A succession of colonial and post-colonial dictators imposed some order, but none effectively brought the country under any meaningful control.

In recent times, the situation has remained unstable. The country has not had a functioning government since the initial outbreak of civil war in 1991, following the removal of dictator Mohamed Siad Barre. The anarchy continued following the ousting of the governing Islamic Courts Union in January 2007 by a United Nations-backed transitional government. The persistent unrest is the major driver behind the piracy epidemic in Somali waters. While military solutions are being used to protect shipping, the only real solution will result from the installation of a stable government and better security for the people, and that seems a long way off.

Piracy has undergone a dramatic and rapid escalation off the Horn of Africa, particularly in the Gulf of Aden and off the Somali and Yemeni coasts. The escalation began in earnest in early 2008 and continued throughout 2009 with no foresee-able end to it in sight. Foreign governments and their navies, shipping companies, and maritime organizations are grap-pling with the problem, which worsened when pirates moved from coastal attacks to strike hundreds of miles offshore.

The piracy problem escalated to such an extent that it prompted the formation of an umbrella organization known as the Round Table of International Shipping Associations. The Round Table is comprised of major shipping groups, in-cluding BIMCO, the world's largest independent international shipping association with 2,720 members. The International Association of Dry Cargo Shipowners (Intercargo), the Inter-national Chamber of Shipping/International Shipping Federa-tion, and the International Association of Independent Tanker Owners (INTERTANKO), which operates 80 percent of the world's tankers, have all joined together to create an alliance with the International Transport Federation (ITF).

As a group, these organizations have considerable clout. They issued a formal request to the International Maritime Organization's secretary general to lobby for and secure United Nations support for an increased naval presence in the Gulf of Aden. The mission was quite simple: Protect the lives of merchant mariners and passengers, and ships and cargoes. The group further asserted that piracy in the Gulf of Aden and in Somali waters was spiraling dangerously out of control, and that more nations needed to commit naval vessels to address the problem. It also stated that naval vessels should be able to effectively and actively stop piracy in any form, and that they should be able to intercept and bring pirates to justice, thereby providing safety and security in one of the world's most strategically important shipping lanes.

A look at a particularly bad day in 2008 when multiple at-tacks on shipping occurred within a twenty-four-hour period is illustrative of how serious the piracy problem had gotten in Somali waters. Early in the morning on that day pirates attacked a United Arab Emirates bulk carrier, but a coalition naval forces helicopter intervened and drove the pirates off. An hour later, pirates armed with automatic weapons and rocket-propelled grenades hit a Philippines-owned chemical tanker. A coalition warship chased the pirates away.

Yet another attack ensued a short time later against an Italian crude oil tanker. The captain of the vessel responded by engaging in evasive maneuvers. The ship escaped. The final attack that day occurred against a Taiwanese container ship. Pirates armed with automatic weapons pursued the vessel, and the ship's crew successfully repelled the pirates by blasting them with high-pressure water jets from onboard fire hoses. Needless to say, the day was stressful for any merchant mariners in the area. Imagine facing pirates with automatic weapons with a fire hose for defense and you'll get a vivid image of how stacked the odds are against merchant mariners voyaging through pirate-infested waters. That day was also busy for the naval forces on patrol.

The situation worsened in Somali waters and in the Gulf of Aden. By the middle of 2009 pirate attacks were being reported almost every day. Some of these attacks were unsuccessful, but extremely violent. There were many other instances where pirates successfully captured ships and crews, and negotiations between the pirates and the shipping companies commenced.

The problem remained largely out of the media until high-profile capture and liberation events grabbed the world's attention. One involved the U.S.-flagged container ship *Maersk Alabama*. Another involved the capture of the Saudi Arabian supertanker *Sirius Star*, which carried a cargo of crude oil worth $100 million. The hijacking of the roll-on-roll-off vehicle carrier *Faina* with its cargo of Soviet-era tanks also hit the news in a big way. These cases will be discussed in further detail later.

Clearly, something needed to be done about the pirates. In October 2008, a draft proposal of a United Nations Security

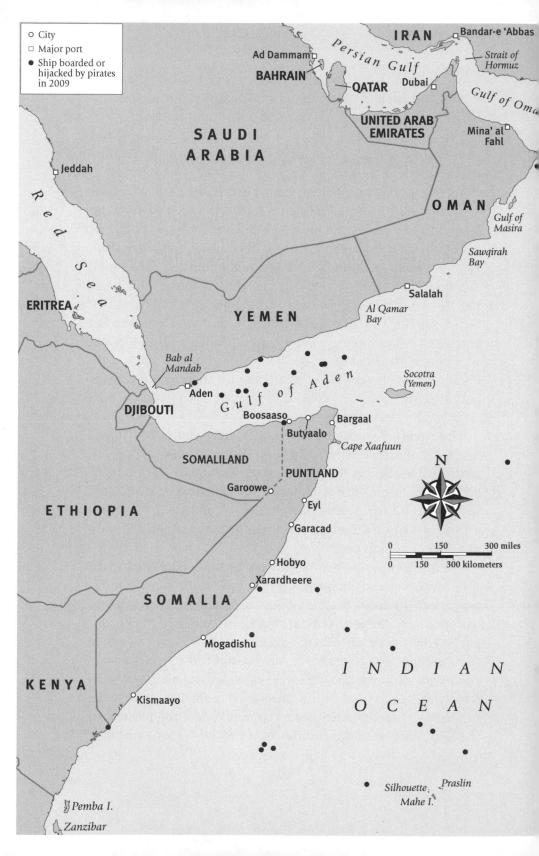

IRAN
Bandar-e 'Abbas
Persian Gulf
Strait of Hormuz
Ad Dammam
BAHRAIN
QATAR
Dubai
Gulf of Oma
UNITED ARAB
EMIRATES
Mina' al Fahl
SAUDI
ARABIA
Jeddah
OMAN
Gulf of Masira
Red Sea
Sawqirah Bay
ERITREA
YEMEN
Salalah
Al Qamar Bay
Bab al Mandab
Gulf of Aden
Socotra (Yemen)
Aden
DJIBOUTI
Boosaaso
Bargaal
Butyaalo
Cape Xaafuun
SOMALILAND
PUNTLAND
ETHIOPIA
Garoowe
Eyl
Garacad
N
Hobyo
Xarardheere
0   150   300 miles
0   150   300 kilometers
SOMALIA
Mogadishu
INDIAN
KENYA
OCEAN
Kismaayo
Silhouette   Praslin
Mahe I.
Pemba I.
Zanzibar

Council resolution started circulating that called on all countries with a stake in maritime safety to deploy naval ships and aircraft to tackle the piracy problem off the Somali coast. The resolution also called on military ships and aircraft to use all necessary means to stop acts of piracy. The resolution expressed grave concern about the proliferation of piracy against vessels off the coast of Somalia, noting that the incidents were becoming increasingly violent and being carried out with heavier weapons. Pirates were becoming more sophisticated, using mother ships and more strategic methods of attack, a clear indication of the worsening situation.

In addition, the resolution urged all states and regional organizations to continue taking appropriate action to protect convoys carrying supplies for the United Nations World Food Program, citing these efforts as vital to bring humanitarian assistance to as many as 2 million Somalis. Several ships carrying food were attacked, garnering more media coverage and further illustrating the dire nature of the problem. Delivery of food aid was suspended for several weeks. The French and Dutch navies started escorting food aid ships in 2007, shepherding them to the entrance of Mogadishu Harbor.

The final United Nations resolution did call on states and regional organizations to take action to protect shipping involved with the transportation and delivery of humanitarian aid to Somalia. In June 2008, the United Nations authorized countries, for a six-month period, to enter the territorial waters of Somalia and use all necessary means to stop piracy. On the legal front, several countries, including the United States and some members of the European Union, also eventually signed an agreement with Kenya, a neighbor of Somalia, to handle prosecutions of captured pirates. The step was necessary because of the difficulties some nations face in prosecuting pirates due to confusing laws, lack of laws regarding the problem, human rights concerns, and fears that pirates, if brought to homeland soil, might claim asylum.

The well-publicized attack on the U.S.-flagged *Maersk Alabama* in April 2009 prompted U.S. Secretary of State Hillary Clinton to introduce plans that included the prosecution and freezing of pirate assets. She outlined measures for shippers and insurers to improve antipiracy defenses. While the use of military force was not called for, the prospect of attacking the Somali pirate shore bases in accordance with United Nations authorization was. The incident also led to urgent meetings among members of the Contact Group on Piracy Off the Coast of Somalia. Members discussed a four-point plan regarding new strategies for securing the release of vessels and merchant mariners captured by pirates.

Just what is the Contact Group? According to a U.S. Department of State fact sheet released on May 18, 2009, the Contact Group was formed in January 2009 "in recognition of the growing impact of piracy on commercial shipping, humanitarian aid, and regional trade in the Horn of Africa." The United States and "its international partners" created the group as an "international cooperation mechanism against piracy, as called for in UN Security Council Resolution 1851." Twenty-eight nations and six international organizations participate in the Contact Group, which has as a primary objective the better coordination of states and organizations in a concerted response to combat the piracy problem.

Unsuccessful attacks on some large cruise ships further highlighted the seriousness of the piracy problem. Had the attacks succeeded it would have created a situation eerily similar to the Palestinian terrorist attack on the *Achille Lauro* in 1985. A ship full of passengers held hostage at the hands of ruthless pirates raises the specter of disaster. Fortunately, as of this writing, such an incident has not occurred. But the potential is there for it to happen, and it demonstrates just how dangerous piracy is for all who venture into waters where pirates are active.

As previously noted, Somali waters and the Gulf of Aden are

among the world's most important shipping lanes because vessels must pass through them to reach the Suez Canal via the Red Sea. Approximately 1,700 ships transit the Suez Canal every month, taking between twelve and eighteen hours to do so. A significant number of merchant vessels travel down from the Persian Gulf as well, many of which head through the Gulf of Aden into the Red Sea. These shipping lanes are significant from a strategic and national security perspective for the many nations depending on them for the movement of commodities such as oil.

The Suez Canal represents a major transit point for merchant ships sailing on voyages back and forth from Asia to Europe, eliminating the need to sail the long way around the Cape of Good Hope at the tip of Africa. The canal is 119 miles in length and starts at the town of Suez located in the south at the top of the Red Sea and it terminates at Port Said in the north at the Mediterranean Sea. The canal is owned and operated by the Egyptian state-owned Suez Canal Authority. The canal took eleven years and 30,000 workers to build, opening to ship traffic in 1869.

In 1956, Egyptian President Gamal Abdel Nasser nationalized the canal, sparking a crisis. The United Kingdom, France, and Israel took control of the canal for a period, citing international need for open and unfettered access to the waterway as the primary cause of the intervention. The Suez Crisis, as it is sometimes called, illustrates the importance of the Suez Canal to world commerce. Choking off or even reducing access to it represents a serious threat to the world economy.

In 2009, two major issues impacted the Suez Canal. The first was that some ships stopped using it and went the long way around the Cape of Good Hope in response to the piracy problems in the Red Sea and Gulf of Aden. The estimated cost for a tanker of maximum size for the Suez Canal to instead travel via the Cape of Good Hope was around $2 million, a significant cost to shipping companies. However, enough merchant shipowners were spending the extra money to use the longer route that it led to a steep decline in canal revenues for Egypt. This seriously impacted the Egyptian economy and its source of foreign exchange. Only tourism revenue and Egyptian overseas worker remittances were greater than Suez Canal revenue generated from ship transits, an indication of the canal's importance to Egypt.

The worldwide global downturn also heavily impacted the number of ships passing through the canal. In 2008, canal revenues exceeded $5.1 billion, but the latest available revenue forecasts predicted a drop to $4.5 billion in 2009 and $3.6 billion in 2010. Piracy, of course, only makes matters worse.

High Suez Canal transit fees also played a big part in shipping company calculations when deciding whether or not to use the canal or take the longer route. In the current economic environment, the high costs of a transit, which average about $250,000, are significant enough to make some shipowners think twice about paying. When bunker fuel prices and the increasing piracy insurance premiums (usually about $20,000 per transit) are factored in to the Suez Canal equation, then the long route becomes somewhat more economically viable. It is still more expensive, but there is a peace of mind dividend. Shipowners and ship crews worry less about piracy on the longer route, and owners aren't forced to buy piracy insurance in most cases.

With rising insurance rates came the economic downturn, which spurred a 90 percent drop in shipping rates. The lower return on a given voyage was also factored into the decision on which route to take. Many shipowners and maritime industry groups have been lobbying Egypt hard for a decrease in Suez Canal transit fees, and in 2009 Egypt agreed not to raise them above current levels. While some shipowners are indeed choosing the longer route, others are braving the pirates and paying to use the Suez Canal. However, many shippers warn that there will be a commercial impact on the consumers of

The guided missile destroyer USS *Cole* sits pier side in Valetta, Malta, March 9, 2009. The USS *Cole* was attacked by suicide bombers on October, 2, 2000 while it was in Aden Harbor, Yemen. Seventeen American sailors were killed. *U.S. Navy photo.*

The merchant vessel *Golden Nori* refuels with dock landing ship USS *Whidbey Island* in the Gulf of Aden, December 13, 2007. Somalia-based pirates seized the Panamanian-flagged vessel on October 28, 2007, holding the 23-man crew hostage in Somali territorial waters until December 12, 2007. *U.S. Navy photo.*

U.S. Navy sailors assigned to a rescue and assistance team provide humanitarian and medical assistance to the crew of the Taiwanese-flagged fishing trawler *Ching Fong Hwa* in the Indian Ocean, November 5, 2007. The vessel was seized by pirates off the coast of Somalia in May 2007 and was released November 5, 2007, with assistance from the U.S. Navy. *U.S. Navy photo.*

Crewmembers assemble on deck aboard a dhow suspected of piracy after being intercepted by the U.S. Navy destroyer USS *Winston Churchill*. *U.S. Navy photo.*

The Russian frigate RFS *Neustrashimyy* steams through the Baltic Sea during exercises supporting Baltic Operations (BALTOPS). BALTOPS is an annual international exercise involving 13 countries. *U.S. Navy photo.*

Maersk Alabama Captain Richard Phillips (right) stands alongside Commander Frank Castellano, commanding officer of USS *Bainbridge* after being rescued by U.S. Naval forces off the coast of Somalia. Captain Phillips was held hostage for five days by pirates. *U.S. Navy photo.*

The guided missile destroyer USS *Bainbridge* tows the lifeboat from the *Maersk Alabama* to the amphibious assault ship USS *Boxer*, in background, to be processed for evidence after the successful rescue of Captain Richard Phillips. Captain Phillips was held captive by suspected Somali pirates in a lifeboat in the Indian Ocean for five days after a failed hijacking attempt off the Somali coast. *U.S. Marine Corps photo.*

A team from the amphibious assault ship USS *Boxer* tows the lifeboat from the *Maersk Alabama* to *Boxer* to process evidence after the successful rescue of Captain Richard Phillips. *U.S. Navy photo.*

The *Maersk Alabama* leaves Mombasa, Kenya, April 21, 2009, after spending time in port after a pirate attack that took her captain hostage. *U.S. Navy photo.*

Pirates transit from MV *Faina* to the coast of Somalia, October 8, 2008, while under observation by a U.S. Navy ship. *Faina*, a Belize-flagged cargo ship, was attacked September 25, 2008, and forced to proceed to anchor off the coast of Somalia. *U.S. Navy photo.*

A montage of Somali pirates after their seizure of the MV *Faina* on September 25, 2008. *U.S. Navy photo.*

The U.S. Navy fleet ocean tug USNS *Catawba* provides fuel and fresh water to MV *Faina* following its release by Somali pirates February 5, 2009, after holding it for more than four months. The U.S. Navy remained within visual range of the ship and maintained a 24-hour, 7-days-a-week presence since it was captured. The Belize-flagged cargo ship is carrying a cargo of Ukrainian T-72 tanks and related equipment. The ship was attacked on September 25, 2008 and forced to proceed to anchorage off the Somali coast. *U.S. Navy photo.*

Sailors from the Norfolk-based destroyer USS *Mason* climb aboard MV *Faina* to conduct a health and comfort inspection of the crew as well as provide them with food, water, and medical support. *U.S. Navy photo.*

the materials that flow through the canal when the increased cost of doing business is passed on.

In mid-2009, East African shippers were hit with an increased piracy surcharge set at $25 per 20-foot container and double that for a 40-foot container on ships bound for the key East African port of Mombasa, in Kenya. These surcharges were expected to double in the relatively near future if the level of attacks kept increasing. This is yet another example of the adverse impacts of piracy on shipping companies.

The narrow entrance to the Red Sea, which obviously must be transited to reach the Suez Canal, is a natural choke point, making it an ideal place for pirates to strike. The total number of pirate attacks in the Gulf of Aden and off the eastern coast of Somalia in the first six months of 2009 exceeded the total for all of 2008, according to the International Maritime Bureau's Piracy Reporting Center. In all of 2008, there were 111 reported incidents of piracy in these waters, including forty-two vessels that were hijacked. In the first six months of 2009, there were 130 reported incidents of piracy, including twenty-nine vessels that were hijacked.

The Gulf of Aden saw a lot of action. In the first six months of 2009, there were seventy-one reported incidents of piracy, including seventeen vessels that were hijacked. In 2008, there were ninety-two reported attacks, and thirty-two of them resulted in the hijacking of the merchant vessels involved. The situation was no better off the eastern coast of Somalia during the first half of 2009, with forty-three reported attacks compared to nineteen in all of 2008. There has also been an increase in the number of vessels fired upon in these regions. In 2008, there were thirty-nine instances of vessels taking fire from pirates. In 2003, there were twenty-one reports of merchant ships that were fired upon.

As the naval presence increased in these waters, albeit at a slow pace and in low numbers considering the vast area in need of patrols (about one million square miles), successful hijackings decreased somewhat in some areas. Warships thwarted would-be hijackers through their presence, and through active disruption of attacks. By late 2009, there were an estimated twenty-five warships from the European Union, the United States, Turkey, Russia, India, and China patrolling in the Gulf of Aden and in adjacent Indian Ocean shipping routes.

Somali pirates reacted by changing their tactics. Part of that change involved (and still does involve) the investment of ransom money in better equipment. Flush with cash paid to them by shipping companies, pirate groups can afford to buy the best new attack boats equipped with powerful engines that can achieve high speeds for more effective strikes and greater range. These boats are also typically equipped with global positioning systems and other electronics. They are often towed behind or stowed aboard larger mother ships that roam the seas in search of targets, often more than 500 nautical miles off the coast. This has taken them away from the steadily increasing naval presence in the Gulf of Aden and made merchant vessel protection and pirate interdiction much more difficult. Almost immediately after a ransom is paid and the hijacked vessels are freed, new vessels are captured as the piracy crews rotate to the next operation.

Pirate groups can also afford to buy plenty of new AK-47 rifles and rocket-propelled grenade launchers, as well as ample stores of ammunition. They can afford to buy rocket-propelled grappling hooks to make boarding ships easier and faster. They can afford to buy and use satellite telephones to coordinate attacks and receive news of the movements of warships. In short, as the piracy problem worsened and more ships and crews were taken, more shipowners were forced to pay ransoms, directly funding the arming and equipping of the very pirates who were attacking their assets. At this writing, the problem has not been solved, putting shipowners in pirate-prone areas like Somali waters and the Gulf of Aden in a very difficult position.

7

Somali Pirates
and their Tactics

Somali pirates work in groups, much like gangs staking out territory within cities. It is estimated that there are ten primary groups of pirates operating in Somalia, with roughly 1,000 to 1,500 members total. Given that there were only an estimated one hundred pirates in Somalia in 2007, that is a massive growth in employment that most Western governments would envy.

The main organized piracy groups are the Somali Marines, the National Volunteer Coast Guard, the Marka Group, and the Puntland Group. The most powerful and influential of these groups is the Somali Marines led by the Somali warlord Abdi Mohamed Afweyne. The National Volunteer Coast Guard is based near the southern town of Kismayo and it was one of the first groups that started operations along the coast, hijacking foreign fishing vessels that were illegally fishing in Somali waters.

Each piracy mission is effectively a separate project or expedition. Each mission requires sponsors or investors prepared to put up the initial venture capital. This capital is required to fund the rental or purchase of the boat, and even the rental of a rocket-propelled grenade launcher and automatic rifles, usually AK-47s. Provisioning and fuel costs are also paid. Added together, the costs to mount a single pirate attack can exceed $10,000. The business model is quite similar to that of some pirate ventures in the distant past.

The financial backers are willing to wait weeks until a team is successful. If their pirates successfully capture a ship and crew and receive a ransom, then they typically receive about 30 percent of the total ransom. Naturally, if the pirates are caught or killed, the backers must foot the bill for all associated expenditures. Thirty percent of a ransom of $2 million (typical these days, but it's increasing) amounts to a payout of $600,000. That is an excellent return on a much smaller investment, which is why backers are easy to find. A typical ransom negotiation takes between six to eight weeks, though in one case the ordeal for the crew lasted ten months. The pirates can afford to wait, and haggle with shipowners over the amount of a ransom. Shipowners often cannot afford to wait, which improves the payout for pirates and their associates.

While the perception in some quarters is that pirate groups just grab any young Somali to join the pirate team, that perception is not entirely accurate. The investor wants to have a reasonable chance of success, so the personnel recruitment process is very important. Pirates are chosen based on their track record. They literally have a career path, working their way into and upward within a pirate group, again much like urban gangs. Young pirates must pay their dues, just like in the corporate world.

Pirates able to demonstrate that they know the ropes, so to speak, in particular those who have been first to board a ship, are in demand. The pirate making the first leap onto the deck of a ship always gets an extra share, typically around $5,000. The extra share is combat pay since being the first to board puts the pirate at risk of being shot, or sent hurtling overboard by a blast from a fire hose and possibly drowning as a result. The first pirate to board is largely responsible for the success of the attack in most cases because when he succeeds any nearby warships usually back off and most crews surrender without putting up any additional resistance.

A United Nations report based on a survey taken ashore in Somalia unearthed the following information on how ransom money is usually distributed. Again, this is quite similar to piracy of the distant past, where there was always a set formula for sharing the spoils of a successful attack. The pirates performing the attack and hijacking the ship receive 30 percent of the ransom, and the land-based militias controlling the shore where the pirates operate and hold the captured ships receive a share of 10 percent. The local community, which includes village clan leaders, elders, and local officials, receives 10 percent, piracy mission financiers receive 20 percent, and the mission sponsor receives 30 percent because he is taking the lion's share of the financial risk. The pirates aboard the ship equally share the cash they rob from the crew, and the first pirate aboard gets the bonus payment of a double share, as noted earlier. If a pirate is killed during the attack, the family of the man receives compensation.

Good public relations can win hearts and minds, and the pirates operating in Somalia know this all too well. One Somali pirate or pirate supporter called in to a talk show aired on a Somali radio station and claimed that the pirates were misunderstood and were just gentlemen who worked on the ocean. The caller stated that many patriots were risking their lives at sea while protecting Somalia's shores. He was quite irritated about all of the negative publicity appearing in the media as a result of the ship hijackings and the hostages being held for ransom. Quite often pirates use the media to ensure that their story is told while they simultaneously negotiate ransom payments with shipowners, hoping that they can influence the outcome. Media reports put pressure on shipowners to settle, and that's not lost on the pirates.

In some cases, pirates have taken strong exception to

being called pirates. One pirate, who claimed to be a spokesman for a pirate group known as the Ocean Salvation Corps, said that he and his men were exacting a tax for the many years that ships have poached fish in Somali waters. He also made an offer to embed journalists with his men to see how they operated. One can easily conjure up images of a CNN or BBC journalist in a skiff as it attacks a merchant ship. Some commentators have acknowledged that there is some truth in what the pirates say, and to some extent there is, or at least there was in the past when the attacks were in protest against illegal fishing. But the large number of hijackings and substantial ransom demands negate any claim that pirates are patriots, or even victims, and many pirates are perfectly willing to say that what they are doing is simply business and all about the money.

When the Somali government collapsed in 1991, there was a period when the waters off Somalia were illegally used as a dumping ground for European toxic industrial waste. It was reported that Italian fishing trawlers would bring down barrels of toxic waste and dump it overboard, and then start fishing, taking home very large catches of illegally caught Somali fish. Containers holding this toxic waste regularly wash up on the shores of Somalia, and regardless of which nation dumped them, they pose a hazard and show a disregard of Somalia's international rights. As noted earlier in this book, the illegal fishing by foreign countries has also violated those rights. So it is unsurprising that in some instances the pirates can grab the attention of the press, even if what they are after is money and nothing else.

Many in the shipping industry believe that a very powerful and influential syndicate of factional leaders and businessmen are at the apex of the Somali pirate business. These people are reputed to have operational bases in Kenya and the United Arab Emirates, although this is strenuously denied. A good proportion of the ransom payments are now thought to be funding drug and weapons smuggling operations, along with human trafficking. There have been allegations that the pirate operatives are also located in London and other financial centers. The hunt is on to locate and identify these people and freeze their assets.

The U.S. Treasury Department's Financial Crimes Enforcement Network has been active in tracking pirate money. It reportedly discovered a money trail linked to Somali and Emirati residents in Dubai. These individuals are thought to be active in arranging for the complex multi-bank transfers of ransom funds, which are rapidly disbursed through many financial institutions around the world. These middlemen also charge a sizeable commission before disbursing the pirate shares of the proceeds back into the *hawala*, the underground cash-based Islamic banking system. There are no written or electronic records for any investigators to follow up on within this system. In spite of requests for United Arab Emirates authorities to assist in tracking and shutting down these financiers, officials have evidently called for more substantial evidence before they will act.

Piracy in Somalia is a very well organized business, and some have correctly called it an industry. This industry is now supported by an extensive infrastructure that includes boatbuilders and repairers, suppliers of food and provisions, security and hostage guards, and a range of other service personnel estimated to number 10,000 to 15,000 people. There is even a boom in restaurants as entrepreneurs cater to pirates and captured crews. The potential to make large sums of money through piracy has resulted in a steadily increasing number of young, poor, and impoverished young Somali men wanting to join the various pirate groups.

The pirate activities within Somalia had a brief cessation in 2006 when the Islamic Courts Union was governing the country. The group seized power from the factional leaders in Mogadishu and quickly gained popular support, and it effectively restored law and order in most parts of Somalia. The total prohibition on piracy was strictly enforced, and the number of incidents dropped substantially.

Once the Islamic courts started to consolidate under militant control, the neighboring state of Ethiopia, along with U.S. support, intervened in December 2006 to oust the Islamic Courts Union. In its place was installed a very unpopular and secular transitional government, resulting in the rise of an Islamist insurgency in the capital of Mogadishu and throughout Somalia. Bloodshed and anarchy was widespread, and it allowed for the resurgence of the present-day piracy problem off Somalia's northern, semi-autonomous region of the Puntland coast.

The main pirate hubs include the fishing village of Eyl, once a sleepy place that has morphed into a boomtown. It's probably one of the busiest ports in Somalia. The villages of Xarardheere and Hobyo regularly host captured vessels. Many of the pirates are able to buy large luxury 4 x 4 vehicles, and there is also a building boom for new luxury homes and villas. The pirates enjoy ostentatious residences. There are also the supporting pirate intermediaries and accountants and various money managers who are busy arranging the ransom deals, and making money hand over fist.

One of the main operating ports is Boosaaso, and this port also serves as a hub for illegal migrant smuggling into the Middle East. The pirate ransom money appears to be trickling down to many levels that include local clans and militias, Islamist rebels, and those in the transitional government. Many Somali pirates are investing their ransom proceeds into the trafficking of a narcotic known as *khat*, along with a variety of other businesses. *Khat* is a mildly narcotic flowering plant indigenous to East Africa and the Arabian Peninsula. It evidently has its origins in Ethiopia, as does coffee. The *khat* users chew the fresh leaves to achieve a mild amphetamine-like high. Some of the business involves the importation of the *khat* leaf from Kenya.

Other pirate investment businesses include the lucrative

charcoal trade with the United Arab Emirates, mining and logging ventures, illegal fishing, and human trafficking. In true gang tradition, there are reports that pirates are also forcibly taking over many local businesses as well. Piracy is socially acceptable in the region, and that does little to discourage young pirates from getting into this prosperous business.

Even the love life of pirates has blossomed under the success of piracy operations. There are now very expensive and ostentatious weddings as pirates marry their second wives, usually the most beautiful women in the neighborhood. Wealthy pirates have attained near celebrity status. All the girls love a pirate in Somalia, if the pirate has money, that is. One local girl was quoted as saying that if she married a man who didn't have enough money, then he would not be able to organize a big wedding for her, and that a big wedding was every girl's dream. Only pirates can afford the luxury of a fabulous wedding, she said, adding that all the girls preferred to be married to pirates.

Piracy activities in some cases have helped resolve long running feuds, and have actually helped some clans to work together, but not everyone ashore is happy with the pirates. Some Somalis say that it is having a very negative local impact. The local economies are being flooded with U.S. dollars, and there is a significant rise in drug and alcohol abuse. It is a case of money equating power, and the pirates are exploiting their newly found influence and affluence.

However, a report indicating a backlash surfaced not long ago. It stated that one of the major pirate strongholds, the town of Hobyo, had been overrun and taken by the local militia. Reports also came out that locals in Hobyo weren't all supporters of the pirate gangs, and the resentment among the people of the pirates and their obvious wealth was fueling support for the Islamic militias. The militias are fighting the Somali central government and they control large areas of south and central Somalia. The pirates have been under considerable pressure by the Shebab, a major Islamic militant group, to disband and cease piracy operations. Whenever pirates have attempted to land in an area under the control of this militia, they have been threatened and chased back to sea. This situation poses a dilemma for Western governments. Whom do they support? Do they support the pirates or the militant Islamist militias? Both potentially pose a threat to global economic activity and also to regional security.

That brings us to another vexing question. Are the pirates really just pirates? Or are they something even more sinister? In May 2009, the Russian Navy captured a number of pirates, and some them were Iranian and Pakistani nationals. Were they terrorists disguised as pirates? That was never proven. There have been several reports that some of the ransom money is being diverted to Somali-based militant groups linked to al-Qaeda. And, not surprisingly, there are corrupt officials within the Somali government as well as Puntland authorities who are actively part of ongoing pirate operations and activities.

Piracy has been largely about money and it is generally believed that there is no overt political agenda behind it. The pirates have gone to great lengths to state this in the media. However, the U.S. government and many others remain unconvinced. After successful hostage rescue operations on the part of France and the United States that involved a number of pirates killed and captured, a new and hardened attitude emerged from the pirates, one not so far removed from terrorism. A pirate leader proclaimed that the French and the Americans would regret the killings. He stated that pirates previously did not kill hostages and only took ransoms. He also said this might change as a result of the pirate deaths. It seems the stakes have been raised for all concerned.

Somali pirate tactics

In the initial stages of the rise in piracy on large merchant ships operating in Somali waters and the Gulf of Aden, the various pirate groups used to attack vessels traveling relatively close to the coast. They used small skiffs equipped with powerful outboard motors or they used fishing vessels. The tactic was simply to drift in the heavy traffic routes, looking like innocent fishermen while the pirates waited for a ship to travel close by. When it did, they attacked. The tactic made sense because the chase would be relatively short. For the merchant ship crew, it was almost impossible to distinguish between fisherman and pirate. For the pirates, the stream of vessels meant targets were plentiful.

As the incidence of piracy increased, merchant ships moved farther offshore. Pirates did the same, extending their operational range significantly by using mother ships. The mother ships were larger vessels such as captured fishing boats, dhows, and traditional sailing vessels. The attack skiffs were hauled aboard and launched when required, or simply towed behind. Pirates used wooden or fiberglass boats with powerful outboard engines. The attack boats were very fast and also relatively difficult to detect on radar. In choppy seas, the boats became almost invisible in the wave troughs. The average loaded oil tanker or bulk carrier travels at around fifteen knots with little additional speed in reserve. A skiff with a 50 hp outboard motor travels at twenty-five knots or more. It was (and still is) easy for pirates to overtake a target. As mentioned in the previous chapter, pirates flush with cash from ransom payments can afford the best in boats and weapons.

Around five years ago, when the piracy epidemic was in its infancy, the International Maritime Organization advised ships to stay fifty nautical miles off Somalia's coast. As the pirates moved offshore, the IMO was forced to advise ships to stay even farther out. Ships are at risk 500 nautical miles offshore, due to the use of mother ships carrying pirate attack boats. There are cases where pirates have attacked even farther out than that. With the extended range through the use of mother ships, pirate attacks have occurred near the Seychelles, off the coast of Oman, and in the southern region of the Red Sea. Pirates have also started operating at night, a major change. Ships are now strongly urged to travel only within the designated Maritime Security Patrol Area, a supposed safe zone where naval patrols are most active. The MSPA is moveable. About half of the world's ship operators decided to exclude vessels from an area 600 nautical miles in width off the coast of Somalia.

Recent statistics indicate that 70 percent of the pirate attacks in the Gulf of Aden were launched against vessels that chose not to transit within the International Maritime Organization's recommended traffic corridor. Many of the crews on these ships failed to take recommended antipiracy measures, whereas among those that did some attacks were aborted. Thus, it appears that staying within the MSPA or other specified traffic zones is helpful, as is taking antipiracy measures and steaming ever farther offshore.

Unlike in the past, the ship's cargo isn't the main target. Pirates do not have the infrastructure to offload much of it. What pirates want is the ransom money, and that requires capturing the ship and crew. When pirates target a potential ship, they often use a VHF radio or satellite telephone to call ashore, providing their group leaders with the name of the ship, along with its International Maritime Organization number. Within minutes, the shore-based pirates can use the Internet to identify the owner of the ship and learn about specific details pertaining to the ship itself that are helpful in planning an attack.

When the pirates are ready to launch the attack, they approach a vessel in their small attack boats at high speeds while firing automatic weapons and rocket-propelled grenades directly at the bridge of a ship. This is naturally frightening for the merchant mariners aboard. Many captains surrender at this point. If he (or she) does not surrender, the pirates keep firing, and in many cases they use an aluminum boarding ladder to clamber up the side of the ship to board, or they use ropes with grappling hooks. In some cases, once a pirate is aboard, he lowers the Jacob's ladder (a ladder pilots use to climb up the side of ships and which is also located near lifeboats) to allow the remainder of the pirates to board. The typical attack lasts only fifteen or twenty minutes from start to finish, leaving the pirates in control of the ship and crew.

While it's an old one from the pirate handbook, another tactic is to issue false distress messages, so that a merchant vessel responds to an apparent yacht or fishing vessel in trouble. The pirates wait for the ship to come to them, and then they strike. Yet another tactic is to approach a merchant ship, intimidating the captain so he (or she) calls for naval support, drawing naval ships away from the real target. As the warships approach the decoy, other pirates attack merchant ships left unguarded.

Naval forces are well aware that the pirates are restricted in their operations during inclement weather, and ships are encouraged to use bad weather to best advantage. Ship captains are advised to plan a route off the eastern coast of Somalia to coincide with the start of the southwest monsoon. It gets windy and rough, which hinders pirates from attacking in small boats. Successful pirate attacks are much more difficult between the months of May and September, so, in effect, there is a piracy season in Somali waters and in the Gulf of Aden. It runs from October through April, ratcheting up and down in the monsoon transition periods.

Merchant ship captains can take a number of antipiracy measures before an attempt to board is made and while a boarding attempt is in progress. Obviously, if a pirate attack boat is observed, increasing speed and engaging in evasive maneuvers is the first step. Usually, the maneuvers entail sharp course changes to make boarding more difficult. Evasive maneuvers will buy time to call for help.

When an attack is clearly under way, most merchant ship

captains issue automatic safety distress alerts using the Global Maritime Distress and Safety System, so the situation is known immediately. They also call for assistance via the ship's VHF radio to alert any nearby warships on patrol. If pirates try to board, blasting them with high-pressure fire hoses has proven effective, though it can be dangerous for the individual doing the blasting. That individual could get wounded or killed, so this measure has its limitations and risks.

Most shipboard safety plans involve locking the ship accommodations, and retreating back to engine control rooms or other safe cabins. These measures have limited effects, though. As soon as pirates get into the bridge and take over the helm, capturing whoever is on the bridge, they will have effective control of the ship. Most shipping companies employ a policy of no resistance once pirates are aboard. In these situations, actual violence against crews is somewhat rare, although threats of violence are always made. Sadly, as the piracy problem continues to escalate in these waters, violence against merchant mariners has been on the increase.

8

Somali Pirate Attacks in 2009

The incidence of pirate attacks in Somali waters and the Gulf of Aden increased dramatically in the first six months of 2009 over totals for the previous year, in spite of added naval patrols and the establishment of traffic corridors, so-called safe zones. While many attacks resulted in the capture of the targeted merchant vessel and its crew, others were unsuccessful because the ship's captain engaged in evasive maneuvers and increased speed, or the crew was able to repel the boarders using a variety of measures, including blasting the pirates with high-pressure fire hoses. Military interventions also stopped attacks in progress or prevented them from happening at all. Below are some of the more notable incidents from that period.

January 2009

In January, there were at least seven reported attacks on merchant ships in Somali waters and in the Gulf of Aden.

On January 1, 2009, fifteen heavily armed pirates attacked, boarded, and captured the St. Kitts- and Nevis-flagged Egyptian general cargo ship *Blue Star*. Twenty-eight Egyptian crewmembers were aboard at the time. The ship was carrying

5,400 tons of urea fertilizer and was traveling east from the Bab al Mandab Strait, which joins the Red Sea and the Gulf of Aden. The ship was sailed to the Somali coast, where the pirates commenced ransom negotiations. One of the hostages reportedly was able to telephone his daughter, asking for help and saying that the pirates were mistreating the crew.

The mistreatment evidently started when the shipowner refused to pay the $6 million ransom. The ransom negotiation process was terminated and the shipowner stopped answering phone calls from the pirates. Claims were made that the shipowner didn't have the money to pay the ransom, and the Egyptian government said it wouldn't pay the ransom either. Nevertheless, the vessel was released on March 4 after a payment of a reported $1 million.

On January 3, pirates in four boats attacked the small Yemeni-owned coastal oil tanker *Sea Princess II*. The pirates boarded and took fifteen hostages. The ship was carrying 2,000 tons of diesel fuel to the disputed island of Socotra. When the tanker was seized it was near Jabal Al Kalb, off the Bir Ali coast. The ship was sailed to Eyl, on the Somali coast.

The ransom negotiations became complicated because three Somali businessmen from Yemen and Somalia owned the cargo of diesel, and because the shipowner left the ransom negotiations to them. They decided to dispatch an armed vessel, acting under the protection of a Letter of Marque issued by the former Puntland government. The last time a ship sailed with a Letter of Marque was probably more than a century ago. Essentially, a Letter of Marque converts a pirate ship into a privateer, granting government approval for its piratical operations. A treaty signed in 1856 and known as the Declaration of Paris prevents many nations from issuing Letters of Marque. Of course, Somalia is not one of those nations.

The privateers effectively steered the tanker down the coast into what were hostile waters for the pirates. The local clans in the area were in opposition to the clans that the pirates belonged to, so the intent was clear. The privateers ran out of fuel before any battle to take the tanker could be organized. The island of Socotra also ran out of fuel as a result of the hijacking. The island suffered electricity blackouts, as there was no fuel for the generators.

After this long and complex series of events, ransom negotiations with a new intermediary commenced. The pirates initially demanded a ransom of $8 million and threatened to execute the crew if the money was not quickly paid. A report emerged that the Somali pirates had executed one of the Indian crew and injured another, and the body of the dead sailor was thrown overboard. The pirates reduced the ransom to $2 million and the negotiations continued. Eventually, a settlement was reached and the tanker was released. The tanker came into Boosaaso Harbor to discharge its cargo and was then scheduled to head to Aden.

On January 29, pirates in a skiff approached the liquid petroleum gas tanker *Longchamp* while it was in transit between Europe and the Far East. Hamburg-based Bernhard Schulte Shipmanagement operated the vessel. The pirates chased the ship, opened fire, boarded, and captured the tanker, taking thirteen hostages. The crew consisted of twelve Filipinos and one Indonesian national. The ship was sailed to the Somali coast and ransom negotiations commenced.

This attack is noteworthy in part because of the cargo (the ship was essentially a giant bomb), and in part because the vessel was traveling in the designated safety corridor in a convoy under escort by an Indian warship when the attack occurred. The captain had delayed the transit through the area for sixteen hours to join the relative safety of a convoy. The attack was successful because the pirates staged decoy raids against two other vessels, diverting the warship and leaving *Longchamp* vulnerable. The ship was released after a ransom was air dropped to the hijackers. The initial ransom demand was for $6 million.

February 2009

In February, there were at least two reported attacks on merchant ships in Somali waters and in the Gulf of Aden.

On February 11, pirates released the Chinese fishing vessel *Tianyu No. 8*, which is owned by China's Tianjin Ocean Fishing Company. The fishing vessel was captured in November 2008 and was released after payment of a ransom. The pirates claimed that the vessel had been fishing illegally. They also sold off the catch, which consisted of fifty-three tons of tuna, twenty-five tons of lobster, and thirty-five tons of shark fins. Some reports indicated that there was illegal ivory aboard.

On February 22, the Greek-owned and Maltese-flagged ship *Saldanha* was attacked and captured while on a voyage carrying coal from Newcastle in Australia to Slovenia. Aboard was a crew of twenty-two, including nineteen Filipinos. The captain contacted a British naval vessel and informed it that his ship had been seized. The British warship *Northumberland* approached, but the pirates warned it off. The warship was also unable to pursue *Saldanha* under British rules of engagement, though a helicopter did fly over the ship. Later that day a skiff believed to have been used in the hijacking was found adrift. The boat contained a large amount of fuel, rocket-propelled grenades, cash, and a ladder. Naval forces used the skiff for target practice, sinking it. The crew of *Saldanha* was freed on April 25 after two months in captivity.

March 2009

In March, there were at least twenty-six reported attacks on merchant ships in Somali waters and in the Gulf of Aden.

On March 3, pirates in a skiff opened fire on the containership *Courier* with automatic weapons and a rocket-propelled grenade launcher. The captain activated antipiracy measures, increased speed, and took evasive action while also calling for help. A warship in the area scrambled an attack helicopter, which soon arrived at the scene and fired warning shots at the pirates. The pirates aborted the attack.

On March 10, the bulk carrier *Mar Reina* was attacked about 385 nautical miles southeast of Socotra Island. Pirates chased the ship in a skiff and opened fire with automatic weapons. The captain activated antipiracy measures and took evasive action. During the action the captain was shot, though he wasn't seriously wounded. The pirates aborted the attack.

On March 11, the oil tanker *Pro Alliance* was attacked by pirates armed with automatic weapons and a rocket-propelled grenade launcher. The pirates chased and opened fire on the tanker, which was carrying 100,000 tons of diesel oil from South Korea to Holland. The captain activated antipiracy measures, increased speed, and took evasive action, as well as calling for naval assistance from coalition warships.

The Yemeni Coast Guard responded. One of its ships stationed at the Ras Amran Advanced Antipiracy Center sailed forty-seven nautical miles to the scene. Two Yemeni Coast Guard officers were aboard the Korean tanker to provide security, as were French and Dutch security officials who had boarded at the port of Nashtoon. The Yemeni officers fired on the Somali pirates, killing one and injuring several others. One of the officers also shot and killed the pirate carrying the rocket-propelled grenade launcher. The pirates aborted the attack. The ship suffered slight damage, including shot-out lights and windows.

Also on March 11, which saw at least three attacks, the 9,000-ton general cargo ship *Chong Chon Gang* was traveling about 360 nautical miles southeast of Mogadishu, Somalia, when pirates in a skiff launched from a mother ship opened fire with automatic weapons and a rocket-propelled grenade launcher. The captain of the Korean vessel called for assistance, activated antipiracy measures, and took evasive action. One member of the crew was injured in the gunfire, though not seriously. The pirates aborted the attack.

On March 19, the Greek-owned bulk carrier *Titan* was attacked by a skiff with six pirates armed with AK-47 rifles and pistols. The ship was on a voyage from the Black Sea to Pusan, in South Korea, with a cargo of iron. The pirates boarded and captured the ship, taking twenty-four hostages. The ship was then sailed to the Somali coast and released in less than a month after the payment of a ransom.

On March 26, the Norwegian-owned, 23,000-ton chemical tanker *Bow Asir* was attacked and hijacked by sixteen to eighteen pirates armed with automatic weapons. The pirates approached in two skiffs, boarded, and captured the ship, taking twenty-seven hostages. The crew consisted of a Norwegian captain, nineteen Filipinos, five Poles, a Russian, and a Lithuanian.

The vessel was hijacked 380 nautical miles off the Somali port of Kismayo, while carrying a cargo of caustic soda. The pirates sailed the ship to Hobyo, Somalia, and ransom negotiations commenced. The shipowners agreed to pay the pirates a reported $2.4 million ransom. The ship was released on or about April 12. Later, it emerged that the Norwegian owners had not informed the European Union and international naval forces that the ship was transiting the area.

April 2009

In April, there were at least thirty-nine reported attacks on merchant ships in Somali waters and in the Gulf of Aden.

On April 6, the Hong Kong-flagged bulk carrier *Shanghai Venture* was in ballast on a passage to India to load coal when pirates armed with automatic weapons and a rocket-propelled grenade launcher attacked it. The pirate boat was initially seen on radar approaching at high speed. The pirates chased the ship and opened fire. The captain activated antipiracy measures and took evasive action, which involved zigzag course changes. Most of the crew locked themselves into the engine room and the bridge, while others pumped ballast water overboard to hinder the boarding attempt. It was estimated that more than ninety rounds were fired at the ship before the pirates aborted the attack. The ship was 248 miles from the nearest naval forces, so help was not available.

On the same day, pirates attacked, captured, and hijacked the 700-ton Taiwanese fishing vessel *Win Far 161* near the Seychelles, more than nine hundred miles from the Gulf of Aden. The Kaohsiung-registered vessel was later used as a mother ship, enabling the pirates to launch attacks on other fishing vessels in the area. The vessel was then taken to Somalia, with thirty hostages aboard, including two Taiwanese, five Chinese, seventeen Filipinos, and six Indonesians. Three other Taiwanese ships in the area that had first reported news of the hijacking took refuge in harbors in the Seychelles. The Taiwanese government contacted U.S. and British forces, requesting assistance. The Chinese Foreign Ministry informed the Taiwanese government that it would make every effort to rescue the ship and its crew, which was somewhat of a diplomatic coup for China.

The piracy incident created considerable political fallout, as Taiwanese lawmakers demanded that their own military intervene. Taiwan's Ministry of National Defense responded, saying that while it could protect Taiwanese fishing vessels, the long distance involved and the absence of diplomatic allies in the region made any efforts complicated. The opposition Democratic Progressive Party stated that the government was harming the public by its ineptitude. It further stated that several piracy incidents had occurred since 2005, and that the military should have been able to come up with a way to protect Taiwanese fishing crews from pirate attacks. Taiwan's deep-sea tuna fishing union called on all its members and one hundred fishing vessels operating in the Indian Ocean to use maximum caution. The Seychelles has been one of Taiwan's main fishing grounds for the last twenty years.

And yet another incident occurred on April 6. Pirates in two high-speed skiffs opened fire on the British-owned and Italian-operated, 32,000-ton bulk carrier *Malaspina Castle*. The pirates boarded and captured the ship, taking twenty-four hostages. The ship was sailed to Somalia and anchored near Eyl, in the Puntland region. In mid-May, the pirates received a $2 million ransom, delivered by a helicopter, and the vessel and crew was released.

The following day, April 7, pirates seized the U.S.-flagged containership *Maersk Alabama*, which will be covered in more detail in another chapter. Suffice it to say here that the attack made worldwide news and ended with the death of three pirates at the hands of U.S. Navy SEALs.

On April 10, pirates attacked and hijacked the Egyptian fishing vessels *Samarah Ahmed* and *Momtaz 1*. The combined total of both crews numbered thirty-four and included three minors on each vessel. The crews were detained for illegal fishing. The vessels reportedly did not have valid Indian Ocean Tuna Commission licenses, and the vessels were reported as confiscated. Later reports indicated that negotiations were ongoing with the owners and that the vessels were being held off Lasqorey village.

Months passed.

On August 12, the Egyptians rejected a $200,000 ransom demand. It seemed to the crews that they would remain prisoners forever. The next day the crew overpowered the pirates and killed two of them in a shootout. Apparently, the pirates were celebrating the payment of a $4 million ransom for the Italian tug *Buccaneer*, which had been held nearby. The five pirates that were guarding the fishing vessels and hostages were evidently drunk, and the fishermen seized the opportunity. The fishermen also captured several of the pirates, while one was stabbed and jumped overboard. Other pirates rescued their cohort in the water.

The crews escaped with their fishing vessels and sailed back to Egypt with their prisoners after enduring four months in captivity. This was an unusual case in that the crews successfully freed themselves from a Somali pirate stronghold without assistance from outside forces or the payment of a hefty ransom.

The aforementioned oceangoing, 250-foot, Italian tug *Buccaneer* was captured the day after the two Egyptian fishing vessels, on April 11. When the tug came under attack, the captain immediately sent a distress call, which a Spanish warship, *Corte-Real*, received. The transmission was terminated after only six minutes.

The tug was attacked while it was towing two 328-foot barges, making it difficult to maneuver effectively to evade the pirates. It took just five minutes for the pirates to board and seize the tug. The shipowners received an e-mail notifying them of the capture of their tug and the crew. The crew consisted of ten Italians, one Croatian, and five Romanians. The tug was taken to Lasqorey village, where ransom negotiations commenced.

The Somali pirates claimed that the barges the tug was towing were loaded with toxic waste, though the Italians strongly denied it. The Italian naval vessel *Maestrale* arrived at the scene of the seizure about two days later. The warship was part of the European Union antipirate mission Atalanta, and there were three Italian frigates involved in the operation. The living conditions on the tug soon degenerated into outright squalor, with several of the crew falling ill. All suffered from mental trauma and depression due to the terrifying events. One of the crew had a heart condition and was low on medication. The five Romanians were taken ashore and held in various locations to prevent any rescue attempts by Italy's Special Forces.

Food ran short, forcing the crew to subsist on rice and bread. Fresh water ran out. Provisions were reportedly sent from Djibouti, but despite assurances that the supplies had arrived at the ship, none ever made it on board. The pirates frequently made the crew stay on the sweltering bridge of the tug, where temperatures hovered at around 105°F. The pirates became exasperated with the lack of progress in ransom negotiations and frequently fired weapons to frighten the crew.

It was stated that there were no ongoing negotiations for the release of the tug and crew, and the captain pleaded for someone to open them. When negotiations did start, an argument broke out among the pirates. A faction that wanted to get a faster but smaller ransom settlement got into a heated exchange with other factions that wanted to milk the seizure for every possible dollar. The heated dispute ended up with one of the pirates shooting another pirate dead with his AK-47 rifle.

In response to this incident, the Italian Senate approved a new emergency piracy law that gave Italy's courts the jurisdiction to try any captured pirates. The Italian and Somali governments, Puntland authorities, and the shipowners continued to negotiate for the release of the tug and crew, which finally happened on August 10. Some reports indicated that no ransom was paid, while other more believable reports indicated that a ransom of roughly $4 million was paid. It was fortuitous indeed for those Egyptian fishing crews, who escaped three days later while the pirates were drunk in celebration of the payment.

On April 14, the U.S.-flagged bulk carrier *Liberty Sun* was attacked by four pirates in a white aluminum skiff. Two of the pirates were armed with AK-47s and the other two were armed with rocket-propelled grenade launchers. A pirate mother ship was observed nearby. The 738-foot bulk carrier was on a passage from Houston, Texas, to Mombasa, Kenya, carrying American food aid for famine-stricken African countries. The cargo consisted of 47,000 tons of bagged corn, corn soya, wheat flour, lentils, yellow peas, and cartons of vegetable oil.

The pirates opened fire on *Liberty Sun* with their rifles and rocket-propelled grenade launchers. The ship's captain increased speed and took evasive action. A rocket-propelled grenade pierced a bulkhead and exploded on the bridge, causing extensive damage and blowing out windows. A small fire started, but it was quickly extinguished. None of the crew was wounded. Indeed, most of them had locked themselves in the engine room. A short time later, the pirates aborted the attack. Not long after the attack, the pirates involved issued a chilling statement, saying that they intended to destroy *Liberty Sun* because of the pirate deaths that resulted from the *Maersk Alabama* incident, which had just been resolved through the use of deadly force.

On April 26, the Yemeni oil tanker *Qana* was attacked and seized by pirates ten nautical miles off the Yemeni coast. The empty oil tanker was on its way back to Aden after discharging its cargo at the eastern port of Mohra. The incident is noteworthy for several reasons, chief among them that no other pirate attack to date had taken place any closer to Yemen. Another is the response from Yemen.

The Yemeni military swung into action. Special Forces were dispatched and attacked the pirates aboard *Qana*, killing five, wounding two, and capturing eleven in a two-day operation. Five of the ship's crew, including one Indian, sustained wounds in the fighting. The operation was notable in that it was the first combined sea and airborne attack on pirates mounted by Yemeni forces. Late April was a busy one for the Yemeni military. On April 26, it also liberated three other small vessels that had been captured at the same time, killing two pirates and capturing four others, while two members of the Yemeni Coast Guard were wounded.

May through June 2009

The attacks highlighted in the earlier months of 2009, especially in April, illustrate the extent of the piracy problem in Somali waters and the Gulf of Aden. They also show how piracy spread to more distant waters, out to 500 nautical miles off the Somali coast and beyond, all the way to the Seychelles. In subsequent months, pirates remained active, plaguing shipping, shooting indiscriminately at sailors, and taking hostages.

In May, the naval presence in these waters had increased to the point where it was forcing pirates to abort attacks in greater numbers as well as forcing them to attack farther offshore. In at least thirteen cases in May, intervention on the part of naval forces stopped attacks in progress. In at least twelve other cases in May, the antipiracy measures taken by the crew stopped attacks in progress. Not every crew was so lucky.

On May 2, pirates attacked, boarded, and hijacked the Greek-owned cargo ship *Ariana*, taking twenty-four hostages. The ship and its Ukrainian crew were on a passage from Brazil to Iran with a cargo of 35,000 tons of soya. The attack occurred at night, quite unusual, north of the Seychelles and roughly one thousand nautical miles from any naval forces.

As usual, ransom negotiations began between the shipowners and the pirates. Some media reports at the time indicated that the pirates were torturing the crew, but these reports turned out to be false. However, there was one incident where a crewmember fought with one of the pirates. During the ransom negotiations the pirates allowed ten of the crew to phone home and encouraged them to speak of their physical problems, execution threats, and the lack of fresh water, fuel, and food to get the families to exert pressure on the owners and the Ukrainian government to pay up.

The Ukrainian government was reported as instructing its foreign ministry to take all necessary measures to facilitate the release of the crew, but it seems they had learned very little from the *Faina* incident, which will be discussed in another chapter. In true bureaucratic style, the Ukrainian Foreign Ministry instructed its first deputy prime minister to set up an operational headquarters to study the situation and to create an action plan for the rescue of the Ukrainian sailors. The staff then issued instructions to the Ukrainian Foreign Intelligence Service, Military Intelligence, the Security Service, and other security agencies, along with the Ministry of Transport and Communications and the Ministry of Foreign Affairs, to help set up the headquarters. Meanwhile, the crew waited for the negotiations to end and the ransom to be paid.

On May 5, the German-owned and Antigua- and Barbuda-flagged general cargo vessel *Victoria* was attacked and hijacked seventy-five nautical miles south of Yemen by eight armed pirates. The vessel was on a voyage to the Red Sea port of Jeddah from India with a cargo of 10,000 tons of rice. When the attack occurred, the ship was traveling within the designated security corridor. The vessel had a crew of eleven Romanians, including a female deck officer. She was serving on the vessel with her father, the chief engineer.

The ship was taken to Eyl, where ransom negotiations commenced. The ship was finally released on July 17 after a ransom payment of $1.8 million was delivered to the ship via a tugboat. The pirates celebrated the delivery of the money by firing their guns into the air, as roughly forty pirates received their share of the loot.

On May 11, the Netherlands Antilles-flagged general cargo vessel *Marathon* was attacked and captured by pirates. The vessel had a crew of eight aboard, and was transiting in a convoy with three other ships. The ship was carrying a cargo of coke. As the vessel had a very low freeboard of less than six feet, it was extremely easy for pirates to climb aboard. One of the crew was wounded and the second engineer was killed when the pirates fired indiscriminately into the cargo hold where the crew was being held.

After the initial hijacking, a Spanish and a Dutch warship arrived at the scene. In one incident, a Somali pirate fell into the water and was subsequently captured, but the circumstances are otherwise unclear. A local boat also attempted to ferry supplies to the ship. However, Spanish commandos intercepted the boat and turned it back. The Sailors' Society

Ukrainian port chaplain was reported as supporting the dead man's widow. The Dutch Defense Ministry was heavily criticized and accused of lying about the death of the seaman, after repeatedly denying what had happened. The vessel was released nearly two months later when a ransom payment of $1.3 million was dropped to the ship via a helicopter.

In June, there were fourteen cases where pirates fired on merchant ships, but aborted the attacks when antipiracy measures were taken and naval forces were alerted. Not all cases were resolved in that manner, though.

Perhaps the unluckiest crew up to that time finally did get a break on June 5 when Somali pirates released the Nigerian tugboat *Yenegoa Ocean*. Pirates had held its ten Nigerian crew as prisoners for ten months, marking the longest period of captivity up to that time. The ship was released off the coast of Caluula, in northeast Somalia. Details regarding the circumstances surrounding the release and the amount of the ransom payment remain unclear, although one report stated that friends and relatives of the hostages had raised $43,000 to free their loved ones. The pirates had initially demanded $1 million and they threatened to execute the crew if the money was not paid. The shipowners didn't have the money, and the Nigerian government failed to respond in any meaningful way, so the crew remained prisoners.

Ultimately, the pirates settled for what they could get after nearly a year of negotiations. It was said that the cost of feeding the crew wore the pirates down. The vessel was attacked and hijacked on August 4, 2008, while returning from Singapore to Nigeria, where it had undergone some repairs. The *Yenagoa Ocean* had berthed in Mogadishu, Somalia, to get medical attention for some of crew when pirates stormed the ship and seized it.

The pirates who seized *Yenagoa Ocean* were members of the Siwaqron clan, and held the ship and crew in the port of Habo in the northern Puntland region. While the pirates held

116

the tug, it reportedly was used as a mother ship and was involved in an attack on a bulk carrier on August 23, 2008, about sixty-eight nautical miles southeast of Al Mukalla, in Yemen. In January 2009, *Yenegoa Ocean* was also reported as being the scene of a gun battle between the pirates who were holding it, and reportedly four pirates died in this incident. The vessel had been shifted from Hawo to Caluula to facilitate the receipt of a ransom, and the negotiations resulted in an argument that quickly escalated into a firefight among the pirates. Following the release of the ship marines from the Dutch naval vessel *De Zeven Provincien* boarded to render assistance. They found one person in need of medical attention. The naval vessel escorted the tug at low speed to a safe port in Yemen.

On June 12, the Antigua- and Barbuda-flagged, German-owned cargo vessel *Charelle* was attacked and hijacked by eight pirates inside the territorial waters of Oman. Reports indicated that the ship was set afire during the attack, but the fire, if it occurred, was extinguished. The attack was unprecedented and marked the first time that armed pirates had attacked a ship off the coast of Oman. The attack occurred only sixty nautical miles southeast of Muscat. The pirates were evidently operating from a mother ship and were using night-vision equipment.

The ship's captain transmitted a distress call, which was acknowledged by the large supertanker *Eli Maersk* that was in the vicinity. The crew of *Eli Maersk* had been commended in 2005 when they rescued thirty-nine refugees from a drifting vessel in the Gulf of Aden. The crew of *Charelle* consisted of three Filipinos and seven Sri Lankan nationals, who were held hostage as the pirates sailed the ship through heavy seas to Eyl. Two warships, one from the Omani Navy, followed the vessel but kept a good distance off. When the vessel arrived at Eyl, ransom negotiations commenced.

This particular hijacking was seen as yet another escalation and expansion of the piracy problem because it marked the first time piracy had spread to the politically and militarily sensitive Persian Gulf region. At that time, pirates were holding fourteen ships and more than two hundred merchant mariners in the Gulf of Aden. Twenty-five percent of the hostages were Filipinos.

9

Piracy Worldwide

Piracy ebbs and flows like the tide. It is fluid, moving from one place to the next as social, political, and economic unrest throws nations into chaos and creates an environment where piracy can flourish. As stability returns to a given region, piracy tends to decrease. When military force is used effectively to combat pirates, piracy also decreases, just as it has for centuries. The Horn of Africa is the most significant hot zone for piracy today, but pirates are active elsewhere as well and have been for quite some time. Below are the regions where pirates are most active and where merchant mariners remain in danger whenever they venture into these pirate-infested waters.

Nigeria

Nigeria is and has long been a hotbed for piratical activities, often ranking as the top piracy location in the world. This may surprise some readers, but the fact is Nigeria rivals Somalia in the proliferation of piracy attacks in recent years. As is the case with Somalia, pirate attacks are on the increase in Nigerian waters, and a significant number of the attacks involve violence against merchant mariners. Guerilla groups as well as pirates are playing a role in the escalation of violence. Interestingly, a significant number of incidents are not reported.

There were fifty attacks reported in Nigeria in 2008, but the actual number is estimated at one hundred fifty or more.

The Niger Delta is the base for the largest oil industry in Africa and is the center of oil production, with daily exports of 2.1 million barrels of oil per day and more than 3,500 oil and gas installations. A member of OPEC, Nigeria is the eighth largest exporter of crude oil in the world. The Niger Delta may be rich in oil, but it is also an excellent place from which to operate, if you're a pirate. There are plenty of places to hide within the 45,000 square miles of mangrove swamps, inlets, and bays.

Nigeria is riddled with crime, and many say the government is corrupt, fostering an environment where piracy can easily thrive. Abductions for ransom are a severe problem. Approximately two hundred foreign nationals were kidnapped between 2006 and 2009, the majority of whom were released unharmed after the payment of a ransom.

The militants behind the kidnappings claim they are fighting for a more equitable share of Nigerian oil wealth. They have resorted to blowing up oil pipelines and to the kidnapping of oil workers, hitting Nigerian oil production hard. Armed robberies and crude oil smuggling are also common.

The oil industry and related shipping are the usual targets for pirates. In recent years, the piracy problem has become so bad that various unions serving merchant mariners have undertaken a campaign to have Nigeria recognized as war zone. The unions are lobbying for combat pay for their members while operating in or traveling through Nigerian waters. Shipowners and operators have fiercely resisted these efforts, which isn't much of a surprise. Many pirate attacks occur in the Lagos anchorage, where the pirates board vessels and often assault the crew before stealing supplies, personal effects, and other items. The following is a sample of incidents that occurred in Nigerian waters in 2009.

In January, pirates hit four oil service supply ships in separate attacks in the channel leading to Nigeria's largest oil and gas export complex on Bonny Island. The attacks caused injuries to the crews, though none of the vessels were actually boarded. Bonny Island is the export point for approximately 400,000 barrels of crude oil per day and eighteen million tons of liquefied natural gas per year, so it is very important. The ships involved in the attacks were there to provide supplies for workers on oil platforms, oil production vessels, and oil drilling rigs offshore. These types of ships are generally working under contracts from major oil companies, and the crews usually include a mix of foreign nationals and Nigerians.

Also in January, ten robbers armed with guns and knives boarded the chemical tanker *Samho Cordelia* while it was at anchor. The bandits assaulted the captain and stole cash and personal effects before escaping. In another attack that month, the Norwegian cable-laying ship *Viking Forcados* was attacked, but none of the crew of fifty-two were injured. Pirates in five speedboats also attacked the fast supply intervention vessel *Bourbon Leda* while it was traveling to the Royal Dutch Shell offshore Bonga oilfield, and militants launched an attack in the Bonny River on a supply vessel that was headed to the Mystras platform. Three of the crew were shot and wounded.

In February, a security vessel was attacked in an oilfield operated by the Canadian company Addax Petroleum. The pirates attacked in two boats early in the morning off the southern Nigerian state of Akwa Ibom. The ship's captain was killed and another mariner was wounded during the attack.

Also in February, five armed pirates aboard a fishing vessel attacked the Russian oil tanker *Khatanga* about twenty miles off the coast. They opened fire using automatic weapons. Most of the crew sheltered in the engine room while the officers on the bridge increased speed and executed evasive maneuvers. The pirates chased the ship for an hour before aborting the

121

attack. The tanker was transporting oil between two Nigerian ports at the time.

In March, robbers armed with guns, knives, and iron bars boarded the oil tanker *Emirates Swan* in the Lagos anchorage. They savagely assaulted the crew, seriously injuring the captain and one of the sailors. Robbers also attacked the chemical tanker *Simon* while it was at anchor. As the crew looked on, a boat with several men armed with automatic weapons, rocket-propelled grenade launchers, and machetes pulled alongside and attempted to board using ropes. The crew raised the alarm and the robbers aborted the attack.

In April, eight masked pirates in a fast boat attacked the Turkish tanker *Aleyna Mercan*. They opened fire and boarded the ship, ordering the crew to stop the main propulsion engine and to shut down the satellite communications system as another boat carrying two more pirates came alongside. They took the chief officer hostage and stole the ship's cash and personal effects from the crew. When they were done with the thieving, the pirates kidnapped the captain and chief engineer, whom they released two days later.

Also in April, two boats with eleven robbers aboard attacked the bulk carrier *Aristeas* while it was alongside at Tincan Island in the port of Lagos. They were armed with machetes and climbed aboard using ropes and grappling hooks. Once the robbers were aboard, they broke into the ship's storeroom and stole some supplies. The ship's duty officer raised the alarm and the crew mustered, and a short standoff ensued, with the robbers threatening the crew with machetes before making good their escape.

In June, the Turkish bulk carrier *Duden* was attacked by armed men at the Lagos outer anchorage. The robbers tried to board using ropes and grappling hooks. As the crew attempted to repel the attack, the robbers opened fire with automatic weapons, injuring three sailors.

In July, the principal Nigerian militant group, the Movement for the Emancipation of the Niger Delta, claimed responsibility for the sabotage of the Chevron Okan oil manifold. They also said they were behind the attack on the Singapore-flagged chemical tanker *MT Siehem Peace* and the kidnapping of six of its crew, three Russians, two Filipinos, and one Indian national. The tanker was taken twenty nautical miles off the coast of Escravos in the Niger Delta, and the hostages were taken ashore. They were released two weeks later.

In August, pirates attached the Lithuanian refrigerated cargo vessel *Saturn* off the Nigerian coast while it was waiting to discharge cargo. The attackers kidnapped the Lithuanian crew, but later released the five sailors unharmed.

East Africa

Various other locations in East Africa besides Somalia and the Gulf of Aden have experienced piracy and armed robbery events over the years. Most notable is the port of Dar es Salaam and capital of Tanzania, a place I have traveled to several times.

On April 9, 2009, the Singapore-registered containership *Ludwig Schulte* was attacked at the Dar es Salaam anchorage. Members of the crew were on watch, knowing the port was prone to robberies, and, sure enough, a group of robbers boarded and managed to steal and then throw one of the ship's life rafts into the sea. The crew raised the alarm, but the bandits retreated and no attempt was made to recover the raft.

On April 21, 2009, the Danish-registered chemical tanker *Gotland Carolina* was attacked in the Dar es Salaam anchorage. The watchkeeper on duty observed a boat on the port side and raised the alarm. Ten thieves were seen on the poop deck. They subsequently jumped overboard and escaped. Investigations revealed that they had successfully broken into the ship storerooms by cutting off padlocks. Some supplies were stolen.

In 2008, pirates attacked the Hong Kong-flagged container-

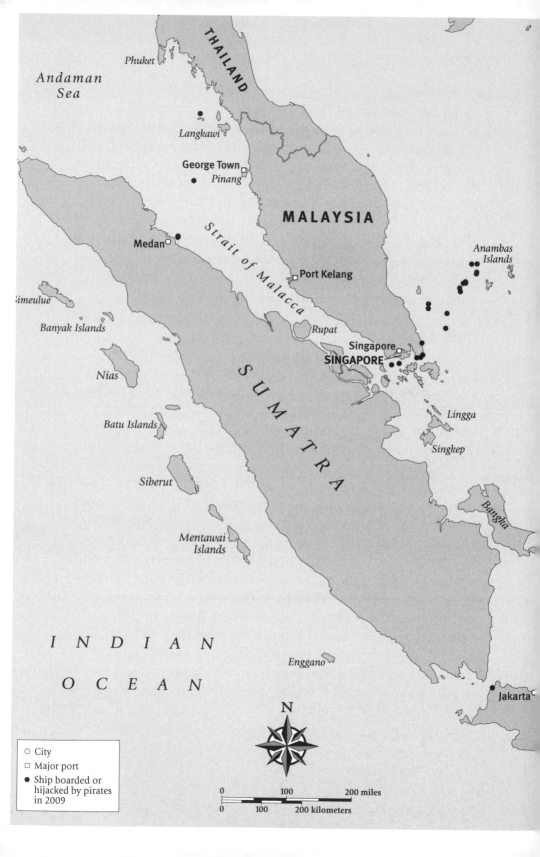

THAILAND

Phuket

Andaman
Sea

Langkawi

George Town
Pinang

MALAYSIA

Medan

Strait of Malacca

Port Kelang

Anambas
Islands

Simeulue

Banyak Islands

Rupat

Nias

S U M A T R A

Singapore
SINGAPORE

Batu Islands

Lingga

Singkep

Siberut

Bangka

Mentawai
Islands

I N D I A N

Enggano

O C E A N

Jakarta

N

○ City
□ Major port
● Ship boarded or
   hijacked by pirates
   in 2009

| 0 | 100 | 200 miles |

| 0 | 100 | 200 kilometers |

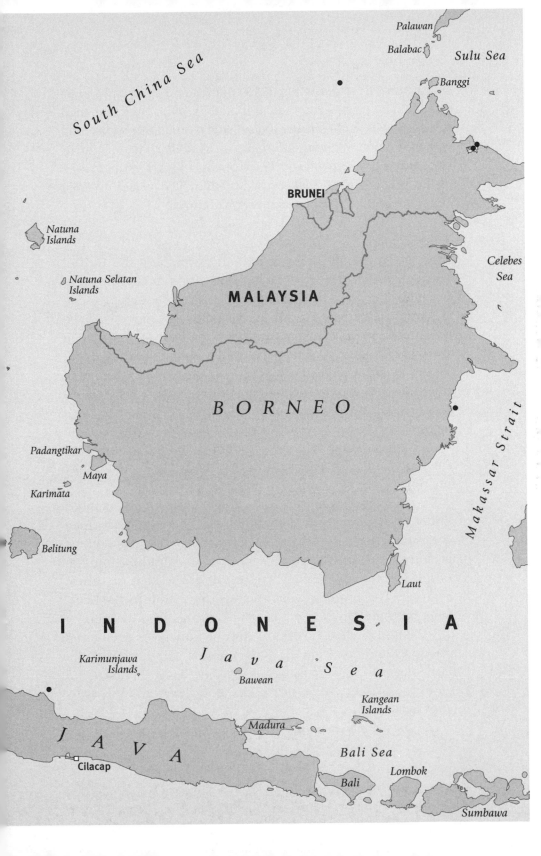

ship *Maersk Regensburg* about 350 nautical miles east of Dar es Salaam. The pirates were using a mother ship. They launched two skiffs with eight pirates aboard, and opened fire on the ship with automatic weapons and rocket-propelled grenade launchers, setting the ship ablaze. The fire was quickly extinguished as the ship's captain took evasive action. The vessel escaped and none of the crew of nineteen was injured.

Asia

Prior to the rise of piracy in Somali waters and the Gulf of Aden, piracy in Asia was a major and longstanding problem. The hot zones were in the Malacca Straits off Indonesia and in the South China Sea. The Malacca Straits are a narrow waterway about 550 miles in length and are the busiest sea route in the world, linking Europe to the major Asian exporting countries of Japan, China, Hong Kong, Taiwan, India, Korea, and other emerging Asian economies. Approximately 50,000 ships pass through it each year, or roughly 600 per day. The strait carries 25 percent of world commerce and around half the world's oil, or roughly eleven million barrels of oil per day! The thousands of nearby islands and many rivers that empty into the straits create an ideal place for pirates to hide.

The Malacca Straits were once home to the infamous Bugis pirates, who came from South Sulawesi. The word bogeyman (Bugisman) derives from the Bugis. Evidently, British mothers in Singapore used to frighten mischievous children into behaving correctly by saying, "Watch out or the bogeyman will get you!" The orang laut pirates also operated in the area, along with the Malay and Sea Dayak pirates from Borneo. In July 2009, a German treasure hunter and diver recovered around $12 million from the sunken pirate ship *Forbes* off the Borneo coast. The ship sank in 1806. The booty totaled about 1.5 tons of silver coins, porcelain, gold jewelry, and many other items.

The piracy problem in the Malacca Straits created quite a

fuss, which isn't surprising given the vital importance of these waters. As the attacks ramped up in recent years, the governments of Singapore, Malaysia, and Indonesia took decisive action, sending naval vessels and aircraft to aggressively patrol the area. Thailand also joined the patrol program, and provided cover for the northern part of the straits and out into the Andaman Sea. The coordinated air and sea patrols significantly reduced the number of pirate attacks, most notably near Aceh, in Indonesia. The tsunami that devastated the area in December 2004 also reduced the number of pirate attacks, killing many pirates and destroying their boats.

The waters around the Philippines in the South China Sea have always been a traditional haven for pirates. However, as with the Malacca Straits, increased air and sea patrols has markedly decreased the number of pirate attacks. The Philippine Coast Guard has reported only two piracy incidents within Philippine waters since 2005, both occurring near the southern island of Mindanao. The most notorious areas in the Asian region are said to be the ports, islands, and anchorages off Indonesia, India, and Vietnam. Between 1980 and 1985, the United Nations reported that pirates had raped an estimated 2,283 women and had kidnapped 592 people, preying upon the Vietnamese boat people that were headed south at that time.

In 2005, Lloyd's of London listed the Malacca Straits as the world's leading piracy hot zone, which resulted in the levying of large insurance premiums amounting to one percent of the value of any cargo transiting the straits. Obviously, the move fanned controversy and anger among shipping companies. Patrols were increased in 2006 as attacks soared both in the Malacca Straits and near the Indonesian island of Sumatra. At this time, the pirates were also becoming more sophisticated and arming themselves with automatic weapons and rocket-propelled grenade launchers. In August 2006, following a marked decrease in the number of pirate attacks, Lloyd's removed the region from its war-risk insurance category.

The number of reported attacks in the Malacca Straits rose from just two in 1999 to seventy-five in 2000. In 2004, there were thirty-eight attacks. The number dropped to just eleven in 2006, to just seven in 2007, and to just two in 2008. However, there are fears in the region that an increase in pirate activity is possible due to the global economic crisis. It was stated that joint counter-piracy operations would continue between Indonesia, Thailand, and Singapore. During the 1997 economic crisis piracy spiraled within the straits.

By the end of June 2009, matters began to change. While any incidents that did occur generally involved robbing ships at anchor, there was a slight increase in incidents that occurred when ships were under way in the Malacca Straits and in the South China Sea. The theft of cash and personal property in these attacks shifted to somewhat more of an emphasis on stealing ship's stores and equipment. Attacks on tugs started to increase, and this was pronounced in Vietnamese waters, in particular at the anchorages of Ho Chi Minh City and Vung Tau. The level of violence also increased, with hostages being taken.

The following accounts of piracy and robbery incidents represent only a small sample of those that have occurred in Asian waters. There are literally hundreds of incidents involving attacks on ships at anchor, while alongside at a berth, or while under way in international and territorial waters. Many attacks involved extreme violence, murder, and the theft of cargoes.

Asian piracy in 2009

On February 16, Malaysian police commandos gave chase to a 24-foot boat loaded with Indonesian pirates, who threw explosives at the six commandos. The commandos returned fire with M-16 rifles. One of the suspects was shot in the hip. The action occurred after pirates attempted to board a cargo ship at night and the ship's captain fired a red flare, hoping to deter the attack. It was then that the pirates noticed the police boat rushing to the scene. The pirates aborted the attack and headed at high speed back toward Indonesia, dumping masks, ladders, and ropes overboard. The pirates were taken into custody and one was hospitalized in Johor.

On February 19, the Singaporean tug *MLC-Nancy 5*, was towing the barge *Miclyn 3316*, when the tug and barge was attacked by twelve armed pirates in daylight in the northern part of the Strait of Malacca.

On April 1, five pirates armed with machetes attacked the Indonesian tug *Terus Daya 23* in the South China Sea off Pulau Aur. The tug was towing a barge at the time. The pirates stole cash and personal effects from the crew before escaping.

On April 7, twelve pirates armed with guns and machetes attacked the Singaporean tug *Prospaq T1* in the South China Sea, close to the Philippines. The tug was on a passage from Singapore to Vietnam, and was towing a very large but empty barge, *Prospaq B1*. The pirates boarded the tug and took the crew of ten as hostages, blindfolding and tying them up using masking tape. They then hijacked both the tug and barge.

The pirates ordered the crew to launch and enter the tug's lifeboat, which they did, and the pirates took off with the tug. The crew was set adrift without food or water. The container-ship *ANL Explorer* rescued the crew a week later and took them to Manila. The crew consisted of six Indonesians, a Malaysian, and three Myanmar nationals. They were said to be hungry and exhausted, but were physically fit.

On April 11, the Malaysian tug *Astaka* was attacked in the South China Sea off Can Tho, in Vietnam. Three hooded pirates armed with guns boarded the tug while it was towing two barges, one loaded with gravel. The pirates took four of the crew as hostages, tied their hands, and blindfolded them before locking them in the captain's cabin. These four individuals managed to free themselves, but the other seven members of the crew were missing. Fearing the worst, they abandoned

129

the vessel and reached shore in a life raft after two hours and raised the alarm with Vietnamese authorities. The tug was discovered ablaze in Can Tho coastal waters. The barge was later located with its cargo off Con Dao island. The seven missing crew have not been found and are presumed dead.

On April 20, eight pirates attacked the chemical tanker *Quds* in the South China Sea off Pulau Mangkai. The pirates were armed with guns and knives and boarded the tanker while it was under way. The pirates took the crew of eight as hostages and stole the ship's cash and personal effects before escaping.

On June 22, the oceangoing tug *Salviceroy* was attacked and boarded by seven pirates armed with automatic weapons while it was under way. The crew barricaded themselves into the cabin and transmitted an alarm. The pirates tried to break into the cabin, but aborted the attack when they were unsuccessful.

On June 28, pirates attacked and boarded two different vessels, which were under way off Mangkai Island, Indonesia, in the South China Sea. The Maltese-flagged general cargo ship *Galax* was attacked and robbed. The Vietnamese cargo ship *Sao Bien 09 Alci* was attacked and robbed.

On June 28, the Panamanian-flagged general cargo ship *White Tokio* was attacked and boarded by pirates while it was under way about thirty-two nautical miles off Pulau Aur, in Malaysia. The six pirates were armed with machetes and steel bars. They boarded the ship and took the captain and the other two deck officers as hostages, and held machetes to their necks before stealing cash and personal effects.

On July 21, six armed and masked pirates attacked the Malaysian vessel *PNG Express* off the Johor coast in Malaysia. The pirates tied up the Malaysian captain and the crew of fifteen Thais before robbing them of cash and personal effects. The Malaysian police, who had received a tip regarding the robbery, arrived an hour later and were able to arrest five of the Indonesian pirates. One pirate escaped by jumping overboard. The police recovered all the stolen items.

On July 12, five masked pirates armed with knives boarded the Singapore-registered tug *Weihai-5* in the Singapore Straits while it was towing the barge *Jovan 1* loaded with a cargo of granite. The pirates ransacked the tug, stealing cash, cell phones, and personal effects from the Indonesian crew of six. The pirates also destroyed all the tug's communications equipment before departing.

On August 2, five pirates armed with knives attacked the Singapore-flagged tug *Tahir* in the middle of the night. The attack is noteworthy because it was the seventh in the South China Sea in 2009, possibly marking a resurgence of regional pirate activity.

South America

Piracy has been and still is a major problem in Brazil, and it is also increasing in other South American countries, including Venezuela, Colombia, and Chile.

Brazil

The major hot zone for piracy in Brazil is the port of Santos. Attacks occur either on anchored vessels or those already alongside at piers. I have been on a ship pirated in this port. It has been suggested that there is considerable local corruption with port and shipping agents who are able to target any ships with desirable cargoes. The problem with countering piracy in Brazil is that there is no coast guard and the federal police do not have patrol boats, although that is changing as the burgeoning oil industry creates another security demand.

On August 10, 2008, a Brazilian naval patrol seized a boat carrying weapons in the Guaruja area, in the southeastern state of São Paulo. The boat was owned by a group of robbers. The naval detachment seized the boat after finding three 12-millimeter carbines, a 9-millimeter submachine gun, and a 40-millimeter pistol, along with ammunition. The thieves were engaged in robbing ships when the navy patrol found

131

them. The five men on the boat jumped overboard and swam to the shore to escape. Four boats were reportedly robbed in Santos Bay in February and March of 2008.

In July 2009, six armed raiders attacked and boarded the 130-foot luxury cruise ship *Aqua* while it was on the Amazon River. The twenty-four wealthy passengers were robbed of money and valuables. The robbers escaped and did not harm the passengers or crew.

Peru

In 2009, there have been several reported incidents of robberies and/or piracy in and around the Peruvian harbor of Callao.

Haiti

The chemical tanker *Iver Prosperity* was in the Port-au-Prince outer anchorage when the sailor on watch observed two robbers on the forecastle deck of the tanker. The robbers were armed with knives. The alarm was raised and the crew mustered. The thieves attempted to steal ship's stores, and then left the vessel.

PART 3

Notable
Pirate Attacks

10

The Hijacking of *Maersk Alabama*

On Tuesday, April 8, 2009, four pirates attacked and seized the 17,000-ton containership *Maersk Alabama*. Given the large number of ships transiting the Red Sea, the characteristic light blue hull livery of the Danish-owned Maersk Line shipping company may or may not have been a welcome sight to the pirates. The ship was operating under the Virginia-based subsidiary of the parent company, Denmark's Copenhagen-based A.P. Moller-Maersk. With a fleet of 543 vessels, Maersk is one the world's largest container shipping companies.

Maersk Alabama had discharged part of its cargo in the port of Djibouti, and was heading to the Kenyan port of Mombasa with a cargo of grain destined for Somalia and Uganda as part of the ongoing humanitarian aid effort to alleviate hunger in these countries. The cargo consisted of 400 containers of food aid, including 232 containers that were part of the United Nations World Food Program.

The ship is relatively small, with a capacity of around 1,100 containers, and it is also slow and has a relatively low freeboard. These characteristics made it the perfect pirate target. The vessel was unlike many of the new generation Maersk containerships, the latest of which can carry 11,000 shipping containers and steam at around twenty-six knots. The Maersk fleet sails under many different flags. The pirates probably didn't know that the ship was sailing under a U.S. flag and had twenty-one American merchant mariners aboard. They definitely could not have imagined the outcome of their attack and that the ramifications of their actions would reverberate around the world, subsequently rallying the U.S. to take decisive action.

Maersk does business with the U.S. Department of Defense, although *Maersk Alabama* was not under a Pentagon contract when it was hijacked. The *Maersk Alabama* is also enrolled in the U.S. Maritime Security Program, which comprises a fleet of militarily useful but privately owned ships. Maersk executives are no strangers to piracy. With a large fleet of vessels, their ships are frequently attacked or are otherwise involved in piracy incidents.

On the day of the attack, *Maersk Alabama* was far out in the Indian Ocean about 300 nautical miles northeast of the coastal town of Eyl, in the northern Puntland region of Somalia, where many hijacked vessels are taken after pirates capture them. As is the case with most crews aboard ships transiting the area, the crew of *Maersk Alabama* would have been exercising heightened surveillance in accordance with standard shipboard security plans. The fact that the vessel was attacked so far out demonstrates the extent to which pirates have increased their operating range.

Maersk Alabama was the sixth vessel within a one-week period to be attacked and seized. It was also only the second containership to be captured by Somali pirates, the previous one being the German *Hansa Stavanger*, which was captured on April 4, 2009. The reason why just two containerships were captured up to that point is that ships of this type usually have relatively high hull sides, making them more difficult to board, and they travel at much faster speeds than oil tankers and bulk carriers. The four pirates who attacked *Maersk Al-*

abama were evidently from a group of seven pirates that had hijacked the German containership earlier in the week.

The attack on *Maersk Alabama* occurred early in the morning, with the pirates opening fire with automatic weapons, shooting at the ship, at the crew, and into the air. As the pirates boarded the vessel, the crew attempted to defend themselves with knives and jets of water from high-pressure fire hoses, which is standard practice. After the successful boarding, the pirate's boat evidently capsized and sank. Once aboard the pirates quickly attempted to take control of the ship and round up the captain and crew who, as per normal procedure, had locked themselves in the engine room and other areas.

The above action on the part of the crew is a fairly standard strategy, and the Maersk standard protocol stipulates that its crews should not attempt to take back a ship once pirates are aboard and have taken control. Most vessels have a safe room system to help the crew evade capture, given that no firearms are carried. In this case, some members of the crew overpowered one of the pirates, took his automatic weapon, and held him in a secure location. The reported story is that the ship's captain, Richard Phillips, talked the pirates into leaving the ship and that he offered himself as a hostage as an alternative to the crew. The three pirates and Phillips then left *Maersk Alabama* in one of the enclosed lifeboats, with a reported nine days of supplies aboard.

This was the beginning of the standoff. The pirates contacted *Maersk Alabama* to discuss an exchange of the pirate for the ship's captain. The ship's crew held the pirate hostage for about twelve hours. During this negotiation and prisoner exchange process the pirate being held on *Maersk Alabama* was handed over. One story says he escaped and jumped into the sea. The pirates subsequently reneged on the deal and refused to return Phillips, choosing instead to flee in the lifeboat. The ship's crew had full control of *Maersk Alabama* and continued to negotiate with the pirates for the release of their captain, offering the pirates food and water. The efforts proved unsuccessful.

Meanwhile, the crew awaited the arrival of the U.S. guided-missile destroyer *Bainbridge*. *Bainbridge* arrived on Thursday, April 8, and a U.S. P-3 Orion aircraft flew reconnaissance overhead. Once on the scene, the destroyer took full command of the situation and FBI hostage negotiation experts were used to support the effort to peacefully resolve the standoff. *Bainbridge* continued to maintain close station just a few hundred yards away from the lifeboat.

Maersk Alabama was instructed to move well away from the lifeboat by officers aboard *Bainbridge*, in spite of the crew's obvious and valid concerns for the safety of their captain. *Maersk Alabama* ultimately sailed from the area for the fifty-hour voyage to Mombasa, Kenya, accompanied by eighteen armed U.S. Navy SEALs as protection against any further attacks from other pirates. The crew was reported as saying that they had avoided capture due the fact that the captain had offered himself as a hostage.

After holding Phillips hostage for two days, the pirates asked for a ransom payment for the captain, along with safe passage as a condition for his release. Phillips attempted an escape by jumping overboard from the lifeboat, but it was reported that the warship was unable to react quickly enough to rescue him. The pirates fired their weapons and Phillips was soon recaptured, fortunately without injury. A two-way radio that had been dropped to the lifeboat to allow communications with the pirates was subsequently thrown overboard, evidently because the pirates were convinced that U.S. forces were using it to secretly communicate with the captain.

At this stage, there was a reported telephone interview with a Somali who claimed he was one of the pirate leaders ashore in the village of Eyl. He stated that the captain was unharmed and that they did not intend to harm him at that point. He also said that the use of force to free the captain would result in his death. The pirate was quoted as saying that he was in contact with the four pirates in the lifeboat via a satellite phone. The pirates had attempted to send reinforcements, but they couldn't get to the pirates in the lifeboat because of the presence of the U.S. Navy. The pirate boats stood off, their crews waiting to see what happened next.

By this time the U.S. frigate *Halyburton* had joined *Bainbridge* at the scene. A new radio was provided for communication, and Phillips made radio contact from the lifeboat. Provisions were also provided. The pirate leader ashore said rather chillingly that if the Americans attempted to use any military force, then nobody would survive. The pirates used the media to great effect and regularly gave interviews to reporters from various news agencies.

It was quite an act of defiance and organization that the pirates managed to coordinate, using satellite phones, and another four foreign vessels that were reportedly held by pirates. These headed towards the lifeboat standoff and the attending warships to support the four pirates in the lifeboat. These ships had a total of fifty-four hostages aboard from a variety of countries, including Russia, the Ukraine, Germany, China, the Philippines, Indonesia, and some others. The pirates were attempting to link up and increase their bargaining power.

The hostage negotiations had the added complication in that allowing safe passage to the pirates would have meant allowing the pirates to transfer Phillips to shore, where he would be difficult, if not impossible, to rescue. The negotiators wanted to avoid that, as it would have immensely increased the bargaining power of the pirates. The pirates had purely commercial goals in mind, and they had a code of conduct that said that no one must get hurt because that would be bad for business. However, when you are stuck in a lifeboat 300 nautical miles offshore, it's not a particularly ideal situation to be in. It should be noted that the only other ship to be rescued using force was a large yacht liberated by French commandos in September 2008.

As the wind and seas increased, the personnel aboard *Bainbridge* managed to convince the pirates to take an 82- to 98-foot towline trailed behind the warship. On Sunday, April 12, the standoff came to a quick and dramatic conclusion. The commander of *Bainbridge* decided that Phillips's life was in grave and imminent danger. Earlier in the standoff, on Friday, U.S. Navy SEALs from SEAL Team 6 had parachuted down near *Halyburton* and transferred across to *Bainbridge*. They were given shoot-to-kill clearance, which President Barack Obama had authorized if it was feared that the captain's life was in immediate danger. The three snipers simultaneously killed the three pirates in the lifeboat.

The remaining pirate, Abdul Wal-i-Musi, who was aboard *Bainbridge* negotiating at the time, was taken into custody. Phillips was rescued unharmed, although it must be said that five days in an enclosed lifeboat is like five days in a gyrating sauna, and most mariners who have only ever done a short sea survival course know how dreadfully uncomfortable those lifeboats can be. There would not be a merchant mariner anywhere that wasn't absolutely delighted with the outcome for both the hostage and the pirates.

Abdul Wal-i-Musi was transferred to New York to face trial on charges that included piracy under the law of nations, conspiracy to seize a ship by force, conspiracy to commit hostage-taking, and other charges related to firearms. On May 18, 2009, a federal grand jury returned a ten-count indictment against Abdul Wal-i-Musi. He was awaiting trial, the first piracy prosecution in the United States for more than a century. Prosecutors tagged the eighteen-year-old Musi as the pirate ringleader. The defense responded that he was just a bewildered teenager. The defense's attempt to convince a judge that Musi was only fifteen and should be tried as a juvenile failed.

The U.S. Navy handed the bodies of the three dead pirates over to Somali representatives. The successful rescue of the captain and the death of the three pirates naturally provoked a strong response from other Somali pirates, notably from pirate leader Abdi Garad, who threatened to attack regional U.S. interests. Somali pirate groups issued explicit warnings that they would specifically target U.S.-flagged ships and exact lethal revenge.

Following the release of *Maersk Alabama*, Somali pirates attacked another U.S.-flagged ship with rockets in an attempt to destroy it as an act of revenge. The attack failed, but further attacks have resulted in more ship captures. During the same period a French naval vessel intercepted a suspected pirate mother ship, and apprehended eleven suspected Somali pirates in possession of weapons.

Phillips returned to the United States as a national hero, and he was honored with a private meeting with President Obama. Phillips continued to draw attention to the piracy issue by appearing before a congressional committee, providing a firsthand account of his harrowing experience. Phillips stated that it was his personal view that vessel crews should have access to effective weaponry so as to defend themselves. His employers at Maersk reiterated their opposition to carrying weapons aboard, or using armed guards on the company's ships.

The issue of escalating the violence was raised, as was the exposure of companies to liabilities relating to weapons aboard merchant ships. These are, of course, real issues to deal with, and the arming of ships is just one of the factors in the whole pirate debate. This policy debate came just days after the crew of a cruise vessel owned by the Mediterranean Shipping Company used firearms to successfully repel pirates. The Maersk Group has reported that it has undertaken additional measures to enhance vessel and crew safety and security. It expanded the sea area off the Somali coast that only allows vessels with a certain freeboard or that are capable of steaming at certain maximum speeds to travel through those waters. The company is also looking at additional antipiracy measures that include access control.

Many issues have been raised with allegations of summary justice with the shooting of the pirates as a deterrent, and that it will aggravate the situation and escalate the Somali problem even further. There is talk about deprivation of human rights and the issues of what to do with pirates when they are captured. There are also comments that pirates will be more willing to use force and also demand higher ransoms. Some commentators state that execution of hostages may also be used to expedite and maximize ransom settlements. At the time of *Maersk Alabama*'s capture, roughly 200 merchant mariners were being held hostage aboard fourteen captured ships, and that number soon expanded to 300 mariners and eighteen ships. In the previous year, more than $100 million in ransom money was paid, and it looked like 2009 would be even worse.

Another factor arising from this case that will concern shipowners is the lawsuit for damages the ship's cook filed in Houston, Texas, after the incident ended. He filed a petition for damages alleging that the Maersk shipping company knowingly put the crew in danger. He also alleged that the shipping company ignored requests from sailors to improve safety measures. What is disappointing about this action is that, as always, the ship's captain, Phillips, will be held accountable for all that happened.

Although the outcome was not decided at the time of this writing, I am almost certain that questions will be raised as to why the captain and crew did not adhere to the Maersk standard procedures. For example, no one was supposed to attempt to take back the ship after the pirates successfully boarded and were in control. Personally, I hope that Phillips is not subject to the typical inquisition that such lawsuits entail. But, then, like the pirates, the cook was after money.

It is somewhat ironic that one of the crew, chiefly the cook, whom Phillips selflessly saved from the pirates appears perfectly willing to subject him and his professional career and standing to further stress. Given that all the crew will probably win large damage payments from lawsuits and that the captain is considering $500,000 in possible book deal offers, the real winners may be the captain and crew after all. One thing is certain, no matter where ships trade, there are piracy risks as much as there are weather risks.

This tale had a further twist when in early June 2009 a story came out in the media indicating that the U.S. military personnel involved in the rescue of Phillips were being questioned after $30,000 dollars went missing from the containership's safe. The very same rescuers who saved the captain were being treated as possible pirates. Legal documents that were filed in the case against the remaining pirate indicate that the pirates ordered Phillips to hand over the money in the ship's safe. Phillips evidently then opened the safe and removed around $30,000 in cash.

The alleged pirate being held for trial and two other pirates reportedly took the cash. Interestingly enough, after the remaining pirate was taken into custody and the other three were killed, the only items that were listed as recovered were the rifles, a pistol, cell phones, and handheld radios. There was no money recorded. The Naval Criminal Investigative Service investigators were questioning military personnel on the warship, Navy SEALs, and the crew of *Maersk Alabama* to determine what happened to the missing cash. In addition to this, investigators found that a Navy SEAL had allegedly taken a pistol from one of the pirates as a souvenir.

As a footnote, *Maersk Alabama* is no stranger to piracy and robbery. In fact, it might appear as though the ship is a target. In November 2006, the ship was six miles off the Tanzanian port of Dar es Salaam waiting to take on a harbor pilot when a robber boarded the ship and was subsequently chased off. In September 2007, the vessel was again attacked while drifting around ten nautical miles off Dar es Salaam awaiting a berth. A member of the crew observed three robbers on the deck and raised the alarm. The robbers quickly disembarked in a small boat lying alongside the ship. The ship used a searchlight to illuminate the 25-foot wooden boat, with an estimated fifteen to twenty men aboard. The robbers had managed to break open a container and some of the cargo had already been removed and left on deck.

In July 2009, the U.S. House Transportation and Infrastructure Committee passed the United States Mariner and Vessel Protection Act aimed at protecting the right of mariners to use self defense against acts of piracy. The act is a direct result of the attacks on the U.S.-flagged vessels *Maersk Alabama* and *Liberty Sun*. The act gives merchant mariners involved in a pirate attack, who either use or authorize the use of force in the defense of a vessel, protection from liability for damages or injuries that result from these actions. The act also instructs the United States to commence negotiations for international agreements through the International Maritime Organization for the provision of similar exemptions from liability in other countries.

The *Maersk Alabama* incident recorded a number of firsts. It marked the first time a U.S.-flagged vessel was hijacked following the establishment of a Maritime Protection Corridor. It was also the first successful seizure of a U.S.-flagged vessel by pirates in about 190 years. The last such seizure was probably at the time of the Barbary Wars in the early 1800s.

On November 18, 2009, pirates once again launched an attack on the *Maersk Alabama* around 350 nautical miles off the Somali coast and this time the vessel returned fire at the pirates. The *Maersk Alabama* had a Vessel Protection Detachment on board and the crew and team successfully repelled the hijacking attempt with no reported casualties. The detachment also reportedly deployed Long Range Acoustic Devices (LRADs) and small arms fire in the defense. The ship was also equipped with water cannon and razor wire to deter pirate attacks. It was noted in the media that this attack was possibly the first to be thwarted by the use of on board armed guards.

11

The Hijacking
of *Faina*

On September 24, 2008, pirates attacked and captured the Ukrainian operated, Belize-flagged, 500-foot Ro-Ro (roll-on-roll-off) vehicle carrier *Faina* about 200 nautical miles off the Somali coast. A company called Tomax Team Inc. owned the ship. The pirates attacked in three fast skiffs and carried automatic weapons, and they belonged to the same clan as the pirates that captured *Sirius Star* (details on *Sirius Star* will be discussed in another chapter). The ship's crew of twenty-one sailors comprised three Russians, seventeen Ukrainians, and one Latvian.

The vessel was on a voyage between Oktyabrsk and the Kenyan port of Mombasa. After pirates captured the vessel, they took it to the village of Hobyo in the Somali central region of Mudug, south of Puntland, about seventy-four miles farther north of the other major pirate stronghold at Xarardheere. Hobyo is a natural port, although there are no port facilities. Initial reports suggested that the pirates were looking for a suitable place to offload the lighter weapons discovered in the cargo (there were heavy weapons as well, including tanks). This hijacking would turn out to be one of the longest and most dramatic of all the hijackings since the piracy problem in Somali waters and the Gulf of Aden began to escalate more rapidly between 2007 and 2008.

Imagine the surprise and delight of the pirates when they inspected the vessel hold and found thirty-three Soviet-era T-72 tanks and assorted other weapons, including grenade launchers and a substantial quantity of ammunition. When word got out about the cargo, the Ukrainian Defense Ministry quickly pointed out that all the weapons had been sold in accordance with international agreements and were being legally shipped to Kenya by Ukrinmash, a subsidiary of Ukr-SpetsExport, which has the Ukrainian arms exports monopoly. The final destination of the cargo was unclear. Some reports indicated that it was bound for Kenya, while others claimed it was bound for southern Sudan. This was a potentially serious embarrassment to the Kenyan government, which had brokered a peace pact there.

A Kenyan government spokesman was quoted as saying that the weapons were for use by different branches of the Kenyan military. One commentator noted that Kenyan authorities had recently seized fifty tanks in the port of Mombasa also allegedly destined for Sudan's People's Liberation Army. Kenya had stated that the shipment was in breach of the Sudan Comprehensive Peace Agreement.

Andrew Mwangura, coordinator of the East Africa Seafarers Assistance Program, was quoted as saying that the pirates aboard *Faina* claimed they had confidential documents confirming that the arms were for delivery to southern Sudan. The pirates suddenly grasped the political significance of the situation and threatened to go public and publish a damning report if the requested ransom wasn't paid. This started a propaganda war between the pirates and the Kenyan government.

In true political style, the Kenyan government was quoted as saying that it would not engage in answering threats from terrorists who had hijacked important military equipment paid for by the Kenyan taxpayer for use by the Kenyan military. The

147

government reaffirmed its policy of not negotiating with pirates, or terrorists, for that matter, and said it would not do so in this case to recover the hijacked ship and military cargo.

It didn't take long for the ramifications of the capture to become plain. Given the nature of the cargo, the attack had taken on a global and regional security dimension, while the pirates just wanted the cash, and probably didn't realize the full impact of the capture. There were many governments who took the view that the problem had escalated to a point where global security was at risk and there was a growing chorus for internationally orchestrated actions to be implemented.

A Russian naval spokesman announced that the frigate the *Neustrashimy* had been deployed the same week to the Somali coast to protect Russian citizens and ships. The week before the attack and capture of *Faina*, the French had started circulating a draft United Nations resolution calling for the deployment of naval vessels and aircraft to the area to combat piracy. The French government had been proactive in interventions to rescue its citizens as well as in the arrest and trial of pirates. The San Diego-based destroyer *Howard* was reported as being on station and was about two nautical miles away and in visual range of *Faina*, which was anchored off Hobyo and in the hands of the pirates.

The destroyer was providing close surveillance to ensure that pirates did not attempt to move any weapons ashore. The pirates issued strong warnings against any military intervention and stated that they would not responsible for the dire consequences that might result from such actions. It was believed that two other pirated vessels, *Capt Stefanos* and *Centauri*, were also anchored at the Hobyo location. One pirate spokesman ashore said that the naval ships used loudspeakers and warned the pirates not to offload the cargo.

Ransom negotiations began, with the initial ransom demand set at $35 million. The size and importance of the captured prize was soon realized and the pirates were reported as

148

preparing for battle if anyone attacked the ship. Reports indicated that heavily armed reinforcements were mobilized in several speedboats heading toward Hobyo. Several enterprising journalists had no problems in reaching the pirates and conducting regular telephone interviews with them regarding the status of the negotiations. As previously noted, the Kenyans officially stated that they wouldn't negotiate with international criminals, pirates, or terrorists, while the pirates were asking for the Kenyan government to exclusively negotiate as the cargo took on a greater value than either the ship or the crew. The pirates also threatened to offload the small arms and secret them off in the countryside.

Seeming to get nowhere, the pirates reduced the ransom demand to $20 million. But even as they issued the new ransom amount three foreign warships surrounded *Faina*. The warships were reported as being one from the United States and two from European countries, although the French, British, Greek, and German governments said they were not part of the operation.

Reports emerged that the crew was held in a single overheated room, and that in spite of the harsh conditions no one was seriously injured. However, the ship's captain, Vladimir Kolobkov, was said to be suffering from heat stroke and that his condition was not good. A later report stated that one of the hostages (unconfirmed by the pirates as the ship's captain) had died of natural causes, possibly a heart attack but not from violence or gunshot wounds.

Interviews with one of the pirate leaders led to the comment that they were not pirates, and that they were just protecting their natural marine resources. They expanded on this theme to state that some countries wanted to make Somali waters a dumping site for Western industrial toxic waste and that the pirates were supported by the local community. As mentioned earlier, these statements hold some truth and the press is quick to pick up on them.

The battle for control of information related to the *Faina* arms shipment continued in Kenya, with the arrest and arraignment in court of Andrew Mwangura, coordinator of the East Africa Seafarers Assistance Program. He was charged with the rather dubious crime of issuing disturbing statements. It was reported that it took eight hours for the Mombasa police to arrest him. Mwangura was the first to publicly declare that the captured weapons on *Faina* were bound for Sudan. He was to spend another five days in police custody for additional interrogation until his case was heard.

Mwangura also stated that three pirates on board had been killed in a shootout between the moderate and hardline pirates, and that no hostages had been killed. The claims and counterclaims about the eventual arms destination continued and the pirates denied that there had been any gun battle or deaths among them. They put the situation in perspective by saying that whoever owned the weapons wasn't their problem, and what they were interested in was getting the $20 million.

To further cloud the issue, the claims that the arms belonged to the Sudanese by both the U.S. and the pirates were denied by spokesmen in Kiev, Nairobi, and Sudan. The pirates also restated that they were sticking to the demand for $20 million. They said the payment wasn't a ransom, but a fine for unlawfully transporting weapons in Somali waters. It is hard not to smile as the pirates further rationalized their actions. The pirates again denied the claim that three pirates were killed during a shootout that purportedly was triggered by a disagreement among them about what to do with *Faina*. One pirate leader claimed that it was propaganda being spread by people who were not aware of their situation. Finally, he declared that they were united in punishing those who abuse Somali waters.

There was a relatively long stalemate in the ransom negotiations, with occasional information leaking out. The pirates had stated that negotiations with the owners of the ship were

150

making progress and that the discussions were encouraging. The Somali government was meanwhile reported to have authorized the Russian Navy to rescue the hijacked ship and its military hardware. While some reports stated a Russian warship was on its way to rescue *Faina*, this wasn't quite accurate, as the ship had been mobilized before the capture as part of the Russian counter-piracy effort.

Meanwhile, back in the Ukraine and Russia, a media campaign was launched urging family members of the captured crew to speak out on television against any use of military intervention, and to urge the Ukrainian and Russian governments to find a diplomatic solution. In July 2008, the United Nations Security Council had adopted a resolution to combat the attacks on and the hijacking of vessels along the Somali coastline. However, the resolution did nothing to persuade the defiant pirates.

The families of *Faina*'s crew tried and were unsuccessful in meeting the Ukrainian President Viktor Yushchenko in Kiev with respect to the ransom demand of $20 million. They vowed that they would not leave until the president met them and they stated that they would sleep on the stairs and collect the ransom money themselves. A Ukrainian news agency made matters worse when it ran a headline saying that the crew might be home by Christmas, but only if the government were to get involved directly in the ransom and release negotiations. It was stated that the Ukraine had not been adequately represented during the three months of negotiations that had transpired thus far.

The pirates were only too happy to confirm the assertion, stating that there had not been one single Ukrainian involved in the negotiation process. There wasn't a Ukrainian anywhere, no negotiator, not even the Ukrainian press, they claimed. For most readers this must seem quite remarkable, given the gravity of the situation. The pirate spokesman said that the pirates would have nothing more to do with the

British lawyer representing the Ukraine in the negotiations. He further stated that they did not want to have direct contact with the Ukrainians, and especially not through a British lawyer, whose only interest was money. In addition, the pirate spokesman also said that *Faina* had run out of fuel, and that while the crew was able to move freely about and were healthy, the situation was going to get worse, and it did.

Just a day following the decision by the Somali government to allow foreign navies to use force against the pirates, the pirates responded. They said that they would fight any forces that attacked or staged a rescue attempt. In addition, they said they had nothing to do with insurgents or terrorist organizations and they only wanted the money. The U.S. voiced concerns that the pirates were after the money as well as some of the military hardware, and that the weapons might be used in an al-Qaeda-linked movement that was currently battling the Somali government. The Somali pirates again announced that a deal to pay the ransom and free *Faina* and its weapons was just days away. They went on to say that a boat would ferry the money from Djibouti.

At this point, the pirates reduced the ransom from $20 million to $8 million, and the pirates warned that the hostages would be executed if their ransom demands were not met. They also repeated the warning about any rescue attempts, as well as their assertion that all they were doing was levying a duty on the illegal transportation of military hardware through Somalia's territorial waters. On January 9, the pirates fired the Somali middleman who was acting as an intermediary in negotiations with the vessel owners, and entered into direct negotiations with them. They also lowered the ransom to $5 million. An onshore associate of the pirates aboard *Faina* was reported as saying that Somali brokers had been delaying the negotiation process by reporting only half or even less of the actual ransom being offered, obviously planning to take a sizeable chunk of the proceeds for themselves.

The hijacked Saudi supertanker *Sirius Star* was held and anchored very close to *Faina*. On the same day that *Sirius Star* was released, the families of *Faina*'s crew again appealed for help. They said that they were not being informed about the progress of the negotiations or the state of health of their loved ones. The pirates responded with reassurances that the hostages were healthy and the cargo was unharmed. They also said the crew would be released. When that might be wasn't clear given the many false alarms about impending releases since the seizure began roughly four months earlier.

The new captain of *Faina* (the original ship's captain had since died of natural causes), former Chief Officer Vladimir Nikolsky, made an appeal by satellite phone for help and pleaded with the shipowners to engage as soon as possible in direct negotiations with the pirates and end the long ordeal. He further stated that the shipowners had made no direct contact with the pirates since the vessel was captured. He asserted that the real shipowner, Vadim Alperin (the man behind the company that owned the ship), did not know the true situation and that his representative had probably been keeping information from him. He also stated that attempts to negotiate the release of *Faina* and its crew had involved many middlemen, who weren't motivated to free the hostages. The pirates were also becoming very frustrated at the lack of progress. Pirate leader Mohamed Abdi was ready to establish direct contact with the owners of *Faina* and was refusing contacts from any other party.

Nikolsky said that the crew was being treated decently. However, the ongoing captivity was taking its toll. The entire crew had been locked in a small cabin for almost four months, a very difficult psychological situation to be in. It was also difficult for them to stay in good shape. The crew had little physical exercise. Half were sick and the other half were said to be going stir-crazy. The body of the deceased captain was being kept stored in the same refrigerator as the food for the crew and the pirates. Nikolsky said that the provisions were very poor, and that they ate only one meal per day in the evening. They were given water and occasionally drank tea.

The frustration with the shipowner increased. The pirates insisted that direct contact with the shipowner was the only solution to resolving the situation. It was also stated that the owner had created a problem for himself by resorting for handling the ransom negotiations to unknown Somali and other foreign intermediaries, who had tried to steal some of the potential cash.

Further reports emerged that there were plans to allow Somali doctors aboard to examine and treat members of the crew who were ill. They had developed rashes and were suffering from diarrhea, and some also had high blood pressure. Reports indicated that the crew's actual condition was unknown and might be worse than thought, and it was even postulated that some chemicals related to the weapons in the hold might be playing a part in the deteriorating condition of the crew. In most hijack scenarios, the crew is allowed on deck, allowed to go fishing, and even allowed to play football on deck. However, given the sensitive situation regarding the military cargo, security was kept very tight.

A report came out that two of the hostages had attempted to overpower two of the pirates who were guarding them. The pirates threatened to punish the men involved. They said that some of the crew was misbehaving and that they had tried to harm two of them. The pirate spokesman said that some of the crew was becoming frustrated, and that the pirates were feeling the same, but that they had never opted for violence. The attempt to overpower the guards was viewed as a serious provocation. Then the pirates announced that they had lowered the ransom demand to $3.5 million and said that an agreement had been made for the release of the ship. Sources were also quoted as saying that there was now deep frustration within the pirate ranks regarding the successive reductions in the ransom payment and all the delays associated with it.

A Russian journalist who had previously acted for the owner of *Faina* published a different version of events. In his reportage, he indicated that American forces had detained two pirates while they were heading for shore in a boat. The pirates reacted by calling in some intermediaries as well as contacting the shipowner to request that they negotiate with the Americans for the release of the two detained pirates. The pirates were advised that this was impossible. The journalist also said that the story about the hostage mutiny attempt was a cover for this incident. If the American forces were holding the two pirates, then any news and information was being suppressed. Nothing further appeared in the media about these developments.

At this time an open letter was sent to the president of the United States by the relatives of the hostages aboard *Faina*. It was released to the general media and added an intriguing, mysterious, and unexplained dimension to the entire saga. The families of the hostages asked the president for assistance in the hostage negotiations and thanked the United States for its initial efforts to help. They stated that the negotiations were proceeding until other parties kept intervening, and they were close to success when another new individual entered the process. They accused a U.S. citizen, Michele Lynn Ballarin, who resided in Virginia, as being the interloper who had hindered the release of their loved ones.

It was further claimed that Ballarin was a respected Somali leader who had established an extensive network of clans and sub-clan leaders in most parts of Somalia, whom the pirates respected. Ballarin claimed in an interview that she could win the release of all merchant ships and all hostages being held at that time. The open letter from the families further stated that Ballarin had effectively stalled and thwarted the negotiations regarding *Faina*, and it also said that Ballarin had sought to step in as a mediator, and on what basis and for what reason wasn't clear. The letter went on to allege that their information was that Ballarin was making promises to the various clan leaders on the various ships that she would be able to help get greater ransom payments out of the shipowners.

The open letter from the families also claimed that Ballarin telephoned the pirates aboard *Faina* every day in an attempt to cancel all the agreements on the negotiating table, hoping to restart the negotiation process based on her terms and conditions. The letter further went on to say that Ballarin's intentions were both immoral and probably illegal, and they implored the president of the United States to stop her from interfering with the negotiations.

The pirates were reported to have allowed the crew of *Faina* to telephone their families, and they reassured their families that they were well, that no one was sick, and that they had sufficient food and water. The families said their loved ones were both cheerful and sounded optimistic. It was confirmed that direct negotiations between the shipowners and the pirates were proceeding, and that the various intermediaries were no longer involved. It was stated that the main problem now was the disagreement between the pirates and those controlling them.

By this time, February 2009, four months had passed since the hijacking. News came out that the $3.2 million ransom had been dropped onto the ship via a parachute. The pirates grabbed the cash and escaped. On February 4, *Faina* was released after 134 days in captivity. It was later announced that Ukrainian business magnate and well-known philanthropist Viktor Pinchuk had paid the ransom. The news prompted politicians to capitalize on the opportunity to bathe in the media limelight at the end of the saga, giving a new meaning to political spin.

For example, Viktor Yushchenko, president of the Ukraine, made many feel-good statements about greeting the Ukrainian sailors, other members of *Faina*'s crew, and the relatives of the former hostages prior to their return home. A spokeswoman for the Ukrainian president stated on February 4 that the ship had been released while a very complex special operation carried out by Ukrainian intelligence, in cooperation with other intelligence assets, was under way. Of course, her statements sounded rather farcical, as the entire chain of events was strictly about paying the ransom and a main complaint was the lack of involvement on the part of the Ukrainian government.

It is hard to see that the Ukrainian government had shown real concern or made a special effort to help its citizens, as the French had shown during cases involving their citizens. The comments from the Ukrainian government must have sounded hollow to the relieved crew and their relatives. The Ukrainian spokeswoman also said that the crew was alive and in good health, and that the ship was preparing to sail to Mombasa, Kenya, where the crew would receive medical aid and physical examinations. The Ukrainian authorities said they were making every effort to repatriate the crew as soon as possible.

The Ukrainian president was seen to be clearly trying to capitalize on events by claiming credit for the ship's release, and one press release said that from the first day of the hijacking the process of freeing the Ukrainians and other members of the crew aboard *Faina* was under the constant oversight of the Ukrainian president. Given some of the comments by pirates and others, the government involvement appeared to have been exactly the opposite, that its efforts were nonexistent. The Ukrainian president had even refused contact with the crew's relatives.

The Bahrain-based U.S. Naval Forces Central Command issued a statement saying it expected to provide humanitarian assistance to the ship and crew. Of course, the controversy over the destination of the cargo again emerged as a hot topic. Demands were made for the Kenyan government to guarantee complete transparency when *Faina* docked in Mombasa. Everyone wanted to know where the tanks and other weapons were going. Kenyan spokesmen again reiterated the concern about paying ransoms and said piracy must not be rewarded. They also stated that genuine talks for the release only really started after four months, and that made a mockery of the Ukrainian claims that they were involved all the time.

Kenya again claimed that the refurbished T-72 tanks, rocket launchers, small arms, and ammunition aboard belonged to the Kenyan armed forces, even though the freight manifest indicated the cargo was bound for southern Sudan. The government of southern Sudan naturally denied any ownership. It is said to be increasing its military capacity ahead of an important 2011 referendum that might resolve some of the issues in that country. Ukrainian intelligence officials then said that they had solid confirmation that the arms on the ship were destined for Kenya. And so the intrigue went on.

A U.S. Navy doctor examined all the crew and said their condition was more or less satisfactory. Evidently, when genuine ransom negotiations finally started some six weeks before the end of the ordeal, they were allowed to start exercising. The U.S. military brought in fresh water, food, and bedding for the crew, which enabled the crew to stop washing in seawater. One unexpected shock for the crew was that their relatives at home were advised that each of the crew's monthly wages would be debited $200 for the cost of the phone calls home from the ship, and the crew subsequently demanded that their rights as set out in the International Transport Workers Federation's collective agreement must be defended.

The unloading of the tanks aboard *Faina* was a major media event, with a receiving ceremony and an effort to restore some international confidence. The Kenyan defense forces enforced strict security and sealed off all roads to the port of Mombasa amid renewed claims that the arms were destined for Sudanese rebels in Darfur. The residents of Mombasa lined the Mama Ngina gardens that overlook the port entrance to welcome the ship, and out of curiosity to view the ship that had embroiled Kenyan politics for so long. There were cheers as *Faina* came down the Likoni channel into Kilindini Harbor assisted by two tugs. Having sailed down the same route several times myself, I know it must have been a welcome sight for the weary crew. *Faina* had engine problems on the way and so experienced some delays in arriving.

It was twenty very tired and strained *Faina* sailors who arrived in the port of Mombasa. The newly promoted ship's captain was quoted as saying that it was very difficult to express the crew's feelings because the voyage was too hard for everybody. He said that they were all happy to be in Mombasa and just wanted to go home. Showing some humor, a Ukrainian official reportedly handed the Kenyan defense minister a plastic model tank, which generated some applause. *Faina*'s first captain on the trip had died of a suspected heart attack during the early stages of the hijacking. Officials stated that as the sailors had spent several months in close proximity to the corpse while it was stored in the ship's refrigerator with the food, they would require a rigorous medical examination.

In Kenya, the controversy continued. The Kenyan government was asked if the weapons were not bound for Sudan, but for Kenya, then why was Kenya arming itself, as it had never gone to war and did not have any current international tensions. Among the cargo were the thirty-three T-72 tanks, spare parts for the T-72 tanks, a ZPU-4 Soviet-built antiaircraft gun, RPG-7V rocket-propelled grenades, spare parts for the rocket-propelled grenade launchers, a BM-21 truck-mounted multiple-launch rocket system, and 812 tons of 125-millimeter ammunition.

The Ukrainian president Viktor Yushchenko announced that all of the crew would be awarded medals for their courage. In a spectacular bit of political spin, he also announced that officers of the Ukraine's special services involved in the *rescue* operation would be given medals, too. One appropriate comment simply was "What Rescue?" The Ukrainian president personally greeted the sailors at Kiev's Borispil Airport and the released hostages were treated as heroes. One sailor downplayed the whole affair and said that they were simply hostages. The body of the deceased captain of *Faina* was flown to St. Petersburg by a Swiss International Airlines flight. It was later announced that an autopsy had been performed which confirmed that the captain's death was due to natural causes. Vladimir Nikolsky and his crew certainly deserved some compensation for their ordeal, but at the time of this writing, it's difficult to say if the crew will receive anything. I certainly hope they won't have to pay the phone bills for calling home from their captured ship.

12

The Hijacking
of *Arctic Sea*

Piracy had not occurred in Scandinavia or in northern Europe and the Baltic Sea for centuries, but that changed on July 24, 2009, when pirates hijacked the general cargo ship *Arctic Sea*. In Sweden, no such attacks had occurred since the sixteenth century. At the time of this writing, Swedish and Russian police were carrying out a major investigation arising from allegations that a gang of up to twelve masked men clad in black and wearing police insignias while claiming to be drug enforcement officers boarded and hijacked the Maltese-flagged vessel. A Finnish company, Solchart Management, owns *Arctic Sea*. The company is associated with another firm, Solchart Arkhangelsk, based in Arkhangelsk, Russia. The English-speaking hijackers were all armed with automatic weapons and handguns.

Arctic Sea was attacked at three o'clock in the morning while it was steaming between the islands of Gotland and Öland in the Baltic Sea, carrying a load of sawn timber to Algeria from the Finnish port of Pietarsaari. Prior to loading the $1.5 million cargo of timber from Stora Enso, the largest papermaker in Europe, *Arctic Sea* had undergone weeks of unspecified repairs at the Pregol shipyard in Kaliningrad, a

Russian port reputedly notorious for smuggling. It was postulated that this repair work had something to do with a secret consignment being carried aboard the ship.

The pirates bound, blindfolded, and gagged the Russian crew of fifteen, all of whom were hired out of Arkhangelsk, and then assaulted them. They struck several of them with rifle butts, while others were beaten so badly their teeth were broken. The crew were intensely interrogated regarding drugs and drug trafficking. The men posing as drug enforcement officers searched the ship and remained aboard for twelve hours before departing in a black high-speed inflatable vessel, which was marked with a police insignia.

There was widespread speculation regarding the motive behind the attack, what the hijackers were searching for, and whether they found it. The hijacking was certainly not random. On the contrary, *Arctic Sea* was precisely targeted. Some speculated that the hijackers were probably searching for drugs, and other reports indicated that the gang might have taken over the wrong ship. An extensive search was under way to find the high-speed inflatable craft used in the attack.

The Russian crew had reportedly complained through the Russian Foreign Ministry about the purported Swedish police action, as they had directly contacted their embassy. The Swedish National Police Board (Rikspolisstyrelsen) denied that the attackers were members of the Swedish drug enforcement authorities and said it only learned of the event through Russian official diplomatic channels in Stockholm. The ship mysteriously continued the voyage without awaiting any official investigation, and it was reportedly almost impossible to contact. There was consternation in many quarters as to why the ship did not report the incident for a week.

The saga didn't end with the initial attack. *Arctic Sea* was last in contact with the British Maritime and Coastguard Agency when it entered the English Channel and called in a routine radio communication on July 28. The British and European coast guards had not yet learned of the attack and short-term hijacking of the vessel while it was off the Swedish coast. After that, the ship was last heard from just after it cleared the English Channel off the French coast on July 30. The signal from the ship's automatic identification system put its position at around fifty nautical miles south of Penzance in Cornwall (another name synonymous with piracy hundred of years ago) on a southwesterly course. The ship AIS system then appears to have been deliberately switched off, so that any tracking and detection was impossible.

When the vessel didn't arrive as expected in the port of Bejaia, in Algeria, on August 4, media outlets such as CNN and the BBC picked up the story. Several Russian agencies were also actively involved in the search for the vessel, including the Federal Security Service (KGB), Maritime Safety Service, and the Russian Navy. The scale of the Russian response provoked some comment as to the motivations behind it. The Russian antisubmarine warfare vessel *Ladny* was reported as having passed through the Strait of Gibraltar in search of *Arctic Sea* and it was reported that the Russians were utilizing all their satellite surveillance capability on the West African coastline.

Two Russian nuclear submarines were also deployed in the hunt for *Arctic Sea*. The Russian Navy chief of staff announced that five Atlantic Ocean-based warships were searching for the missing vessel. Dmitry Medvedev, Russia's president, ordered the defense minister to use every means necessary, including the use of force, to find *Arctic Sea* and its Russian crew. A Russian naval task force consisting of the vessels *Azov*, *Yamal*, and *Novocherkassk* sailed for the Atlantic to join the hunt. Even the Swiss police were reportedly investigating the attack, and a crisis headquarters was established in the ship's flag state of Malta.

The media frenzy continued, with some claiming that there were actually two hijackings, the second occurring off

Portugal, although it was probable the ship was hijacked off Sweden and still remained in the control of the attackers who seized it.

The reasons behind the hijacking and whatever was on the ship that provoked such an event was being widely speculated on within the media and maritime circles. It was clear that the attack and hijacking were well organized and executed. Many commentators said the episode was probably related to a very large drug or illegal arms shipment.

Given the rapid and large-scale Russian military response, which far exceeded the level of response regarding the pirates in the Gulf of Aden, one could be forgiven for thinking that they were chasing a stolen nuclear warhead. If true, that is a rather chilling thought. Finnish authorities discounted the idea that *Arctic Sea* was carrying nuclear materials and said that experts in Finland had tested the vessel for radiation before its departure, which in itself raised a curious point. Why test the ship for radiation, unless possible terrorism was feared? The whole search had a *Hunt for Red October* feel about it.

Arctic Sea had a limited amount of bunker fuel on board, so authorities were checking ports and coastlines in Spain, Portugal, and Morocco to see if the ship was there. The suspicion was that the ship was probably bound for a North African port. The cooperation between NATO and the Russian Navy was also unprecedented and considered a first, much in keeping with the many naval firsts that pirates in the Gulf of Aden had instigated.

As usual, every maritime security expert was rolled out on the various media channels to provide opinions about the incident, and the politics started. People wanted to know how such a thing could happen and how the perpetrators could get away with it. They wanted to know how *Arctic Sea* could have sailed through the most monitored and controlled waterway in the world, the English Channel, without being intercepted or seen. There were many more similar questions. The maritime trade unions demanded that authorities, including Interpol, explain why it took a week to raise the alarm about what had happened off Sweden.

On August 16, *Arctic Sea* was finally sighted around 400 nautical miles from the Cape Verde Islands, an archipelago lying roughly 280 miles off the African country of Senegal. To add to the mystery, an unspecified cash ransom demand was made to the shipowners in Finland, which the Finnish police confirmed. Rumor had it that the ransom demand was for around $2 million. However, there were doubts as to whether the demand was genuine. Of course, the act of pirating a ship in the Baltic Sea and sailing it thousands of miles into the Atlantic before issuing a ransom demand was an extraordinary and unheard of occurrence.

On August 17, the Russian antisubmarine warfare vessel *Ladny* intercepted *Arctic Sea* off the Cape Verde Islands. The crew was found unharmed and then transferred to the warship, and eight alleged pirates were arrested. The hijackers were from Latvia, Estonia, and Russia, and they were captured without any resistance. The crew was interrogated regarding the events that occurred off Sweden and up until the Cape Verde Islands. The media frenzy continued, as speculations about the actual events surrounding the hijacking circulated. Even the Russian president commented publicly. In Finland, the police investigation was casting doubt on the actual circumstances and motives behind the hijacking. It emerged that initially the hijackers had posed as a broken down vessel requiring assistance to get aboard.

The conspiracy theories continued to rage and the suspicion that the ship was carrying weapons, including nuclear warheads, became a main topic of debate. Some commentators said the Russian government was involved in the events and initially questioned why it made no response, and then only did so after the families of the crew launched public appeals for their rescue. Russia was criticized about the very limited information being released, and there were accusations that the whole affair was being covered up. The Maltese Maritime Authority announced that *Arctic Sea* had never really disappeared, and this fueled speculation about Russian secret security service involvement. Russian authorities denied being involved in any way and strongly denounced the claims about nuclear weapons or other secret cargoes.

Russian television showed the pirates taken ashore in handcuffs. It was postulated that the ship was hijacked because Western intelligence agencies had learned of the illicit cargo, whatever it was, and the alleged "hijacking" was executed to prevent a Western country from taking the ship and its cargo. The whole episode was becoming more like a Hollywood movie script. One member of the crew was reported as saying that an electronic distress call advising they were being hijacked was sent and the captain was forced to reply to the response that all was normal and that the call was a joke.

The crew and the alleged hijackers were transferred to Russian military aircraft in the Cape Verde Islands. Eyebrows were raised as to why three military aircraft were required take a small group of men back to Moscow. Also, the question was asked as to why one of Russia's largest heavy lift aircraft was used as part of the operation. *Arctic Sea* remained drifting about 200 nautical miles off the Cape Verde Islands with four of the crew in charge. One report stated the alleged hijackers claimed to be environmentalists and scientists, and had been captured in error, that they were merely sheltering from bad weather and had requested fuel from *Arctic Sea*.

One television station in Russia that covered the arrival of the hijackers showed images of the heavily tattooed hijackers and stated that only professional criminals were tattooed in that way. Russian authorities continued the interrogation of the hijackers, and held the crew in the Lefortovo remand prison to determine whether they were involved in the incident. The anxious relatives of the crew were kept totally in the dark about what was happening. The crew was not allowed to call them.

Meanwhile, *Arctic Sea* was being towed some 4,000 miles to the Russian Black Sea Port of Novorossiisk for further investigation and would bypass the Algerian port that the cargo of timber was destined for. This was even stranger, as it would have been quicker and easier for the ship to sail under its own power, and the replacement crew that was to make the passage never arrived. Something like that had never happened in the piracy incidents in Gulf of Aden and elsewhere, adding to the intrigue. One commentator said the Russian government had effectively hijacked the ship again and was making sure no one was going to be able to observe what was happening.

The Russian and Ukrainian media had a field day and fueled more speculation that also surfaced in some Arab media. Some of these reports said that Israeli Mossad agents were behind the hijacking, and that the vessel was secretly carrying X-55 cruise missiles and S-300 antiaircraft rockets to Iran, which were stowed in secret compartments. The alleged missile cargo was to be transshipped in Algeria before going to Iran, a practice used in the past. The speculation was that the secret shipment details were leaked to Western intelligence services, and that when the Russians learned of the leak, Mossad activated the hijack operation. This story was supposedly given credence when there were reports that the Israeli Prime Minister Benjamin Netanyahu had made a secret visit to Russia in early September to outline concerns about the shipment. Of course this raised the issue as to how these people managed to get hold of Russian S-300 missiles without Russian government knowledge.

After the alleged hijackers arrived in Moscow, two of them filed papers protesting against their arrest. Given that they faced a twenty-year jail term, this is not surprising.

By early September the eleven crew who had been taken to Moscow were released from custody. During a media broadcast on television one of the eight alleged hijackers was then recognized as being the CEO of Pakri Tankers, which had recently gone bankrupt which added further intrigue to the already mystifying episode. A Russian journalist fled the country after he reportedly had received death threats for contradicting official reports of the authorities.

By mid-September Russian investigators announced they had nearly completed the investigations on the *Arctic Sea* and they would soon hand over the ship to the Las Palmas representatives of the Republic of Malta, the vessel's flag state. This of course caused some consternation as the ship was supposedly under tow to the Black Sea. The vessel had been kept well out to sea the entire time guarded by the warship *Ladny*. Of course the immediate reaction to this revelation was to heighten suspicions that the Russians were hiding something as they spread misinformation, and the Russians vehemently denied that illegal arms were involved. The only inconsistency to be released by the investigators was that the cargo was in fact pine timber and not mahogany as stated on the cargo manifest. The cargo was scheduled to be offloaded in Las Palmas when the ship was handed over.

The saga continued when the news emerged that the owner of the *Arctic Sea* had declared bankruptcy. The bankruptcy was evidently declared on the day the Russian naval ship intercepted the *Arctic Sea*. The Finnish ship managers criticized the Russian authorities for the lack of communications on the issue. The bankruptcy also meant there were no funds for bunker fuel and the ship remained anchored some 17 nautical miles off the port in international waters with its four remaining crew and Russian investigators. In spite of an agreement for one of the company representatives to visit the ship, they refused him access. All efforts to get written undertakings on the handover of the ship back to the owners met with silence. The Maltese authorities refused to accept the ship back and this caused criticism by the Russians who in spite of the events over recent weeks stated that Malta's refusal was illogical and inconsistent with international laws of the sea and conventions. But then the whole episode was inconsistent and illogical in the extreme.

The Spanish authorities who had previously granted permission for the Russian frigate *Ladny* and its accompanying tug and the *Arctic Sea* to call at Las Palmas then revoked the permission. The Spanish foreign ministry held intensive discussions with the Russian and Maltese ambassadors. Meanwhile the media went into overdrive and continued speculation that the ship was part of Russian state-sponsored arms trafficking and they were trying to covertly deliver S-300 air defense system missiles to either Iran or Syria. The Russian foreign minister robustly dismissed this speculation. The Russians blamed the Maltese for the impasse. It was stated that the request to call at Las Palmas was revoked the same day as the Russian investigators reportedly offloaded evidence from the *Arctic Sea* to the Russian warships and the permission to berth was also revoked as the ship had eleven military personnel still on board.

For the remaining four crew, the situation was also dire and no different than if they had been hijacked by Somali pirates, only this time they were the captives of Russian authorities. The wives and families of the four men published an open letter to the International Transport Federation, the Red Cross Society and the respective governments of Russia, Spain, Malta and Finland. They stated that after two months since the hijacking and five weeks after its recapture, their husbands were held on board at sea with virtually no communications with their families though there was nothing incriminating or suspicious on board. They also explained the individual health issues that all of the men were experiencing and that they required medical assistance. They said Russian authorities had stated the crew members were free to leave the ship, however they could not as the hijackers had destroyed all their passports. The authorities could have remedied this situation very quickly of course. They also asked the same questions as to why a replacement crew hadn't been flown out to take the ship over. All of this simply added to the mystery. The media pondered on what evidence was found and removed and why it took so long to complete an investigation.

It was announced late October that the *Arctic Sea* would be handed over to Maltese authorities in Valletta. The ship returned under tow as the steering gear was reportedly damaged. The ship was also checked for radiation before being allowed entry. The entire saga remains a mystery with claim and counterclaim without anyone really explaining the circumstances or motivations and eventually this may filter out. It will make a great movie.

13

Other Notable Hijackings

The hijacking of *Sirius Star*

On November 15, 2008, six pirates attacked and captured the supertanker *Sirius Star*, which is owned by Saudi Aramco and operated by the subsidiary Vela International. The ship was flagged in Liberia and had a crew from Great Britain, Croatia, Poland, Saudi Arabia and the Philippines. A group of pirates in a skiff managed to slow the ship down while another group of pirates boarded using ropes and grappling hooks. They seized the ship in just sixteen minutes. The pirates were armed with AK-47 automatic rifles and a rocket-propelled grenade launcher.

This particular act of piracy sparked a global response in the media because it involved one of the largest ships in the world worth roughly $150 million. Built in 2007 in South Korea, the vessel is 1,080 feet in length, about three times the size of a large U.S. aircraft carrier. Also, the ship's cargo of about two million barrels of crude oil worth an estimated $100 million was newsworthy. To put two million barrels of crude oil into perspective, consider that it equals about 25 percent of Saudi Arabia's daily oil production. The attack actually impacted the world's oil markets, reversing declining oil prices, which closed up on the day of the attack as jitters about the security of oil supplies were manifested in the oil futures markets.

It's interesting to note that *Sirius Star* was too big to transit the Suez Canal, so it wasn't heading to the Gulf of Aden and the Red Sea. Instead, it was on a voyage from the Persian Gulf to Europe via the Cape of Good Hope. Thus, the implications of the attack are far reaching because it is an indication that piracy in the waters around the Horn of Africa can disrupt one of the key oil routes from the Persian Gulf to Europe, to the United States, and elsewhere. There was some justification to the fear about oil security in the markets.

Also newsworthy was the fact that the ship belonged to a Muslim country and was seized about 500 nautical miles southeast of the Kenyan port of Mombasa. The attack was the farthest out to sea of any hijacking, and it stunned most security and maritime industry experts. Senior U.S. Navy officers were quoted as saying they were surprised by the hijacking, and astonished at the clever tactics employed, not just by the capture of such a large prize but also of such a strategically important one. Those more concerned with terrorism also found good cause for alarm.

After the tanker was seized, the pirates sailed it to the Somali pirate base of Xarardheere, about 186 miles north of Mogadishu, and anchored the vessel there. The pirates contacted the owners of the ship and began ransom negotiations. The pirates demanded an initial ransom of $25 million to be paid within ten days and they threatened disastrous consequences if the operating company Vela International did not comply. A pirate spokesman in Xarardheere said there were no plans to either destroy the supertanker or cause any harm to the ship's crew. The Somali pirates said they would fight back if there was any military attempt to rescue the vessel and its crew.

The Saudi Foreign Minister, Prince Saud al-Faisal, stated that he was opposed to any negotiations with the pirates, and that piracy was an evil that had to be eradicated, the same as terrorism. Most everyone supported his view. Arab countries bordering the Red Sea met to formulate a common antipiracy strategy. There was talk about getting the Somali government to release the tanker by force, but Saudi Arabia vetoed that action. The pirates reiterated their warning against an attack and said that not only would it risk the lives of the hostages, it would also risk the sinking of the tanker with the resulting environmental disaster that would follow.

The chairman of Lloyd's of London insurance was quoted as saying that it was highly likely the owners of *Sirius Star* would pay the ransom demand. Another senior official stated that there was no real alternative, if lives were to be saved. While most shipping industry people agreed with the various governments that ransoms should not be paid, the choice between that and having the hostages murdered was an easy one to make. Most shipping experts ruled out any rescue attempt because it represented significant risks to the crew and to the fully laden oil tanker. NATO also announced that there were no plans to rescue the hijacked tanker.

The region where the attack took place was a long distance from where NATO warships were performing piracy deterrence patrols. The U.S. 5th Fleet based in Bahrain also declined to comment on any proposed military intervention. Numerous maritime and industry groups made public calls for the United Nations to initiate an international naval blockade to bring a halt to the piracy, and some proposed that a coordinated naval action off the Somalia coast was required. As noted previously, this eventually was done. It is safe to say that the *Sirius Star* incident helped move matters forward, albeit at a slow pace.

The audacious seizure of such a large tanker so far out to sea caused some panic. Many shipping companies announced that they would start routing ships via the Cape of Good Hope. This was a potential economic setback for Egypt, which stood to lose a major source of foreign currency income if a significant number of ships stopped using the Suez Canal (this did come to pass). The Norwegian shipping company Odfjell, one

173

of the world's largest shipping groups, announced that it would suspend routes that transited through the Gulf of Aden, and that it would route many of its fleet around the Cape of Good Hope. Another of the largest shipping companies, A.P. Moeller-Maersk of Denmark, announced similar intentions.

If most companies started routing ships around the Cape of Good Hope, commercial traffic in one of the busiest shipping routes in the world would become a mere trickle, until the piracy problem was resolved. The adverse impact such an eventuality would have on world trade is obvious. It would mean significantly higher costs to ship goods by sea and would increase delivery times for those goods. Ironically, though, the situation actually might have benefited shipping in some respects at a time when the global recession was causing mass idling of merchant vessels, because the longer route required longer voyages and therefore longer charter durations. As 2009 unfolded, this actually did happen, to a certain extent.

The hijacking of *Sirius Star* further aggravated the Somali political situation. It was reported that additional well-armed reinforcements had joined the pirates already holding the vessel. There were also local reports that clan militias and Islamist fighters had arrived in the village and the surrounding area. The Islamist Shebab group, which controls a large area of Somalia, had stated its strong opposition to piracy, which under Islamic law is classified as a capital offense. Its possible involvement posed the likelihood of further fighting ashore. Another militia, the Islamic Courts Union, was quoted as saying it would attack and free the ship.

A local Islamist militia leader was quoted as saying that Saudi Arabia was a Muslim country and that it was a major crime to hold Muslim property. The leader repeatedly warned that those who were holding the ship must free it unconditionally, or armed conflict would ensue. The successful release of the crew and ship would have been an ideal outcome for the

174

shipowners, but the risks were high, and they did not want the situation to escalate. It appeared that the threats on the part of the militias were hollow, though. An Islamist official in Xarardheere stated that Shebab fighters arriving in the area had no plans to attack the pirates. Some local residents said that it was simple greed that had attracted all the additional people to the village.

As a result of the local Islamic militia threats to free the ship and hostages, the tanker was reportedly moved to a safer location. A pirate said that they were moving the ship from time to time and from place to place for tactical reasons, and that it was like a war game, but they would not be taking the ship too far. The pirate also warned that they still had enough people on the ground and on the ship, and that no one could terrorize them, not even the antipiracy militia groups. The pirate leader declared that any attempt to take the ship by force was futile.

Tensions ashore continued to increase between the pirates holding *Sirius Star* and the Islamist Shebab fighters, despite contradictory reports that Shebab had no intentions of attacking the pirates. Nevertheless, as the November 30 deadline for the ransom payment approached, word came from the Shebab militia that it would attack the hijackers. The pirates declared that they were not frightened of Shebab, and they stated that they were the Shebab of the sea. They also warned that if anybody attempted to attack them, it would be suicidal. The pirates said that they still expected a favorable reply from the shipowners. In the meantime, the days ticked by.

The regional political tensions also ratcheted up a notch. The Ethiopian prime minister called for tougher international actions against piracy. He also claimed that Ethiopia's longtime enemy, Eritrea, was actively supporting the pirates. He further stated that by directly and conspicuously supporting extremists in Somalia and exacerbating its woes, Eritrea was responsible for the rampant piracy in the region. He demanded that the international community do more to prevent the ongoing piracy crisis in the Gulf of Aden. The Ethiopian Foreign Ministry stated that the international response had not been sufficient, given both the seriousness and the magnitude of the problem. However, there was and still is a general consensus that the piracy issue cannot be resolved until the relentless fighting and civil war within Somalia between the many clans, Islamic groups, Somali government forces, and Ethiopian troops is ended with a genuine political settlement.

Sirius Star was released after two months of protracted negotiations. The pirates stated that no member of the ship's crew or any of the pirates had been hurt during the hijacking. While the exact amount of ransom paid was not confirmed, it is thought that the pirates settled for about $3 million, far less than the $25 million they had initially demanded.

The story of the hijacking of *Sirius Star* didn't end there. It took on all the characteristics of a Hollywood action movie, with a twist at the end. The ransom payment was dropped via parachute onto the ship by a light aircraft, and photographs of the drop hit the news. After receiving the ransom, the money was counted and divided between the six hijackers. The pirates then left the vessel in a relatively small boat and headed toward shore, along with other pirates, at high speed, hoping to avoid capture by nearby naval forces. The boat was severely overloaded.

A large, fully laden oil tanker has a very deep draft, so it must be anchored some distance offshore, as was the case with *Sirius Star*. A strong wind was blowing and seas were rough, and as the boat sped through the waves, it capsized and sank. The group's $300,000 share of the ransom was lost. Three of the surviving pirates in the boat were in the water for several hours, and they swam ashore without any of the ransom money. The body of one of the drowned pirates washed up on the beach a few days later with $153,000 of the ransom.

The *Zhen Hua 4* incident

On December 17, 2008, nine pirates in two fast skiffs attacked the Chinese merchant ship *Zhen Hua 4* in the Gulf of Aden. The pirates successfully boarded the ship, and tried to take control and take the crew hostage. However, the crew had entirely different ideas. A battle ensued that could have come from any great action movie. The ship's captain, Peng Weiyuan, immediately sent a distress message to the International Maritime Bureau's Piracy Reporting Center, which alerted coalition naval forces and requested assistance for the ship. The captain also called the ship owner, Shanghai Zhen Hua Port Machinery Corp, and initiated carefully prepared antipiracy measures.

The pirates did not know that the captain had a plan to repel and deal with pirates. The crew had performed many drills to address the various contingencies that might occur. They had reviewed pirate attack strategies and how to identify pirate boats. The crew had removed the ladders leading from the main deck to the crew's cabins, and as the attack commenced, some of the crew locked themselves in safe rooms. Other members of the crew prepared fire hoses, while still others started preparing gasoline bombs (Molotov cocktails), which were made using empty beer bottles. This type of plan was and still is unusual.

The on-deck attack began when seven pirates armed with automatic weapons and rocket-propelled grenades tried to break into the cabins. As they did so, the ship's crew heaved gas bombs at them. Some of the pirates weren't wearing shoes and burned their feet in the burning gas on deck. The pirates stopped trying to break into the cabins and shouted to the crew to give them shoes and fuel. About thirty minutes after the assault began, the pirates evidently asked for a ceasefire.

Two helicopters, including one from the Malaysian Navy, arrived at the scene and opened fire on the pirates, without killing or wounding any of them. When the helicopters flew away, the pirates pressed on with the attack. By this time, the attack had lasted for two hours. The sailors continued to resist. The crew was aware that once the pirates got inside the cabins, the fight would be over, that they would be taken as hostages, and that their captivity might last for many months. The second officer shouted to the pirates that a warship was coming soon, but they didn't seem to care.

The crew continued to desperately fight back, throwing more Molotov cocktails at the pirates. Finally, the pirates gave up the attack. The ship was steered toward an approaching Malaysian warship. As the pirates retreated, the pirate leader was reported to have given a thumbs-up sign in recognition of the crew's courage. The crew also threw shoes and some Chinese cigarettes to the pirates before they departed in their boat. The attack lasted for four hours!

The crew returned home to Shanghai as national heroes, as is appropriate, with hundreds turning out to greet them. One of the great outcomes was that the crew's employer paid them a total of $300,000 ($10,000 each) in recognition of their bravery in warding off the attack. Captain Peng Weiyuan received a gold medal. This attack galvanized the Chinese to take action against pirates. China announced that it would deploy two destroyers and a supply vessel to Somalia to support international antipiracy efforts. It was stated that about 20 percent of Chinese ships transiting the Somali coast had suffered pirate attacks in 2008.

The *Svitzer Korsakov* hijacking

On February 1, 2008, the new Danish-owned ice-class ocean-going tug *Svitzer Korsakov* was on its maiden voyage when nine heavily armed pirates attacked it eighty-five nautical miles off the Somali coast. The pirates boarded using steel ladders and lines with grappling hooks. The crew was rounded up and made to lie face down on the deck while some of the pirates threatened to shoot and kill them, as others ransacked the cabins.

The 115-foot tug was built in St. Petersburg, Russia. It was on its way to work at Sakhalin Island, between Russia and northwest Japan, where the Gazprom Sakhalin II oil and gas project was ongoing. Aboard the tug was a crew of six consisting of a British captain, an Irish chief engineer, a Russian chief officer, and three Russian sailors. After the successful attack, the crew was taken hostage and the tug was sailed to and anchored near Eyl, in Somalia. A U.S. naval vessel was nearby and was later reported as having fired on one of the pirate boats in an attempt to prevent a resupply effort. A ransom demand was made and negotiations commenced.

The crew was kept under strict control and was not allowed to sleep in their cabins. Food was limited. After media reports came out regarding the hijacking, a spokesman for the hijackers said during a telephone call to Radio Garoowe in Puntland that they were not pirates. He asserted that the Russian-registered vessel was responsible for some of the environmental destruction that had been happening along the coast of Somalia, that it was part of the fleet of foreign ships dumping hazardous waste in Somali waters. The group holding the tug was known as the Ocean Salvation Corps, Somali nationalists claiming they only attack to protect Somalia's environment and fishery.

A number of questions arose regarding the attack, such as why the relatively slow vessel did not follow recommended routes with an escort and why it did not stay well offshore. The ship and crew were released on payment of a ransom on St Patrick's Day after forty-seven days in captivity.

The *Hansa Stavanger* hijacking

On April 4, 2009, pirates attacked the 20,000-ton German containership *Hansa Stavanger* about 400 nautical miles off the Somali port of Kismayu. The ship was hijacked and the crew of twenty-four were taken as hostages. The hostages included the German captain, five other Germans, three Russians, two

Ukrainians, two Filipinos, eleven Tuvalu, and one Fiji national. Rocket-propelled grenades and automatic weapons fire struck the vessel during the attack. The pirates were aboard within minutes of coming alongside.

The German frigate *Rheinland-Pfalz* was on its way to Mombasa, Kenya, when it responded to the distress call from *Hansa Stavanger*. As the frigate closed on the containership, the pirates held an AK-47 to the captain's head, forcing him to radio the warship and tell it to turn around. If it did not comply, he said the pirates would kill him. The frigate turned away. The captain informed the shipowners in Hamburg of the seizure and the pirates immediately requested a ransom of $15 million. The ship was then sailed to Xarardheere Bay in Somalia. A week passed without any contact from the shipowners, and the pirates became increasingly nervous. On the eighth day, the shipowners contacted the vessel and ordered the ship's officers not to negotiate with the pirates, saying they must leave that process to them.

The shipowners used a British-based company to carry out the negotiations, and they immediately offered a sum of $600,000. The pirates reduced the ransom to $6 million and threatened to destroy the ship if their demands were not met. The negotiations frequently broke down and stalled. Whenever a warship closed in on the vessel, virtual panic ensued and there appeared to be little command structure among the pirate gang. The pirates frequently fired weapons without warning or reason, and were almost constantly chewing *khat* (a mild narcotic that produces an amphetamine-like high).

On April 20, the negotiations had completely stalled and the pirates were becoming extremely frustrated. The crew was all assembled and informed that they would be executed one at a time. The pirates pulled the captain out of the line, taped his eyes closed, and dragged him out on deck. The pirates screamed and then fired their weapons next to his head. Back in the United Kingdom and Germany, those responsible for negotiating with the pirates seemed to care little about the safety of the crew.

Reports emerged that conditions aboard were becoming serious for the hostages. The drinking water ran out, food was rationed, and some crewmembers became sick. The crew was kept on the ship's bridge under armed guard, while the pirates slept on deck where it was cooler at night. The supplies of food and water were not sufficient to sustain sixty pirates and the ship's crew. A number of goats roamed freely about the ship's deck, awaiting their slaughter by the pirates.

As the negotiations continued to start and stop again, the third officer had a heart attack, which he barely survived. The desperate captain implored the company to negotiate an end to the situation, saying that the crew was mentally exhausted from the continual psychological terror. Some of the crew had developed fevers and several of the pirates were clearly suffering from tuberculosis. The vessel's medical locker was by this time empty.

The German Association of Captains and Marine Officers strongly criticized the shipowners Leonhardt & Blumberg, but received no response from them, which was sadly typical in these cases. The negotiations continued to go badly, and the condition of the crew worsened. The German government finally decided to act in earnest to free the ship, mobilizing the German federal police counterterrorism force, GSG-9, to the area.

Acting under instructions from the German interior minister, GSG-9 was to perform an assessment on the feasibility of any rescue attempt. On April 25, the 200 personnel attached to the deployed GSG-9 team carried out exercises in preparation for the attempt aboard the U.S. Navy's helicopter carrier *Boxer*, well out of range of the ship. The pirates observed aircraft buzzing *Hansa Stavanger* and they became increasingly agitated. They took defensive positions and switched on all the deck lighting at night. The pirates transferred three Germans and one Russian member of the crew ashore, where they were subjected to humiliation, starvation, and mock executions as a deterrent to any rescue attempt. The German government got the message and eventually ordered GSG-9 to abort the mission, fearing a bloodbath. Negotiations for the release of the ship and crew stalled yet again.

At last, after a period of more than two months, with the crew suffering acute physical and psychological duress, a settlement looked likely by mid-June. Two days before the anticipated payment of the ransom, a senior pirate leader came aboard and declared that a greater sum was required, in particular for the hostages being held ashore. There was to be no negotiation. Meanwhile, the political issues continued back in Germany, with politicians criticizing the government for the poor communication and for bureaucratic delays between the military and GSG-9. The ordeal dragged on for the hapless crew and their desperate families.

By mid-July and more than three months since the hijacking occurred, the families of the crew started to appear in the mainstream media, begging for some action to free their loved ones unharmed. The shipowners did not give any information to the families and they also refused to budge in their negotiations with the pirates. At about this time, a media report emerged that the ship had been released, but the report was soon dismissed as false. And still nothing happened to move the situation forward to a positive end.

At the end of July, the families and friends of the hostages launched a public online petition to pressure the shipowners to do something to end the crisis. I signed that petition and approved of the global campaign under way to apply pressure on the shipowners to act on behalf of their employees. The families planned to present the petition on August 4, marking the end of four long months since the crew was hijacked and taken hostage.

On July 27, a $3 million ransom was reportedly agreed

upon and some of the pirates evidently went to await the delivery of the cash. Without any warning, members of the pirate group demanded another $500,000 to $1 million. Of course, the additional demands infuriated the shipowners. They stopped accepting calls from the pirates and stood firm on the $3 million. Yet another standoff ensued.

On August 3, it was announced that a ransom of $2.75 million had been paid to the pirates, dropped from a light aircraft onto the ship via parachute. After the pirates counted and distributed the cash, they left the vessel and disappeared with their loot. The German Navy moved in. The release of the hostages and the vessel came exactly four months after the hijacking. The ship, with its 1,070 containers, headed to Mombasa, Kenya. Two German warships escorted it. The vessel had to steam at slow speeds, as the hull was heavily fouled with shell growth after sitting at anchor for so long. The crew was well, but exhausted. One of the hard things the crew reported was that the pirates stole their toothbrushes and toothpaste, so none of them had brushed their teeth for four months. On its arrival in Mombasa, *Hansa Stavanger* berthed at the same quay where *Maersk Alabama* had been only hours earlier, after suffering its own ordeal with pirates.

The controversy continued. Evidently, a dispute between the shipowners and the owners of the cargo arose because of the crisis, and the two parties fought it out. Widespread criticism spread regarding the slow and seemingly inept measures taken to resolve the situation, one that put and kept the crew in real danger for four months. Blame was heaped on the ship insurers, the shipowners, and the German government, the latter for its unsuccessful military rescue plans.

There was significant German political fallout, particularly in view of the fact that the German government had been adamant that no ransom should be paid. German politicians criticized the ransom payment and stated that it encouraged further attacks and hijackings. One senior politician called for the increased use of military force in ending the hijackings, and another said the West was funding the hijack industry, which was indeed true, though no one had a choice if lives were to be saved. It seemed to many that the German politicians viewed the crew and ship as expendable, all for the greater political good. The world's merchant mariners welcomed the crew home, happy that they were out of danger and no longer suffering. Based on this incident, the next German crew that is taken hostage may not fare well at all.

The *Iran Deyanat* hijacking

On August 14, 2008, an estimated forty pirates armed with automatic weapons and rocket-propelled grenade launchers attacked and seized the 44,468-ton Iranian bulk carrier *MV Iran Deyanat*. The pirates were reported to have fired their weapons continuously until the ship submitted.

The Islamic Republic of Iran Shipping Lines, a state-owned company operated by the Iranian military, owns and operates *Iran Deyanat*. The vessel was on a voyage from the port of Nanjing, in China, to the port of Rotterdam, in the Netherlands, by way of the Suez Canal. Loaded with 42,500 tons of iron ore and industrial products, the ship was captured about eighty-two nautical miles southeast of al-Makalla, in Yemen. At the time, the pirates viewed the capture as just another handsome prize that would yield a large ransom payment. They were in for an unpleasant surprise.

After the pirates seized *Iran Deyanat*, they hijacked it. Trouble started almost immediately. The ship had engine problems. The weather turned foul and the seas turned rough. The ship was also short on drinking water. It was stated that within days, some of the pirates started to develop mysterious health complications, including skin burns and hair loss. Other sources said that some pirates had died. Unable to make their intended destination, the pirates took the ship to Eyl, where it was secured by a much larger contingent of pirates, about fifty

The German ship MV *Hansa Stavanger* anchors in the coastal port town of Mombasa, Kenya on Saturday, August 8, 2009. The nightmare of being held hostage in Somalia is over. The container ship with approximately 1,070 containers was sea-jacked by Somali pirates on April 3, 2009, 400 km off the southern Somali port of Kismaayu. *AP/Wide World Photos.*

The Liberian-flagged oil tanker MV *Sirius Star* is at anchor Wednesday, November 18, 2008, off the coast of Somalia. The Saudi-owned very large crude carrier was hijacked by Somali pirates on November 15, 2008, about 450 nautical miles off the coast of Kenya and forced to proceed to anchorage near Somalia. *U.S. Navy photo.*

A small aircraft is observed by the U.S. Navy as it flies over MV *Sirius Star* during an apparent payment via a parachuted container to pirates holding the *Sirius Star*. *U.S. Navy photo.*

The visit, board, search, and seizure team assigned to the guided missile destroyer USS *Mahan* conducts a training exercise with the Royal Navy frigate HMS *Portland*. *U.S. Navy photo.*

The guided missile cruiser USS *Cape St. George* steams in the Indian Ocean supporting maritime security operations in the U.S. Fifth Fleet area of responsibility. *U.S. Navy photo.*

A suspected pirate vessel ignites in flames before burning to the waterline. USS *Gonzalez* and USS *Cape St. George* were conducting maritime security operations in international waters off the coast of Somalia and attempted to perform a routine boarding of the suspicious vessel towing two skiffs. The suspected pirates opened fire on the U.S. Navy ships and the ships' crewmembers returned fire. One suspect was killed and 12 were taken into custody. *U.S. Navy photo.*

Members of a U.S. Navy visit, board, search, and seizure team from guided missile cruiser USS *Gettysburg* and U.S. Coast Guard Tactical Law Enforcement Team South, Detachment 409, approach a suspected pirate mother ship in the Gulf of Aden, May 13, 2009, after responding to a merchant vessel distress signal while operating in the Combined Maritime Forces area of responsibility. *U.S. Navy photo.*

The U.S. Navy visit, board, search, and seizure team aboard guided missile cruiser USS *Gettysburg* detains suspected pirates in the Gulf of Aden, April 17, 2009. *Gettysburg* is deployed as part of Combined Task Force 151, a multinational task force conducting counter-piracy operations in and around the Gulf of Aden, the Arabian Sea, the Indian Ocean, and the Red Sea. *U.S. Navy photo.*

Members of a visit, board, search, and seizure team assigned to USS *Gettysburg* and U.S. Coast Guard Tactical Law Enforcement Team South Detachment 409 detain suspected pirates after responding to a merchant vessel distress signal while operating in the Gulf of Aden, May 13, 2009. *U.S. Navy photo.*

The Maersk ship *Liberty Sun* is docked in Mombasa, Kenya, April 21, 2009, after a failed pirate attack. *U.S. Navy photo.*

The Royal Australian Navy Adelaide-class guided missile frigate HMAS *Sydney* and the Anzac-class frigate HMAS *Ballarat* perform formation maneuvering with the guided missile destroyer USS *Mahan*. *U.S. Navy photo.*

The visit, board, search, and seizure team assigned to the guided missile cruiser USS *Chosin* practices boarding techniques, December 3, 2009, in the Gulf of Aden. *Chosin* is the flagship of the Combined Joint Task Force 151, a multinational task force established to conduct counter piracy operations off the coast of Somalia. *U.S. Navy photo.*

U.S. sailors with the visit, board, search, and seizure team from guided missile cruiser USS *Chosin* keep watch over the crew of a suspected pirate dhow as fellow teammates conduct a search for weapons and other gear, November 12, 2009, in the Gulf of Aden. *U.S. Navy photo.*

U.S. Navy sailors with the visit, board, search, and seizure team of the guided missile cruiser USS *Vella Gulf* apprehend suspected pirates in the Gulf of Aden on February 11, 2009. The *Vella Gulf* is the flagship for the Combined Task Force 151, a multinational task force conducting operations to detect and deter piracy in and around the Gulf of Aden, Arabian Gulf, Indian Ocean, and Red Sea. *U.S. Navy photo.*

Zodiac commando boats arrive at French cruise ship *Le Ponant* off Somalia's coast, Saturday, April 12, 2008. Helicopter-borne French troops swooped in on Somali pirates after they released 30 hostages from the yacht, seizing six of the pirates and recovering sacks of money, apparently ransom paid by the yacht's owners to win the captives' release. The pirates had boarded the 88-meter (288-foot) French luxury yacht *Ponant* a week earlier, capturing its crew. *AP/Wide World Photos*

This undated photo provided Friday, April 10, 2009 by the French Navy shows people aboard the French sailboat *Tanit*, off the coast of Somalia. France's Navy stormed the French sailboat held by pirates off the Somali coast in an assault triggered by threats that the passengers would be executed. One hostage was killed in the rescue operation. *AP/Wide World Photos.*

aboard and fifty ashore. The number of pirates involved was curious, given that the ship was a bulk carrier.

Reports from the shipping company's website said the ship arrived in the Gulf of Aden on August 20 (the capture occurred six days earlier) and was expected to arrive at the Suez Canal on August 27. The passage from the Gulf of Aden to the Suez Canal usually takes about four or five days at most, so the extra days added to the schedule was peculiar. More than 50 percent of the crew were Iranians, which was highly unusual, even for an Iranian vessel. The crew comprised thirty men, a Pakistani captain, an Iranian engineer, thirteen other Iranians, three Indians, two Filipinos, and ten Eastern Europeans, possibly from Croatia.

News about the illnesses and deaths and the possibility that something in the cargo was toxic quickly reached the Puntland government in Garoowe. The government promptly dispatched a delegation led by the minister of minerals and oil to investigate. During a six-day negotiation several members of the pirate group became ill and died, further fanning fears about the nature of the cargo. The delegation concluded that the ship was not carrying a normal shipment.

The pirates refused permission to inspect the vessel, and they threatened to blow up the ship if the authorities attempted to use force to gain access for an inspection. Eyl city officials formed a committee to negotiate with the pirates. The pirates said they had tried to inspect seven cargo containers after the health issues emerged on board, but the containers were locked. Incidentally, containers are a curious deck cargo to have on a bulk carrier.

When asked, the crew maintained that they didn't have the lock access codes for the containers. The captain and the engineer were contacted to determine the nature of the cargo, particularly the contents of those containers. Unofficial sources stated that the containers were packed with dangerous chemicals. In Mombasa, Kenya, Andrew Mwangura, coordinator of the East African Seafarers Assistance Program, was among those who said the cargo was toxic. The Iranian shipping company denied that the vessel was carrying a dangerous consignment and threatened legal action against Mwangura for saying so.

The pirates set the ransom at $2 million and the Iranian government was said to have given $200,000 to a local broker to facilitate the payment and the release of the ship. Iran later said that it had not agreed to the price and had not paid the pirates or the broker anything. On September 10, the U.S. Department of the Treasury sanctioned the company in an attempt to get answers, but the Iranians dug in their heels, saying they would not deal with the pirates, and, besides, even if they did want to come to an arrangement with them, the U.S. Navy was hovering around, which made the situation impossible to resolve.

What proved even more perplexing was a claim in the Iranian media that stated the U.S. had offered a $7 million bribe to the pirates in return for the privilege of searching and inspecting the ship. The Pentagon and the U.S. Department of State obviously refused to comment. To this day, the nature of the cargo remains a mystery, but officials in Puntland and Baidoa said they were absolutely convinced that the ship was carrying weapons to Eritrea for Islamist insurgents. Whether they are right or not is subject to question.

On October 13, the ship and crew was released. There was an almost complete absence of international press coverage of the entire incident, which is somewhat puzzling given the mystery over the ship's supposedly lethal cargo. The capture of *Faina* seemed to eclipse the importance of this strange episode.

Speculation did continue to circulate. One blogger evidently reported that the ship was a dirty bomb on its way to an Israeli coastal city, where it was to have been blown up, showering the city with radiation. The blogger said that Iran had purchased radioactive sand from China that was subsequently sealed in barrels. Obviously, you can't believe everything you read on the Internet, but the blogs got a lot of attention.

There were alternative claims as well. Some said that the whole incident was an Israeli operation. Iran's state radio was reported as saying that a ransom had been reluctantly paid to free the ship and the crew. The head of the Iranian shipping company announced that they had been in telephone contact with the pirates to arrange food and water supplies before the final release. The shipping company subsequently ordered all its vessels to install barbed wire along the decks as an added anti-boarding measure.

When *Iran Deyanat* finally arrived in Rotterdam, the ship was subjected to scrutiny and further speculation. The port authorities found nothing suspicious after their thorough inspection. Whatever was aboard that caused the illness and deaths appeared to have vanished, if it ever was there at all. Some postulated that the mysterious cargo had been offloaded in Eritrea after the ship resumed its voyage. *Iran Deyanat* also made maritime news in 2007 when it was forced to anchor in a bay in the United Kingdom after suffering engine problems during heavy weather in the English Channel.

PART 4

Piracy and Yachts

14

Reducing Piracy Risks

Every year throughout the world pirates or armed robbers attack more than 3,000 yachts and small boats. The vast majority of these incidents are never reported and fewer still are recorded as actual piracy. Few reports reach the International Maritime Bureau's Piracy Reporting Center or other international maritime organizations, which are mainly concerned with commercial shipping. When an act of piracy or armed robbery occurs and involves a yacht, it is typically reported to local authorities that may or may not do anything about it.

As a longtime cruising yachtsman, I find that when discussing ocean voyaging in the various parts of the world with other offshore passagemakers, it doesn't take long for the topic of piracy and robbery to come up, and for very good reason. It's frightening to think you or your spouse or crew might be assaulted or killed, either at anchor or on the high seas. While the above statistic of 3,000 or more annual piracy incidents against yachts is sobering, it is only an estimate. The problem could well be more widespread, or it could be somewhat less widespread. However, piracy against yachts does occur, and it will continue to occur in many places where cruising is popular.

In recent years, Venezuela has consistently ranked highest among hot zones for piracy and armed robberies against yachts. Many of these attacks have involved violence and sometimes murder. Indonesia is also high on the danger list. Somali waters and the Gulf of Aden are extremely hazardous, but the number of yachts transiting the region remains low compared to the Caribbean, so fewer sailors are at risk. Obviously, areas where pirates are active and where there are large numbers of yachts will see more attacks than areas where there are fewer yachts. Piracy and armed robberies against yachts have occurred in South and Central America (Caribbean, Atlantic, and Pacific sides), Indonesia and the South China Sea, Somali waters and the Gulf of Aden, parts of the South Pacific, and parts of the Mediterranean.

Whereas the owners of merchant vessels carry hefty insurance policies to cover all kinds of risk, including the payment of a ransom, a yacht owner won't have such coverage. Nevertheless, hostages have been taken and ransoms have been paid. A yacht also doesn't have a large crew to repel boarders, and the yacht itself is extremely vulnerable to gunfire, is typically quite slow, and has very low freeboard, making it easy to board from a fast skiff with no ropes, grappling hooks, or ladders. In short, a yacht is the perfect target for pirate attacks.

When the statistics are analyzed, the single greatest robbery and piracy exposure situations are faced while a yacht is lying at anchor. Serious injuries or death sometimes occurs, usually when someone resists the attack or confronts the assailants. The basic fact in cruising is that you want to stay away from expensive marinas and drop the hook in a tranquil bay away from crowds. In many cases, this is absolutely fine, but there are places where certain anchorages present opportunistic criminals with an easy chance to commit armed robbery. What security measures can you take? As the skipper of a yacht, you need to plan ahead regarding antipiracy measures. As with any merchant ship, the plan has to include a multi-layered approach to handling piracy and robbery.

Reducing piracy risks when anchored

Like merchant ships and even ashore at home, you need a sanctuary to retreat to when under attack. A yacht is a special challenge, as it often only has two or three cabins and it is also generally made of fiberglass. The first instinct when you hear those heart-stopping footfalls on the deck above you is to go up and check it out. That is probably the worst thing you can do. It is better to lose a dinghy or an outboard engine than to lose your life. Unfortunately, attackers generally want your money and other valuables, not the dinghy. They have to come below to confront you and ransack the yacht to find the cash and valuables they want. Therefore, it is essential to stop them from coming below.

Few yachts have any provisions for enhanced physical security. Indeed, most crews leave the washboards out at the top of the companionway steps at night, an open invitation for pirates to come below. Some people, including myself, prefer to close up the boat and secure themselves below. Yet, in the tropics that is not desirable because it gets hot and stuffy below. There are viable solutions, though.

On one of my yachts, I had a drop-in and lockable stainless-steel washboard grill for the companionway that allowed ventilation while preventing any access from the cockpit. The forward hatch presents a challenge, but similar arrangements are possible. If the pirates or robbers can't get below, it is far less likely that you or your crew will be harmed. I do not hold to the view that one should allow the pirates or robbers to come below, and give them all they want. The fact is whatever you give them is never enough and they invariably resort to violence when they don't get as much as they expect to find. I would prefer to stay locked below and throw some sacrificial cash out through the protective washboard grills. While you are hunkered down below you have time to get on the VHF radio and summon help.

Audible alarms and lighting play a big part in yacht protection plans. Many yacht owners do not want to switch the deck lights on at night since they consume lots of electricity. However, installing high-powered LED deck lighting is a way around the problem. With LEDs, leaving the deck lights on all night won't overly drain the batteries. A well-lit yacht has the potential to deter attackers. They like to board quietly in the dark and then escape with a minimal chance of detection. If they see a yacht that is lit and one that is not, they'll go to the darkened boat first.

It is also a good practice to install a panic button below that is used to activate spotlights and loud sirens. Spotlights and strobes can be installed on the mast under the spreaders and in any other suitable location. The same goes for high-decibel sirens, which can be installed on the mast and in the cockpit. The idea is to attract attention if you are boarded in the middle of the night, or in broad daylight, for that matter. The loud noise and bright lights will also help to disorient attackers, and, hopefully, will deter them from pressing on with the attack.

There are measures that involve the rigging of high voltage wires around the perimeter of the boat. Insulated outriggers are bolted or fastened to the lifeline stanchions. The outriggers have a wire strung through them, usually a polyester string with an integral conductor. A battery-powered, high-voltage fence energizer is used to apply a pulse to the wire. A secondary ground wire is also rigged. Any intruders who grab the wires while trying to board will get a severe electric shock. Merchant vessels are using such systems.

There are occasions where in the daytime while at anchor people in canoes, fishing boats, and other craft will approach your yacht. A group of boats traveling toward you is always something to be suspicious of. Relaxing in the cockpit during the early evening is another period that this technique is sometimes used. The people in the boats will often start a conversation and offer to sell you fish or ask for something, but once they manage to get up close, the guns come out and the attack begins. If you are in a high piracy area, you always need to keep an eye out for potential threats. If the situation feels threatening, have a plan to retreat below and quickly lock yourselves in. Rehearse the drill, as practice makes perfect.

Reducing piracy risks when under way

You may be attacked while you are in transit between ports, either under power or under sail. Handling such an attack is problematic. If you are passing through a high-risk area, then traveling in company with other yachts is wise. You need to have a group strategy to handle any threats. If you are traveling on your own, then you have to look at things differently. It is essential to keep a careful watch for rapidly closing small boats. The earlier you detect a threat, the earlier you can initiate defensive plans. So many times you hear accounts from people who were attacked saying how quickly a boat was on them. If you are not looking, then the pirates are always a surprise when they show up!

When an attack appears imminent while you are under sail, the first task is to get the engine started and to drop the mainsail fast. The headsail can also be furled within a minute. A modern yacht under power is very maneuverable and evasive actions can be effective in preventing a boarding. Putting the helm hard over with the engine at full throttle will give you a tight turning circle, making boarding difficult, if not impossible. It's worth practicing this maneuver to see how your yacht responds and to determine how maneuverable it is.

If your sails are up when an attack occurs, your boat will be far less maneuverable. However, there are some good arguments for keeping the main up and allowing the mainsheet to run out. As you turn the vessel in a tight circle, the boom will slam hard over from side to side, and that may deter any boarders. I think it's an interesting idea to consider.

Another technique, often used by fishing vessels in the

Gulf of Aden, is to turn the yacht into the wind under power. The yacht will tend to pitch and hobbyhorse in the swells and waves, making any boarding from other boats very hazardous. One problem with this technique is that the person at the helm will be exposed to weapons fire. Sitting down low while steering is recommended. One sailing friend of mine set up an autopilot control below, allowing him to take evasive action without having to do so from the cockpit. A pitching vessel also makes accurate gunfire very difficult for pirates.

In some cases, yachts have successfully rammed the attacking craft. This is not easy, of course, but it's better than being captured and is often enough to stop the attack. The aim is to continue the evasive maneuvers long enough for the attackers to decide that it's just too much of a hassle to continue the attack. I have a friend who installed reinforcing in the bow and a stainless-steel protective strip down the bow just to make ramming pirate boats a viable option.

Carrying guns aboard

To arm or not to arm is a subject that soon emerges as a major topic when pirates and armed robberies come up in conversations among cruisers. Most boaters state that they want to carry a firearm and I know several who do. But carrying firearms aboard brings with it many legal issues, and these issues are prevalent in many of the countries situated in the most popular cruising grounds. If you conceal a weapon, fail to declare it, and it is discovered, you're in for a world of problems that can include jail.

Then, of course, the question arises as to when do you use a gun. If you use firearms to defend the yacht while it is in international waters, you may not end up being prosecuted. However, if you shoot at, wound, or kill a pirate or armed robber in territorial waters, before you know it a police or navy boat turns up and the next thing you know you are in jail on attempted murder charges. Bear in mind that many of these robbers have connections with local authorities.

And then there's another major consideration. Chances are you will simply be outgunned. The pirates may have three AK-47s and you have a pistol or a shotgun. The contest is somewhat unequal! Also, in many cases by the time you get to your weapon the pirates are already on board. Firearms have the potential to escalate the situation, causing a major fire-fight in which someone may be killed. Carrying and choosing to use a firearm in the defense of a yacht is a personal choice, but one thing is clear, if you do carry a gun aboard you have to know how to use it and must be willing to use it.

15

Notable Yacht Hijackings and Murders

Any encounter with pirates or armed robbers while cruising is a frightening experience, and there are literally hundreds of cases on record. As previously noted, most incidents involving yachts go unreported, so the record is far from complete. Every now and then a case arises that receives widespread media attention because of its brutal nature or because the victims of an attack are famous. The tragic death of the renowned New Zealand sailor Sir Peter Blake is a good example of the latter. Below are some of the more notable, or nefarious, cases of recent piracy against yachts. Most of the ones highlighted here occurred in Somali waters and the Gulf of Aden. Incidents of piracy against yachts that occurred elsewhere will be covered in more detail in another chapter.

The hijacking of *Le Ponant*

The French-flagged yacht *Le Ponant* was attacked and seized about 250 nautical miles off the Somali coast in the Gulf of Aden on Friday, April 4, 2008. The 850-ton, three-masted luxury passenger yacht was on a delivery voyage to the Mediterranean Sea from the Seychelles with a crew of thirty aboard. They were all taken hostages. The crew consisted of twenty-two French nationals, six Filipinos (including one woman), one Ukrainian, and a Cameroon national.

Prior to the attack and hijacking the vessel was scheduled to commence a voyage from the Egyptian port of Alexandria to Valletta, in Malta, on April 21. The owner of the yacht is the Marseille-based cruise operator Compagnie des Iles du Ponant, one of France's leading cruise vacation companies and a subsidiary of CMA-CGM, one of the world's largest shipping enterprises. This incident received worldwide attention in the media, in part because it involved a beautiful sailing yacht, and in part because the story had a dramatic ending.

After the pirates were captured, details of what happened emerged with more clarity. The pirates, who were members of one of Somalia's sea militias, took two speedboats from a village, presumably with the use of force, ostensibly to go out fishing and to defend Somalia's territorial waters. Some reports stated that the militiamen were probably the Somali Marines, who had a reputation for being well organized and had warlord protection, along with a completely separate business structure for handling and negotiating ransom demands.

Initially, the pirates attacked and captured a Yemeni trawler, taking the crew of twenty-seven as hostages. The fate of this crew remains unclear. The pirates used the captured trawler as mother ship. They encountered *Le Ponant*. Obviously, sighting the yacht would have been the equivalent of winning the lottery for the pirates, or so they probably thought. Three pirates immediately got into a speedboat and raced toward *Le Ponant*, opening fire with AK-47s while the yacht's skipper, Patrick Marchesseau, and his crew tried to repel the attack on the vessel with fire hoses. It was a pretty unequal contest, of course.

An additional six pirates joined in the attack in another boat, reinforcing the first three pirates. The nine pirates easily stormed the yacht and overpowered the crew, taking control. The Yemeni trawler was abandoned once the pirates realized they had a potentially valuable ransom opportunity, and they decided that they were all needed to maintain effective control of the yacht.

A French frigate was diverted from its usual patrol area to track the progress of the yacht, and an aircraft was scrambled out of the large French base in Djibouti to fly over the vessel. A Canadian Navy helicopter from the vessel *Charlottetown* also joined the French forces in the tracking and surveillance of *Le Ponant*. The helicopter took surveillance images of the yacht, which were passed on to the Combined Task Force 150, an international coalition of vessels tasked with monitoring and inspecting vessels in the area.

Le Ponant was sailed south by the pirates from where it was captured and anchored off the village of Garaad. Garaad is in northeastern Somalia, in Puntland, a self-proclaimed semi-autonomous region located to the south of the main pirate port of Eyl. The yacht was kept under constant surveillance by a French naval vessel. Following the arrival and anchoring of the yacht, the female crewmembers were separated from the men and secured in another area of the yacht for the first two days of the weeklong ordeal.

Interestingly, about seventy local villagers reportedly assembled to offer protection services for both the yacht and the crew. There was a genuine fear that other rival clans might attack and steal the prize. As a result of these fears, additional automatic weapons were brought aboard and a total of approximately thirty pirates and the newly employed villagers were put on guard duty. The pirates even brought goats aboard and had a barbeque. At the moment, the situation was relatively relaxed. The pirates were comfortable and familiar with typical ransom negotiations.

The pirates were reported as being very strict at trying to maintain discipline among the pirate group and the villagers. For example, when one pirate discharged his weapon by accident and nearly shot *Le Ponant*'s doctor, the pirate leader immediately sent the offender ashore as punishment. The pirates were very focused on not harming any of the captives and were following a code of conduct, including a prohibition against any form of sexual assaults on the female hostages. A copy of this pirate code was later found on *Le Ponant*.

In spite of the relative ease aboard the yacht, the pirates obviously remained on edge and discipline occasionally unraveled. One pirate allegedly shot one of the villagers dead. Evidently, the hapless villager was killed because he refused to give the pirate some *khat*, a mildly narcotic plant that furnishes an amphetamine-like high.

At a very early stage, the French government was involved with the negotiations for the release of the yacht, at the most senior level. Various senior French government ministers appeared in the media. The French government said it had been in contact with the pirates and Foreign Minister Bernard Kouchner stated in a radio interview that resolving the issue might take some time and that the objective was to avoid bloodshed. He also said that negotiations were under way, but he did not elaborate on the details, though most commentators believed the negotiations involved a ransom payment. French Prime Minister Francois Fillon was quoted as saying the defense and foreign ministries were working to secure the release of the yacht and its crew. The French Defense Minister Hervé Morin was quoted as saying that there would not be any military intervention unless the safety of the crew could be guaranteed.

The Puntland region information minister issued a warning to the French government against paying any ransom, and further stated that the payment of money would only encourage the pirates to continue their criminal acts. He further urged the U.S. Navy and other Western forces to take the yacht by force. This was an easy comment for him to make. After all, none of his citizens were in danger. The ransom was reportedly set at

$2 million. Each villager was to receive $50, while each pirate would get between $11,000 and $20,000.

During the negotiations a French warship maintained close surveillance on the yacht, along with members from the Groupe d'Intervention de la Gendarmerie Nationale, which is considered Europe's top Special Forces unit. Members of the unit had been flown to and stationed at the French naval base in nearby Djibouti. Djibouti is the largest French military base outside France, and it is located in a former small colony at Somalia's northern border. Djibouti is strategically important within the Horn of Africa region. It lies at the junction of both the Red Sea and the Gulf of Aden, the main shipping lane to and from the Suez Canal and Indian Ocean.

A French military source issued a report indicating that the hostages had been freed following negotiations and that no military intervention had been required. The French President Nicolas Sarkozy released a statement announcing the successful liberation of the crew, who had been held hostage for a week by the Somali pirates. President Sarkozy also offered thanks and deep gratitude to the French armed forces and to the government services that had permitted a rapid resolution of the hostage incident. It was in fact a remarkably quick outcome, as ransom negotiations often take many months.

Details of the hostage liberation were released only after President Sarkozy personally met the families of the hostages to give them the news first. The French Foreign Minister Bernard Kouchner also stated that preparations were being made to repatriate the former hostages back to France as soon as possible. One news report stated that no French government funding was used for the ransom payment. However, it was possible that the money came from *Le Ponant*'s owners.

The vessel owners CMA-CGM announced that *Le Ponant* was due to arrive in Djibouti the following Tuesday, with or without the crew. The spokesman for the owners was also quoted as saying that he did not know any details regarding crew repatriation. He stated that it would take several sailing days for the vessel to get to Djibouti, and that it was possible the skipper would stay aboard with a navy crew to bring the yacht back under a naval escort. The yacht's skipper, Marchesseau, was quoted as saying that he had managed to contact authorities without the pirates knowing about it, in spite of warnings not to do so.

The crew was transferred to the French helicopter carrier *Jeanne d'Arc* and was scheduled to fly to the French military base in Djibouti and then travel back to France. The freed hostages arrived back in Paris and received medical examinations and psychological evaluations. The arrangements for the six Philippine nationals, the Ukrainian, and the Cameroonian were not revealed.

Like any good adventure tale the French came up with an unexpected and welcome end to the saga. About an hour after receiving the ransom, the pirates left the yacht and went ashore. Unknown to them, the French military was maintaining surveillance. French Special Forces aboard a helicopter intercepted a vehicle as it left the area, capturing six people. They also recovered a portion of the ransom.

The French military announced that the successful operation had been carried out with authorization from Somali authorities. The commandos fired warning shots near the vehicle, but no rounds were directed at the pirates. The pirates were arrested and transported immediately by helicopter to *Jeanne d'Arc*. The pirates were then transferred to the ship *Jean Bart*, which was sailing toward Djibouti.

French defense personnel reported that President Nicolas Sarkozy had ordered that the pirates be captured alive if possible without causing collateral damage, so that they could be brought to justice. The French defense minister announced that the French would not tolerate extortion attempts. It was also stated by the French defense minister that it was the first time a country had refused to be extorted, and took matters into its own hands.

The French foreign ministry announced that it would prefer to see the pirates brought to France for trial. Several commentators discussed the potential legal problems were this to happen. The French government was not concerned, as it had authorization from Somali authorities to carry out the arrest operation. Some of the legal challenges in prosecuting the pirates were that they carried out the offenses in international waters, were taken to Somali territorial waters, and then captured in Somalia. Two of the captured Somali prisoners were understood to be members of a militia, while three were villagers. The sixth person was reported to be the driver of the vehicle.

The governor of the Mugug region in Somalia, where the capture took place, proclaimed that four of the men were innocent and were just *khat* traders doing business with the two pirates. He was also reported as saying that three people were killed during the French raid. However, the office of President Sarkozy categorically denied the assertions and it was restated that not a drop of blood was spilled.

The six suspected pirates arrived aboard a military transport plane at Le Bourget airport near Paris and were transferred to a detention center in Paris. French justice officials were quoted as saying that they hoped to try the pirates on the charges of organized criminality for the hijacking of the French-flagged yacht, the taking of hostages (including French nationals), and also the taking of the hostages with the intent to secure a ransom. The pirates faced a possible life sentence.

At the time of this writing, the trial had not been completed. It will be of interest to everyone to see how the trial turns out, given the legal complexities of dealing with pirates. Like most mariners, I congratulate the French on the speed at which they resolved the crisis and on the decisive action taken against the pirates after the release of the crew.

After this incident, pirates threatened to kill any European they captured unless France returned the six suspected pirates captured by the French commandos. The pirates further stated that if other European Union countries refused to negotiate for the release of their compatriots, they would target all Europeans, saying they would behead every European hostage.

The hijacking of *Rockall*

On June 23, 2008, pirates attacked the German-registered yacht *Rockall* and took the three members of the crew as hostages. In a comparatively rare event, the attack and hijacking occurred off Somaliland, a somewhat more stable and prosperous area of Somalia. I was reading a newspaper in Abu Dhabi at the time and a long article carried the following banner headline in large red text: "One Crazy Sailor!" The story was about 62-year-old Jurgen Kantner and his wife Sabine Merz, who had survived the pirate attack on their yacht and a subsequent two months of captivity. The pirates took them inland and secured them in a mountain hideout to prevent any possible rescue.

The couple was subjected to severe deprivations and mock executions during their fifty-two day ordeal, until a ransom was paid. At one stage, it was reported that Sabine Merz was running out of her medicine to treat her diabetes and an intermediary managed to get some to her. It was also stated that she had been roughly treated during the kidnapping. The area where the couple was held was likened to the Tora Bora complex in the mountains of Afghanistan, where the Taliban often take refuge. They were moved almost daily to make rescue attempts difficult. The report stated that they were almost constantly intimidated and harassed, and at times they just wished someone would bomb the pirates and they could all die together.

The couple, and the third individual with them, was released in August 2008 after a reported ransom of about $800,000 was paid. After returning to Germany the couple decided to go back to Somaliland to reclaim their yacht. The boat was anchored between two Somali naval vessels, in the Somaliland port of Berbera, and the couple, especially the skipper, become minor celebrities. The locals evidently called Jurgen "the mad German sailor". He was quoted as saying, "My boat is my life, and I don't want to lose her!" He expressed some concern about sailing from the port and possibly encountering pirates again, and he said he would have to devise a plan. Meanwhile, he repaired the yacht and was preparing to sail on. Jurgen and Sabine epitomize the spirit of cruising.

The hijacking of *Carré d'As IV*

On February 9, 2009, six pirates attacked and captured the Venezuelan-flagged and French-crewed yacht *Carré d'As IV*. The 52-foot, two-masted yacht was on a passage from the Cocos (Keeling) Islands to Aden. The crew had departed from Tahiti and was sailing to La Rochelle, France, on the Bay of Biscay. The pirates took the crew as hostages and sailed the yacht to Eyl, in Somalia. Naturally, the French government demanded that the hostages be released immediately.

There were suggestions that the pirates did not realize that French nationals were aboard and that the hijacking would prove to be a big mistake. It was further reported that the hostages had not been taken to Eyl and that the couple, Jean-Yves and his wife, Bernardette Delanne, had been put ashore near Alula and taken into the Xaabo mountains. The reports also suggested that the yacht was being used as a decoy vessel to attack other ships. An alert was issued, along with a description of the yacht. These claims and assertions proved unfounded, as events will show. The initial ransom demand was reportedly for $1.4 million. In addition to the ransom, the pirates insisted on the release of the six Somalis taken captive and transferred to France for trial subsequent to the hijacking of the yacht *Le Ponant*.

An elite thirty-man contingent of French Special Forces, known as the Hubert Commandos, were air dropped some distance away from *Carré d'As IV*. The commando team then swam to the yacht and stormed aboard. One pirate opened fire and was killed. In just ten minutes, the rest of the pirates had been captured and the hostages were freed. No commandos were injured. French President Nicolas Sarkozy stated that the operation was a warning to all those engaged in piracy and hostage taking, and that France would not accept the notion that crime pays. Most mariners applauded France's second successful and decisive strike back at the pirates. The captured pirates joined the previous six awaiting trial in France.

This hijacking did not end with the capture and transfer of the alleged pirates to France. In July 2009, two Frenchmen who were training Somali government forces were kidnapped from their hotel in Mogadishu, Somalia. It was announced by a Shebab spokesman that they would be tried and punished under Sharia law for spying and aiding the enemy of Allah. The principal reason behind the kidnapping was to pressure the French into releasing the twelve pirates being held in France for trial for their part in the French yacht hijackings.

The hijacking of *Tanit*

On April 4, 2009, pirates attacked and captured the French-flagged yacht *Tanit*. The crew of five was taken hostage and yacht was then sailed to Somalia, where ransom negotiations commenced. The skipper of the yacht was Florent Lemaçon, of Vannes, who was sailing with his wife and three-year-old son.

The French military launched a rescue attempt in which Lemaçon was killed, along with two of the pirates. Three other pirates were arrested and three crewmembers and the child were liberated. What remains unclear is whether the pirates executed the skipper or if he was unfortunately caught in the cross fire during the action. Later reports stated that he was killed as he tried to lower himself down a hatch when the gunfire began.

France has always taken a tough stance with pirates. However, in this case it was revealed that French negotiators did discuss the payment of a ransom with the pirates, but the pirates refused to name a price. It was believed that given the nature of the pirates and that they had made no demand for money, the hostages were in imminent danger and would likely be taken ashore, where rescue would be difficult, if not impossible. In keeping with the French policy of never allowing French citizens to be taken ashore as hostages, rescue by military intervention was deemed necessary.

During the rescue operation the pirates fired at the eight French commandos with AK-47 rifles as they boarded the yacht. Up to seventy commandos were standing by on three French frigates. The three pirates taken prisoner in the operation were transferred to France for criminal proceedings. The *Tanit* rescue marked the third time within a year that French forces staged recovery operations and freed hostages from pirates. However, it was the first time a hostage had been killed.

The murder of Sir Peter Blake

One of the most publicized incidents of piracy against yachts occurred on December 6, 2001, when Sir Peter Blake was shot to death. I was working in Brazil at the time of this tragic event and remember the shock at hearing the news. The renowned New Zealand yachtsman and environmentalist, and winner of the America's Cup in 1995 and 2000, was killed during a pirate attack in Brazil. He died aboard his 118-foot yacht *Seamaster*, which was anchored off Macapa in Amaoa, one of the jungle states that border the Amazon River.

Seamaster had just concluded a three-month expedition on the Amazon River and had arrived at the town of Macapa on the Amazon Delta. The yacht was requested to drop anchor a few hundred yards off the small fishing village of Fazendinha. The crew was awaiting clearance from Brazilian customs officials before departing Brazil for Venezuela. The crew all went ashore for a meal to celebrate the conclusion of the expedition, and upon returning to the yacht they sat out on deck enjoying a few cold beers.

A band of river pirates known as the Water Rats attacked the yacht at around nine o'clock that evening. The Water Rats didn't expect too much resistance, but they met some very tough New Zealanders. The six or eight pirates came up over the rail wearing balaclavas and helmets after reaching the yacht in a rubber dinghy. One of the crew squirted beer into the face of one of the pirates and was pistol-whipped in the face for his efforts.

It was reported that Sir Peter Blake went below to get his gun, while others say he was already below. As he was coming up the companionway steps, he encountered a pirate holding a pistol to the head of one of the crew. The pirate was shouting, "Money! Money! Money!" Another pirate, who was out on bail for a previous robbery, also had a gun. Blake fired at the pirate and hit him in the hand, blowing off one of his fingers. Still another pirate, also out on bail for robbery, returned fire, shooting twice and hitting Blake in the back. Blake died instantly.

The pirates grabbed whatever they could, including money, cameras, and other items. They stole Blake's wristwatch. They also took Blake's rifle, and then escaped in their own boat, along with one of the yacht's inflatable boats and a spare outboard motor. They fired at the yacht and slightly wounded one of the crew.

Water Rats, or *ratos de agua*, is what Brazilians call the pirates operating on the Amazon River. Although the robbers are almost always armed, in general robberies are executed without harm to people aboard their yachts. The aim is to get money or goods for resale to fund drug habits. It is said that like on most of their other night raids the Water Rats didn't expect armed resistance. Many say that the decision to defend the yacht probably cost Blake his life. Brazilian federal police stated that the pirates were only after valuables and cash, and would have left on their own after they got what they wanted. As I said, I was working in Brazil at the time and we had a policy of always having some money in a pocket to hand over to robbers, as well as a policy of putting up no resistance. Several robberies ashore that I knew about showed that the robbers would shoot and kill immediately any time resistance was offered.

The outcry over Blake's murder was intense at an international level. The Brazilian President Fernando Henrique Cardoso issued orders that the criminals be promptly identified and arrested, and he said that Brazil deeply regretted the tragic death of New Zealand's renowned explorer, yachtsman, and environmentalist. The police captured the pirates within twenty-four hours. They were subsequently sentenced to about thirty-two years in prison, with the pirate who fired the fatal shots getting a sentence of thirty-six years, nine months. It was stated that the yacht crew had always been very vigilant when traveling on the river and had always maintained careful watches, and that they had only relaxed when they returned to Macapa.

Sir Peter Blake was buried in Warblington churchyard, near Emsworth, in Hampshire, England, where he, his wife Pippa, and their children had settled. Many New Zealanders often leave New Zealand coins on his headstone as a tribute to the man and all of his achievements. The headstone bears the words from John Masefield's famous poem, *Sea Fever*: "I must go down to the sea again, to the lonely sea and sky, and all I ask. . . ."

Blake's yachting achievements bear restating here. He skippered *Team New Zealand* to a five-to-zero victory over the three-time champion Dennis Conner and *Young America* in the 1995 America's Cup in San Diego, California. Peter Blake also became the first non-American contestant in 149 years to defend the cup by defeating Italy's *Pravda* with a five-to-zero victory aboard *Black Magic*. He also won the Whitbread Round the World Race aboard *Steinlager 1* in 1989, and he competed in five of those races. He won the Jules Verne trophy awarded for circumnavigating the globe on the catamaran *ENZA New Zealand*, which set a record for a fast passage of 74 days, 22 hours, 17 minutes, and 22 seconds.

Blake also sailed in the most infamous Fastnet yacht race in history aboard the 77-foot maxi yacht *Condor of Bermuda*. The race, held in 1979, was sailed in dreadful Force 10 conditions, in which twenty-four yachts were abandoned, five other yachts sank, and fifteen sailors died. *Condor of Bermuda* won line honors ahead of Ted Turner in the 61-foot *Tenacious*, which won the race on corrected time. In addition, Blake sailed in five Sydney-Hobart races, five Fastnet races, in the double-handed Round Britain Race, on three Trans-Tasman races, and in several other major events as well.

16

Yacht Piracy Worldwide

Piracy against yachts can occur just about anywhere, though as previously noted some regions are hotter than others. Incidents of piracy and armed robbery have been reported in remote places like coastal Central America and in the islands of the South Pacific, and in not so remote places like the Greek isles. A look at a small sampling of incidents from around the world illustrates the typical behavior of pirates and some of the measures yacht crews have used to avoid harm and to defend their yachts.

Somali waters and the Gulf of Aden
Much of this book has necessarily focused on the increased piracy in the Horn of Africa, and for good reason. Below are just a few examples of attacks on yachts that occurred in 2009, and one very intriguing account of two yachts that successfully fought back in 2005.

The Seychelles maritime research yacht *Indian Ocean Explorer* was attacked on March 28, 2009, off the Seychelles and southern Somalia. The pirates boarded and hijacked the yacht, along with its crew of seven. The skipper contacted the yacht owners to inform them of the hijack situation. The yacht was sailed to the Somali coast. The crew were released in June without their yacht. The pirates set fire to the yacht and destroyed it after receiving $450,000 instead of the $1 million they demanded. The pirates burned the yacht to ensure that it could not be recovered. These actions made the episode virtually unique, as the vessel and crew is usually considered a single package for negotiation purposes.

The yacht *Grandezza* was attacked in March 2009 in the Gulf of Aden. Pirates armed with automatic weapons attacked in skiffs and chased the yacht, opening fire on it. The skipper contacted coalition warships for assistance, increased boat speed, and took evasive action. The pirates attempted to board the yacht using an aluminium ladder, but were unsuccessful and the ladder fell into the sea. A coalition helicopter arrived and the pirates aborted the attack.

In March 2005, the U.S.-flagged steel yacht *Gandalf* was attacked about thirty nautical miles off the coast of Yemen and south of Al Mukalla while sailing in company with another steel American yacht, *Mahdi*. The yachts were en route from Salalah in Oman to Aden. Initially, two 25-foot fishing boats equipped with outboard motors approached the yachts, but the boats left without attacking. Several hours later two larger vessels equipped with inboard diesel engines approached, and the four men in each of these boats opened fire with AK-47s. Both yachts were hit with many rounds.

The crews transmitted Mayday calls requesting assistance from patrolling naval vessels on all VHF channels and HF frequencies, including two HF emergency frequencies supplied by the U.S. Coast Guard. *Gandalf*'s skipper, Jay Barry, started evasive maneuvers and actually rammed his yacht into the hull of one pirate boat, causing serious damage and apparently injuring two of the pirates. Aboard *Mahdi*, the skipper, Rod Nowlin, an ex-U.S. Navy sailor, returned fire with a 12-gauge shotgun loaded with buckshot.

The pirates stopped firing when fire was returned and the pirate skiff helmsman took cover behind the steering console. Nowlin kept firing and the engine aboard the pirate boat

Areas in which several cases of yacht piracy have been repor

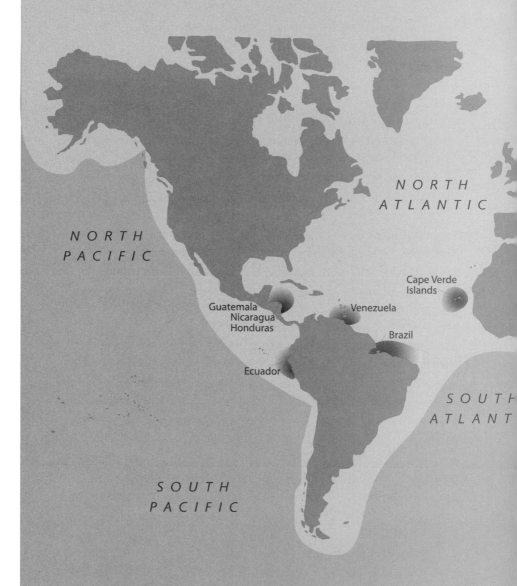

NORTH
ATLANTIC

NORTH
PACIFIC

Cape Verde
Islands

Guatemala
Nicaragua
Honduras

Venezuela

Brazil

Ecuador

SOUT
ATLANT

SOUTH
PACIFIC

PACIFIC
OCEAN

Philippines
Sulu Sea

Gulf of
Aden

Socotra

Somalia

Indonesia

INDIAN
OCEAN

started smoking. *Gandalf* was then turned and rammed into the fiberglass pirate skiff, almost cutting it in half and capsizing it. The second boat attacked *Mahdi*, with the pirates continually firing and trying to board the yacht. The pirates were already on the bow when Nowlin shot them both with his shotgun and they fell back into the skiff.

As the skiff veered away from the yachts, the driver was also shot. The pirates discontinued the attack, most likely because they were unable to keep firing, having sustained casualties. Their boats were also disabled. The crews took a moment to photograph the pirate boats, and then the yachts escaped at maximum speed. On arrival in Aden, both skippers reported the attack to Yemeni authorities.

In late October 2009 the British sailing yacht *Lynn Rival* was hijacked while on a passage from Victoria in the Seychelles to the Amirante Islands and then on to Tanzania. On being attacked they initially activated an emergency distress beacon. The abandoned yacht was later found by a British naval vessel. The two crew, Rachel and Paul Chandler, were not injured in the fighting and were initially transferred to a captured container ship before being taken ashore to a more secure area, and this followed similar actions on previous yacht incidents. The pirates initially demanded a ransom of $7 million dollars; however they were soon made aware that there were no financial resources to meet even a small part of the demand. This demand was modified when the pirates started debating between themselves whether to press for the ransom or to exchange the hostages for comrades being held by UE forces after they were captured following a hijack of a Spanish fishing vessel.

South and Central America
The yacht *Pico Alto* was attacked in February 2009 off Itaparica Marina in Brazil. Two robbers came out to the yacht in a small boat and boarded the yacht while it was anchored. The

skipper confronted the two men and was shot and killed. The men then jumped overboard and swam off, leaving their boat. Nothing was stolen. Police later arrested two suspects.

The French yacht *Maclow* was attacked in December 2008 in Bahia de Todos Os, in Santos, Brazil. Two armed attackers boarded the yacht while it was at anchor and assaulted the two sailors on board. They stole equipment, cash, and personal effects before escaping. The two injured crew required medical treatment ashore.

The U.S. yacht *Sarana* was attacked in November 2008 while it was anchored off Pedernales, Ecuador. Five bandits in a small fishing boat came out to the yacht and boarded. They assaulted the crew and stole personal effects and equipment. The crew aboard another yacht reported the incident to the U.S. Coast Guard vessel *Alameda*, which contacted Ecuadorian authorities. The attackers took two hostages.

Pirates attacked the British yacht *Raven Eye* eight nautical miles off Puerto Santos, Venezuela, in 2008. The six pirates arrived in a pirogue-type fishing boat. All were armed with guns and knives, and one was dressed in a military uniform, while two others wore masks. The couple sailing the 41-foot yacht were Peter and Betty Lee from Stockport, in the United Kingdom. They were in the midst of a voyage around the world. They later stated that the attack happened quickly, which is typical.

The skipper took evasive action and rammed the yacht into the fishing boat. The pirates opened fire with pistols, forcing the couple to surrender in fear of their lives. The pirates boarded the yacht, tied up the skipper, and forced him to lie face down on deck while one of the pirates held a pistol to his head. Two pirates armed with pistols took his wife below, frequently holding a pistol to her head as they ransacked the boat. They were extremely aggressive and kept demanding money.

The couple's dog sensed the danger and attacked the men in an attempt to protect its owners. One of the pirates shot the

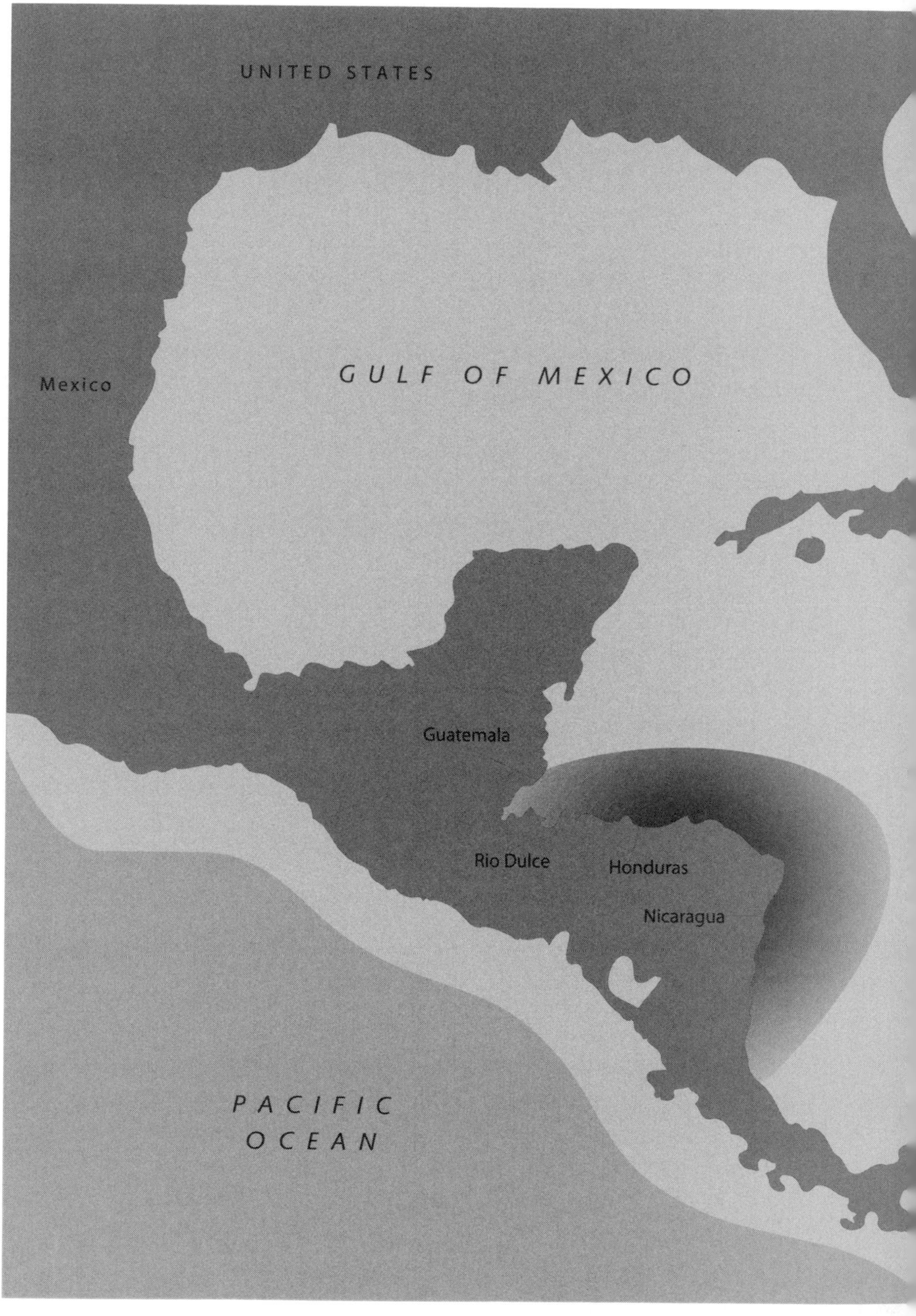
UNITED STATES
Mexico
GULF OF MEXICO
Guatemala
Rio Dulce
Honduras
Nicaragua
PACIFIC
OCEAN

Particularly dangerous areas in the Caribbean

NORTH ATLANTIC

Cuba

Haiti

Dominican
Republic

maica

Virgin Islands

Antigua

Guadeloupe

Dominica

Martinique

St. Lucia

Barbados

Grenada

CARIBBEAN SEA

Tobago

Trinidad

Colombia

Venezuela

dog and stabbed it between the shoulder blades. When the pirates were only able to find a couple of hundred dollars, they then tried to steal the wife's wedding ring, roughing her up still more, which resulted in her sustaining cuts and bruises. The pirates left with all they could carry. When Peter and Betty Lee arrived in Trinidad, they spoke to another British couple who had been robbed in the same area. Shaken but undeterred, Peter and Betty Lee said they intended to continue their circumnavigation.

The French yacht *Ti Ve* was attacked in Bahia de Robledal, Isla de Margarita, Venezuela, in 2008. Five pirates boarded the yacht and assaulted the crew, shooting and seriously injuring one of them. They stole equipment and personal effects before escaping. The incident was reported to local authorities, which launched an investigation.

In January 2008, a yacht was boarded off Isla de Margarita, Venezuela. Five bandits armed with guns boarded the yacht at Bahia De Robledal, assaulting the crew and demanding that they give up all of their property. One of the crew was shot, but survived the bullet wound.

On September 14, 2008, the catamaran *Chrysalide* was attacked by several armed men near La Guaraia in the vicinity of Caracas, Venezuela. The yacht was anchored outside Marina de Caraballeda. The victim was a well-known charter skipper and French citizen who was shot four times in the head and killed after he resisted the robbers. The motive appeared to be robbery because some cash was stolen.

Asia

The British yacht *Mr. Bean* was attacked in March 2009 in the South China Sea off Koh Tong (Tong Island), Satun Province, in Thailand. The attack came at night while the yacht was anchored near the Thai and Malaysian border in the Andaman Sea. A British couple, 64-year-old Malcolm Robertson and his wife, Linda, owned the yacht and had been slowly cruising around the world since 1998. They left the United Kingdom in June of that year and after more than a decade of sailing had nearly circumnavigated the globe.

The Robertsons were sleeping in separate cabins and evidently Linda heard someone up on deck. Then she heard a commotion and Malcolm calling for her to get off the boat. When she came out of the cabin, she saw three teenage boys armed with knives and hammers. Blood was everywhere. The boys tied Linda up and held her hostage for twelve hours.

Malcolm had evidently confronted the three robbers as they attempted to steal the dinghy. The boys beat him with a hammer and cut his throat before throwing his body overboard. When the attackers left the vessel in the dinghy, Linda managed to free herself, weigh anchor, and get *Mr. Bean* moving under power. She approached some fishing boats and asked for help, tying up alongside one of the vessels. The fishermen called the police.

A boat with Turatao National Park rangers arrived quickly, and soon after the Thai police and Royal Thai Navy showed up, too. They immediately launched a manhunt and captured the three murderers in short order. They were still wearing some of Malcolm's clothes. Linda then had to endure the anguish of traveling to shore on the same boat as the teenage pirates. Some reports say a mob attacked the pirates when they were brought ashore. The three boys were Burmese and they confessed to the killing. Some reports linked them to the many Rohingya refugees fleeing the Myanmar military campaign.

About a week later, fishermen recovered Malcolm's body about ten nautical miles off Lipeh Island. Subsequent reports indicated that robbers had boarded the yacht in the past and that the Robertsons always had cigarettes and alcohol to hand over. My sincere condolences go out to Linda. As a footnote, the region around the Tarutao National Park, off Satun, was a thriving center for piracy during World War II. The former guards and the prisoners from two jails on Turatao turned to piracy and they were finally stopped by British troops during the Malayan insurgency.

Recently, the International Maritime Bureau released an alert regarding a 45-foot sloop that had been observed anchored in Sihanoukville Harbor in Cambodia. The yacht appeared to have been occupied by squatters, and makeshift awnings had been erected, along with a cooking area. The suspicion was that pirates had captured the yacht, which was well prepared for blue-water voyaging. The details and fate of the owners was unknown and the IMB was seeking information.

In 2007, the yacht *Dilan* was attacked about forty-eight nautical miles southeast of Pulau Repong, in Indonesia. The pirates approached in two boats and initially took up station behind the yacht, following it. The yacht crew broadcasted an alert on the VHF radio and a nearby ship relayed the message to the Singapore authorities, which in turn notified the Maritime Rescue Coordination Center in Jakarta. A warning to all vessels in the area was issued via the NAVTEX and Inmarsat C's SafetyNET system, both of which are useful in the quick conveyance of threats to shipping. The attempted attack was aborted after evasive actions were performed.

In 2007, pirates attacked the German yacht *Freiheit* off the Anambas Islands, in Indonesia. A boat carrying four pirates approached the yacht, and, when they were almost alongside, a pirate in the bow threw a small anchor with a light messenger line onto the yacht to assist in the boarding attempt. The skipper increased the yacht's speed and started zigzagging. The pirates continued the attack and finally aborted the attack when the engine of their small boat failed.

The Mediterranean

Piracy hasn't completely disappeared from the Mediterranean, though it is far less common than in other regions of the world. One piracy event involved a British couple sailing a chartered yacht around the lovely island of Corfu, one of my personal favorite sailing places. Masked men carrying assault rifles and grenades attacked and boarded the yacht, stealing personal possessions and boat equipment, including navigational gear. The pirates took the couple as hostages, but the couple was rescued after the Greek Coast Guard arrived. The pirates were assumed to have come from nearby Albania.

On July 27, 2000, the Greek yacht *Erato* was attacked near Nafplion, a port situated on Greece's Peloponnesian Peninsula. The armed robber attacked while the yacht was at anchor and attempted to hijack the boat, demanding that the crew take him to Morocco. The man took the family of four as hostages, and, when the Hellenic Coast Guard arrived at the scene, he opened fire. One officer was shot in the stomach. The robber was shot and killed. The family was rescued without injury.

In another incident near Corfu, Albanian pirates shot and killed the British skipper of a yacht as he tried to repel an attack. Tourism is big business in the Greek islands. In response to this and other attacks, the Greek government sent naval patrols to deter Albanian pirates from crossing the narrow Corfu Channel to attack the many yachts that cruise there in the summer.

The Cayman Islands-registered 180-foot luxury yacht *Tiara* was attacked off Porto Vecchio in the Golfo De Porto Novo, Corsica, in August 2008. Four masked and armed robbers approached the anchored yacht in a fast dinghy at about midnight. They robbed the German passengers of about $204,000. The thieves also reportedly robbed the nine passengers of their jewelry, although others dispute this. One report also said that artworks on the luxury yacht were stolen. There were no reported injuries to the crew and passengers or any damage to the yacht. The chartered yacht was bound for the resort harbors of Sardinia. The passengers were reportedly wealthy members of the German financial world. *Tiara* is decorated in Art Deco style and has five cabins and a marble bathroom. Local police investigated the incident.

17

No End in Sight

Clear and present danger

The monsoon period is traditionally a quiet time for piracy as the seas are too rough for small skiffs to make successful attacks. By the end of September 2009 the monsoon season had largely subsided and it didn't take long for the pirates to launch a season opening attack. There remained only four ships being held by pirates as the protracted ransom negotiations dragged on. The continuing success of coalition naval forces in thwarting attempted pirate attacks started to show. The pirates appeared to be getting increasingly desperate for a successful hijacking.

The first post monsoon attacks occurred when seven pirates attempted to board and seize a Bahamian-flagged ship. The South Korean Navy vessel *Munmu The Great* answered the distress transmission and came to the rescue of the ship. A team of special forces in high speed semi-rigid boats supported by a Lynx helicopter intervened to stop the attack and then detained the boat along with the pirates. They found AK-47 casings and a knife and after issuing warnings they released the pirates. The weapons were presumably thrown overboard by the pirates to get rid of any evidence.

Pirates then attempted to board the Turkish bulk carrier *El-giznur Cebi*. A Turkish warship passed a message to a German

NATO warship. A helicopter was quickly scrambled and the pirates in two boats quickly abandoned the attack.

One of the detained vessels is the Taiwanese fishing vessel *Win Far*. The vessel was captured some 20 weeks previously and was reportedly being used as a mother ship for other pirate attacks, and this included the attack against the *Maersk Alabama*. When a U.S. Seahawk helicopter flew over the captured vessel in late August on a routine surveillance mission the pirates opened fire with a heavy caliber weapon. Fortunately the chopper wasn't hit but it did show a change in behavior and a sign of increasing stress.

By mid-September the Ukrainian crew of the *Ariana*, which had been held for more than three months, were issuing public media requests to speed up the negotiations and also to help evacuate one of the two female hostages being held on board, as she had developed life-threatening health problems. The negotiations with the Greek shipowners had stalled and no real progress was being made. The crew pleaded for Ukrainian government intervention and involvement with the negotiations. The pirates then threatened to start executing Ukrainian crewmembers when the ship's fuel supplies ran out and the Russian Seamen's Trade Union was openly urging the Ukrainian President Viktor Yushchenko to take immediate action to help in the release of the crew.

Similarly negotiations continued for the Turkish bulk carrier *Horizon 1* which had been seized in early July. The pirates were demanding $20 million dollars for the ship's release and negotiations had stalled. The ship was finally released mid-October. In September pirates freed the Greek-owned ship *Irene* a long five months after the hijacking. The pirates had requested a ransom of nearly $3 million dollars and it is presumed a ransom was ultimately paid for the ship and crew release.

The ramifications of some hijackings continue long after the event, and this was the case with the *Hansa Stavanger*.

The shipowners are now demanding that the cargo owners pay for the ransom that was handed over to release ship and cargo. The ship is still at anchor in Mombasa and the issue has gone to the courts as they seek to recover around $3.6 million dollars. The shipowners now want the cargo and cargo owners arrested so that it can continue its voyage down the East African coast.

Meanwhile back in Copenhagen, three Danish crewmembers had been pursuing a lawsuit brought against shipowners by the Seaman's Union. This related to the previously hijacked *Danica White* and the crew demanded additional compensation. However the court ruled against them and they had unsuccessfully argued that the shipowners were responsible for the capture of the ship and crew by Somali pirates in 2007.

As the monsoon southwesterly winds that create the rough seas had abated, the hijackers pursued their attacks with renewed vigor. One alleged Somali pirate was shot dead when a skiff being pursued by a helicopter from the German warship *Brandenburg* refused to stop. The helicopter had filmed the boat occupants throwing boarding ladders and weapons over the side. After the skiff was boarded additional weapons were found and the injured person later died on the German warship.

A North Korean ship was attacked, and the crew retaliated with improvised Molotov cocktails and fired rocket distress flares at the skiffs. The pirates aborted the attack when they encountered fierce resistance. The ship was drifting at sea while doing some engine repair work when it was attacked by ten pirates in two boats, all wearing military clothing. They opened fire at the ship using rocket propelled grenades and automatic weapons. One of the crew was also injured in the attack and a U.S. warship arrived on the scene shortly after the pirates had departed. Pirates also started attacking the seventeen-strong Indian Ocean-based Spanish fishing fleet again, and four unsuccessful attacks occurred since the monsoon started to subside.

There are now some 30 naval vessels in the Gulf of Aden area awaiting the expected resurgence in pirate activity. This is a considerable improvement over the 20 that were in the area during the attack peak period in May. The coordinated responses between all these international navies is probably unprecedented. The Australian warship *HMAS Toowoomba* intercepted a pirate skiff and confiscated an RPG and automatic weapons as they were stalking the *BBC Portugal*. They threw the boarding ladder overboard when the naval vessel approached.

Another pirate gang attacked the Russian oil tanker *Prisco Alexandra* with a full cargo of 41,000 tons of aviation fuel. Like in most cases the pirates opened fire at the outset of the attack, a dangerous action given the nature of the cargo, but the captain of the tanker started maneuvering and they were unable to get on board. Again the naval forces intervened with the South Korean destroyer *Dae Jo-yeong* coming to the aid of the oil tanker.

Pirates again had to deal with the combined efforts of naval forces when they attacked the Italian ship *Southern Cross*, which was transiting the Gulf of Aden around 80 nautical miles south of Al Mukkala. When the ship came under fire as the pirates attempted to board the vessel the distress message was received by the Norwegian warship *HNOMS Fridtjof Nansen*. A South Korean warship *Dae Jo-yeong* scrambled a helicopter to the scene. The pirate skiff then abandoned the attack as the ship also commenced antiboarding maneuvers that gave them additional time and made boarding impossible. The EU NAVFOR German naval vessel *FGS Bremen* then scrambled a helicopter to hunt the pirate skiff down. When they located the culprits the *Fridtjof Nansen* launched fast boats with a boarding team, and the pirates were seen throwing weapons over board into the sea. The skiff was later released and another attack failed due to the well coordinated naval action. At the same time elsewhere in the region the attacks also continued and were a sign of the intensity that was ramping up now that conditions had improved for the pirates.

The Turkish Naval Frigate *TCG Gediz*, which is part of the NATO force, intercepted and arrested seven pirates, further ratcheting up the pressure on them. The pirates were aboard a skiff and were setting up to attack two Panamanian-flagged ships. The frigate scrambled its helicopter and then Turkish commandos subsequently boarded the skiff and took the pirates into custody.

In another more sinister post-monsoon incident in September 2009, Somali pirates actually boarded the Panama-flagged *Barwaqo* while it was heading into Mogadishu Harbor. The pirates promptly murdered the Syrian captain when he refused to alter course away from the port. The ensuing firefight with pirates resulted in one policeman and three crew being wounded. African Union peacekeeping mission troops and Somali police rescued the vessel from the pirates.

At the beginning of October the pirates made their first successful post-monsoon attack when they hijacked a 100-meter Spanish fishing vessel the *Alakana* and the crew of thirty-six in the area between the Seychelles and Somalia. The vessel had reportedly been attacked in September but had escaped. The crew included nationals from Spain, Indonesia, Ghana, Madagascar, Senegal and the Seychelles. Two of the suspected pirates were later arrested by the EU NAVFOR Spanish warship *Canarias*.

This raised the current pirate ship tally back to five vessels including a Taiwanese fishing vessel along with ships from Germany, Turkey and the Ukraine. It has since been reported that a number of Seychelles-based Spanish tuna trawlers are now employing former British Army Gurkha soldiers, as the

Spanish government does not allow the use of Spanish troops for protection. In another development the Spanish courts announced they were to release one of the alleged pirates captured following the trawler hijacking as he was apparently below 18 years of age.

Pirates still continue to confuse merchant and naval vessels. Five Somali pirates were captured after firing on a French naval vessel. They attacked at night about 300 miles off the Somalia coast. The target was the French naval command and supply vessel, the *Somme*. There were also additional attacks on various merchants at night in full moon conditions but all escaped. The French defense forces were also once again in the media spotlight when soldiers successfully defended two fishing French tuna trawlers the *Drennec* and *Glénan* from a pirate attack in the Indian Ocean and the eleven alleged pirates were pursued and captured. In a combined operation with the Seychelles coastguard vessel *Topaze* they also captured two small boats and the suspected mother ship some 200 nautical miles north of the Seychelles. In what is a typical challenge they reluctantly had to later release the suspected mother ship and crew as they did not have sufficient evidence to hold and charge them.

Pirates then managed to seize on October 16 the Singapore-flagged container ship *Kota Wajar* and its twenty-one crew 550 miles off the Somali coast while on passage to Mombasa. This made it the first successful commercial ship hijack since early July. This hijacking also sent chills around the maritime community as it showed a change in tactics by pirates who were striking well away from patrolled areas and well out into the Indian Ocean. The vessel was then taken to the Hobyo area in Central Somalia to await ransom negotiations. On her arrival the captain of the *Ariana* anchored nearby requested some fuel from the vessel as she had none left and stated that one of the two Ukrainian female crew on board was seriously ill, and also that the vessel's Greek owners had effectively abandoned

229

them. At the same time the *Charelle* issued a MAYDAY call to naval vessels as they had exhausted all food and water supplies and fuel was also nearly gone and ransom negotiations had broken down.

The next vessel to be hijacked was the Chinese bulk carrier *De Xin Hai* which was hijacked 550 nautical miles northeast of the Seychelles and 700 nautical miles off the east coast of Somalia. The official warnings started specifying that ships stay at least 600 nautical miles offshore and in effect the pirates were now threatening the sea routes from the Persian Gulf down to the Cape of Good Hope, which is a major oil supply route. The pirates issued warnings that they would start executing the Chinese crew if any rescue attempt was made, and China declared they would do all they could to rescue the ship and crew.

This hijacking was followed up by the capture of the British yacht *Lynn Rival* making three successful seizures in quick succession. In this new activity well off the coast an unsuccessful attack were reported on the Italian-flagged ship *Jolly Rosso* using RPG and automatic weapons. Almost simultaneously another attack on the bulk carrier *Al Khaliq* was successful and the pirates sailed the ship towards the coast. The next successful hijacking didn't take long as the Thai cargo ship *Thor Star* was hijacked 200 nautical miles north of the Seychelles. In November the U.S.-flagged bulk carrier *Harriette* successfully repelled an attack around 350 nautical miles off Mombasa.

The battle at sea is escalating and is a dark omen for the future. The Norwegian warship *HNOMS Fridtjof Nansen* was performing fishing vessel inspections off the Somali coast when it came under sustained and heavy gunfire from a dhow at night. The men on the dhow were using heavy caliber weapons and Kalashnikov rifles. The Spanish government has authorized the private security firms on Spanish fishing vessels to use heavy caliber weapons to repel pirate attacks. The attacks will continue and the challenge of policing such vast sea areas is now facing naval forces and shipowners. With no political solutions in sight the hijackings will continue. Some will end tragically and seafarers will start losing their lives. The pirates have changed tactics and have adapted to the heavy naval presence and in doing so they are threatening the security of the Western Indian Ocean. The number of hijackings steadily increased and at the end of November 2009 pirates seized one of their largest ships to date, the oil super tanker *Maran Centaurus* with 2.2 million barrels of oil. The ship was hijacked more than 750 miles out in the Indian Ocean while she was on her way from Saudi Arabia to the United States. The capture has shaken the maritime world and this is the largest ship since *Sirius Star* was captured. Fighting villainy on the high seas is going to require a lot of resources and will be both long and arduous, with many casualties along the way.

Appendix A

Yacht Transit Advice in Somali Waters

The following are condensed recommendations for yachts transiting the Gulf of Aden, Yemen, and Somali regions up to 600 nautical miles offshore. The International Sailing Federation offers additional guidelines in cooperation with the Maritime Security Center Horn of Africa, which was established by EU NAVFOR Atalanta. Check the sailing federation's website for the latest information. The Maritime Security Center liaises with the various naval vessels from several nations conducting antipiracy patrols for the protection of merchant vessels, as far as surveillance and support is practical. There is no guarantee that any yacht or merchant vessel can be adequately protected.

Although it is unpleasant to consider, thought should be given regarding the feasibility of paying a ransom if you and the crew are taken hostage. Do you have the financial resources or capability to raise a million dollars or more in cash? Who will handle the raising of a ransom? Governments do not pay ransoms on your behalf, so you can't count on assistance from your home country.

If a yacht crew decides to take the risk and transit through the area, they should make their plans known with as much

233

notice as possible to the United Kingdom Maritime Trade Organization in Dubai and the Maritime Security Center. U.S.-flagged vessels should contact the Maritime Liaison Office of the U.S. Navy in Bahrain at the following e-mail address: marlo.bahrain@me.navy.mil, or call +973 3940 1395 (twenty-four-hour watch). Also contact the United Kingdom Maritime Trade Organization in Dubai. E-mail: ukmto@eim.ae, or call +971 50 552 3215. The Maritime Security Center's contact information is as follows. E-mail: postmaster@mschoa.org, or call +44 (0)1923 958547, 39, 35.

You will need to provide the following information. Also make sure someone ashore has all the details, plus crew information. Yacht name; MMSI number; national registration number, if any; home port; flag state; call sign; LOA; number of persons on board and whether male or female; Satcom-C number, if any; satellite phone numbers, if any; MF/HF details, if any; normal and maximum cruising speeds; color of topsides; color of deck; color of hull; rig details; sail numbers and insignia; e-mail addresses being used on board, if any; captain's name, nationality, and passport number; yacht club or association, if any; the contact person ashore who can be reached twenty-four hours a day, seven days a week and who has all boat and crew details; the dates and places of intended passage.

A yacht should register at least two weeks before entering the area. Yachts coming south through the Red Sea should report before reaching Bab al Mandab and also should register before reaching Safaga/Jeddah. Following registration, the Maritime Security Center will e-mail yacht piracy alerts until the yacht is clear of the area. The center will also pass details of yacht movements to naval vessels patrolling in the area.

While transiting the area all yachts should monitor VHF channel 16 and VHF channel 8 and file movement and status reports as advised by the Maritime Security Center or by any patrolling naval vessel. In an emergency, use VHF channel 8 and VHF channel 16, or the telephone numbers given below, as all are on twenty-four hour watches.

Merchant ships are being advised to use the Internationally Recognized Transit Corridor to receive maximum naval patrol protection. Yachts are advised to transit either within or close to this corridor. The IRTC is very similar to a traffic separation zone, and the two, five-mile lanes are separated by a two nautical-mile separation zone. The IRTC coordinates are as follows:

Westbound lane, northern boundary: 12° 00' N, 45° 00' E, 14° 30' N, 53° 00' E. Southern boundary: 11° 55' N, 45° 00' E, 14° 25' N, 53° 00' E.

Eastbound lane, northern boundary: 11° 53' N, 45° 00' E, 14° 23' N, 53° 00' E. Southern boundary: 11° 48' N, 45° 00' E, 14° 18' N, 53° 00' E.

The course eastbound is 072° True and westbound 252° True.

Yachts are advised to transit either in the two nautical-mile buffer zone or close to the outer limits of the lanes. This maximizes the chances of being heard on any VHF call by both naval and merchant vessels. However, be warned. Being heard is not guaranteed. It is also advised that yachts join the IRTC as early as possible before the IRTC start position to maximize protection. Yachts are also advised to travel as far as possible at night with *no* navigation lights turned on. Run under power with no sails up to reduce visibility. The practice of forming small groups or convoys in Djibouti, Aden, and Salalah is encouraged by naval authorities, and the advice is to limit groups to five yachts because this is the most practical for close formation when yachts are typically short-handed.

The carriage of firearms is not recommended because the

risk of escalation in violence is considerable. Most yachts do not carry an automatic identification system transponder. However, when a yacht has a Class B transponder, the crew should keep it on so naval vessels can identify your yacht. If you choose to travel outside areas where naval vessels are patrolling, then it is best to switch it off. Do not use EPIRBs and PLBs, as these are emergency location devices. If you have a search and rescue radar transponder, switch it off. Pirates also carry radar on some mother ships. A radar target enhancer should also be turned off. A yacht crew can reduce radar visibility by taking down the radar reflector.

It is absolutely important to be thoroughly prepared for the transit. Make sure that all boat equipment is in perfect order. The engine is the main concern, as you will be running it at maximum speed for quite some time. Check that seawater pumps and strainers are in perfect condition. Check that fuel filters are in perfect condition and service your engine. You cannot afford a breakdown since it may jeopardize you and the yachts you are traveling with. Make sure that radios and satellite telephones work properly, and check all connections and aerials. Check that batteries are serviced and ready, and make sure the water tanks are full, with a few extra jerry jugs as a reserve.

Carry as much spare fuel as you can. You will need it for the sustained period of motoring at maximum speed. Hide your cell phones, a portable VHF radio, medical supplies, vitamin supplements, and water purification tablets on board, in the unfortunate event you are seized and taken hostage by pirates. The transit will be all motoring or motor sailing. My own view is that unless the sail is giving a lot of extra speed, then keeping a low profile is the best tactic.

During the transit maintain the very highest standard of watchkeeping and vigilance. Every person must be constantly scanning the surrounding waters and horizon with binoculars. Relaxation is not an option. Every boat must be treated as a potential threat. Innocent looking fishing boats may have pirates hiding out of sight. Any high-speed boat or group of boats approaching must be treated as potentially hostile. Pirates use very small skiffs limited by sea conditions. Generally, they find it hard to operate in Force 3 winds and above.

There are also few attacks at night, so darkness and winds above Force 3 will improve safety. As the visual horizon of a pirate in a skiff is less than five nautical miles, they will sight a merchant ship well before a yacht. A white or colored hull is far more visible than a blue or black hull. Consider using water washable paint or some other media on the hull to camouflage the large white or colored hull areas. Even bright orange life rings are highly visible, so survey your boat for potential items that have high visibility.

Every member of the yacht crew must know the response plan. Attacks happen so fast that there is no room for discussion, and skippers should carry out drills before departure. If there is any doubt as to the intentions of approaching boats, use the VHF radios and satellite phone to raise the alarm. The earlier you summon assistance, the less time you have to hold off an attack before help arrives. It takes time to get a chopper in the air and to your location, so vigilance and early detection are the key.

When making routine VHF radio calls, never give your position. However, if you are genuinely under attack, position details are essential. Have someone assigned to stay below and keep calling on the radio and phone. They need to be calm and measured so that the authorities have accurate information. When under confirmed attack you are allowed to issue a Mayday call on VHF channel 16 and VHF channel 8, or HF DSC and Sat-C, if you have it. If you have a satellite phone, call the United Kingdom Maritime Trade Organization in Dubai. Have its number programmed for speed dial, and have the number clearly posted at the navigation station. If there is time, also call the Maritime Security Center and the Maritime Liaison Office of the U.S. Navy in Bahrain.

You need to delay, or, if possible, force the pirates to abandon the attack. This may be difficult if you are under fire. The judgment has to be made regarding the safety of yourself and the crew. Swift and decisive evasive maneuvers often work, as does heading into the wind and waves to make boarding difficult, especially if you are zigzagging the yacht.

If you can't hold the pirates off and they get aboard, it is essential that the skipper and crew remain calm and compliant, and that no resistance is offered. While fighting back is instinctive, it's better to stay alive. The pirates will be pumped up and probably high on *khat*. The pirates no longer want some cash and valuables. They want you, the crew, and the boat as hostages. They generally will not harm hostages, unless pushed to do so. Do not be tempted to use firearms! It is also advised that you do not use pyrotechnics or flash photography. In general, you will be outgunned. Pirates in these waters are usually armed with AK-47s and sometimes rocket-propelled grenade launchers. If the military takes action against pirates on your boat, lay low on the deck and put your hands over your head, so the military knows who you are.

Appendix B

Pirate Attack Incidents Summary

There are so many piracy incidents and hijackings that it is quite impossible to list them all. The following summaries extracted from IMO piracy reports are listed by date, and whether they were successful or not. They illustrate the absolute relentless nature of attacks by pirates on merchant shipping within the Gulf of Aden area.

The number of pirate attacks off the Somali coast rose to unprecedented levels in the year 2008. Pirates made a total of 111 attacks and seized an incredible 42 vessels, most of these in the Gulf of Aden. When converted to percentages, that's a very high success rate. They also raised an estimated $150 million dollars in ransom money, all cash!

Notable incidents in the period 2004 to 2008

The following are some of the dramatic incidents that occurred in the period leading up to the current piracy epidemic.

In August 2005 three Taiwanese fishing boats, the *Chung Yi 218*, *Cheng Ching Feng* and *Hsin Lien Feng 36* were hijacked off the Somali coast. The pirates threatened to kill all the 60 crewmembers unless the demand for a ransom payment of $500,000 per vessel was not paid by the deadline.

There was a touch of irony when, in April 2006, eight pirates in two skiffs attacked, fired on and subsequently seized along with its twenty-five crew the 350-ton South Korean *Dong Won (628)*, owned by Dongwon Fisheries. The company is renowned for illegal fishing. The Korean Foreign Minister Ban Ki-moon (now UN Secretary-General) announced to the media that the crew were all safe and that some had been able to phone home to families. The Somali pirates demanded $400,000 for the release of the fishing vessel. Local village elders said the payment was a fine for illegal fishing and not a ransom and in this case one could be forgiven for thinking they might be right, and in some quarters there was little sympathy. When the fishing vessel was attacked, about 60 nautical miles off the Somalia coast, it requested assistance from coalition naval vessels. The Dutch frigate *HNLMS De Zeven Provinciën* and the guided-missile destroyer *USS Roosevelt* responded to the distress call. By the time the warships had arrived at the scene the pirates had taken control of the fishing vessel, and then headed into Somali territorial waters.

On November 1, 2006, the Dubai-based 80-meter dhow *MV Veesham-I* was hijacked by six pirates, while carrying a cargo of charcoal from the Somalia port of Al Maan to Salalah in Oman. They took the fourteen crewmembers hostages. Following the seizure a U.S. naval vessel and Somali patrol boats tracked the vessel to the port of Obbia. The pirates issued a $1 million dollar ransom demand, and the ransom was negotiated down to $150,000. The dhow was then surrounded by Islamic Court militiamen, intent on boarding the ship. The Islamic Courts have vowed to wipe out piracy off Somali coastal waters. This attack occurred after a seven month period of low pirate activity and was the first since the Islamic Courts had taken over. As the dhow slowly headed towards the pirate port, the captain maintained contact by satellite phone. Eventually, some forty heavily armed members of the Islamic militia stormed the dhow and in the resulting shootout

240

two of the pirates were seriously wounded and all eight pirates were captured. The crew was unharmed in the attack. In a later press conference the Union of Islamic Courts supreme leader openly expressed their satisfaction and happiness over the successful rescue operation.

In August 2006 a group of Somali fishermen rescued four Thai crewmen off the Puntland coast. The four crew were then taken to the Puntland capital of Garoowe. It was suggested that the sailors would be held in custody as hostages in negotiations for the release of three Somalis who were serving three-year sentences in a Thai prison. The Somalis maintained that the pirates in the Thai prison were wrongfully convicted. It was also stated that the Thais may face charges of illegal fishing.

In another interesting episode in 2006, the Iraqi captain of a United Arab Emirates-owned 3,000 ton vessel and its seventeen crew were rescued from attacking pirates by U.S marines from the *USS Roosevelt*. The ship was carrying a cargo of charcoal. The enterprising captain had fabricated sails from old cloth after the ship's engines had failed. The outcome had an unhappy ending for the captain at the hands of the Seychelles court system. The courts ordered the sale of the Dominican Republic-registered vessel so that debts of around $300,000 for the ship towage and unpaid crew wages could be settled. The captain had stated that the Americans were the only people prepared to offer help while others encouraged them to abandon the ship after it developed serious mechanical problems. They were then towed in by port authority tugs, with a crippling towage bill.

On February 26, 2007, pirates armed with AK-47 automatic weapons and RPG's attacked and hijacked the UN chartered Saint Vincent and the Grenadines-flagged *MV Rozen* off the coast of North Eastern Somalia following its discharge of 1,800 tons in food aid to the towns of Boosaaso and Berbera in the Puntland region. The ship was headed back to Mombasa in

Kenya when it was attacked and managed to raise the alarm before the pirates severed all communications. This incident raised serious concerns that piracy would re-emerge again. For the shipping company, Motaku, this was the third attack and hijacking within two years of a WFP chartered vessel. The Somali pirates had also seized three Motaku vessels in 2005, and in one case they held the ship and crew hostage for nearly 100 days. The WFP stated that there were serious concerns about piracy undermining food relief deliveries and aggravating the humanitarian catastrophe ashore. A U.S. warship headed towards the captured ship and she was subsequently anchored off Bargol ahead of ransom negotiations. The Somali authorities were then able to arrest four men who were allegedly members of the pirate gang who had hijacked the ship while they were ashore getting provisions, and another two were arrested separately, leaving four left on board. The ship was subsequently surrounded by three Somali Police boats and a US naval vessel was in the area monitoring events.

On May 15, 2007, the Tanzanian-flagged and Korean-owned fishing trawlers *Mavuno I* and *Mavuno II* were attacked and seized by pirates while on passage from Mombassa to Yemen. The ransom demanded was $700,000, however the ship owner didn't have the funds to pay and sought Korean government assistance, without success. The hostage crew was kept on board in extremely poor conditions. They were soon out of food and fuel, and subsisted on meager rice handouts from the pirates. The South Korean government maintained its stance of not negotiating and not paying any ransom demands and they were heavily criticized in the Korean media for not making any effort to assist in freeing the four Korean seafarers. Trade unions and other groups lobbied extensively but the government maintained its position. This is of course consistent with the South Korean governments appalling attitude and official stance towards seafarers in general.

In May 2007 the Taiwanese fishing vessel *Ching Fong Hwa*

242

168, was attacked and captured with two Taiwanese and twelve Chinese crewmembers. The fishing vessel was seized around 220 nautical miles off the Somali coast when around 15 pirates came aboard with automatic weapons and an RPG. The pirates attacked using three skiffs and were aboard within minutes. They immediately went to the captain's cabin, and he was heard to shout for the crew to run. However the pirates began firing their weapons and so escape was not possible, and they shot one crewman in the back; fortunately he survived. The ordeal for the crew continued, and they developed scurvy due to the poor diet, and were subjected to frequent mock executions and also violent beatings and death threats. The beatings were often because the crew could not understand pirate orders and instructions in either Somali or broken English. The Somali pirates then lined up the crew and randomly selected one of them and then executed him. They further threatened to kill more hostages unless the ransom demands were met. The pirates regularly forced some of the crew to telephone their homes in an effort to get relatives to apply more pressure on the ship owners to settle the ransom demand of a $220,000. After being paid the agreed ransom, the pirates then reneged on the release and demanded a greater ransom. At this stage the US Navy moved in and demanded that they release the hostages. After some protracted negotiations the pirates agreed to leave the ship. One released Chinese sailor who was held hostage for the 202 days vowed that he would never go back to sea again. The American destroyer *USS James E. Williams* provided badly needed supplies and medical assistance aid to the crew of the *Ching Fong Hwa* after they regained control, and escorted her out of Somali waters.

In October 2007 pirates successfully attacked and hijacked the Japanese owned 6,253-ton chemical tanker *Golden Nori*. The Panama-flagged tanker was on a voyage from Singapore to Israel with a cargo of 10,000 tons of highly inflammable benzene. Two U.S. naval vessels sailed in close to the hijacked vessel and attempted to block supplies from reaching the pirates on the ship in an effort to force the release of the vessel. The *USS Porter* opened fire to destroy the pirates skiffs tied to the ship. With a cargo of benzene that was somewhat fraught with risk. The effort proved unsuccessful and the ship anchored off the port of Boosaaso while ransom negotiations continued. The *Golden Nori* was eventually released six weeks later in mid-December without harm to the crew after a ransom was paid.

In November 2007 the North Korean vessel *Dan Hong Dai* was attacked by pirates, around 60 nautical miles off the coast off Mogadishu, where it had discharged a cargo of sugar. The destroyer *USS James E. Williams* responded to the scene and a standoff ensued with the pirates being ordered to surrender. The North Korean crew fought back, overpowered the Somali pirates who had seized their vessel, and regained control of the ship. In the fight, three of the crew were seriously injured, two Somali pirates were killed and five captured.

Notable 2008 Incidents

The following are some of more dramatic incidents that occurred in 2008 when piracy started to achieve worldwide attention. There were many incidents where ships came under sustained fire and escaped, and also cases where naval intervention helped.

The cargo ship *MV Jaipur-1* was captured on October 10, 2007, and fourteen Indian hostages were reportedly facing death by starvation. The ship is owned by Dubai's Al Rashid Shipping Company and was held in Mogadishu. The pirates apparently had dumped their food and drinking water overboard, and stolen all their personal money. They also threw the medicine supplies overboard and demanded $20 million as ransom. One of the crew had kept his family informed of the dire situation with a hidden cell phone. The shipowners had after four months effectively abandoned the ship and crew.

In April 2008, some 110 Somali troops stormed a Dubai-flagged ship *Al-Khaleej* and liberated the hostage Pakistani crew and arrested seven pirates after a brief but fierce fight. The *Al-Khaleej* had been carrying food and new motor vehicles for Somalia from Dubai when she was attacked and captured by pirates a few days earlier around four miles off the port of Boosaaso. The seven pirates had masqueraded as fishermen, desperate for fresh drinking water. When they got alongside they boarded and seized the vessel. The crew attempted to hide, but were soon rounded up. The large force of security officers from Puntland came to the vessel in two boats, before boarding and then engaged them in a firefight. After the ship was brought into the port of Boosaaso, seven pirates were observed being taken away in chains, three of them bleeding from wounds sustained in the fight. The Puntland security minister was quoted as saying that seven pirates would face the death penalty and it is presumed that they were executed.

On May 28, 2008, the German-owned cargo vessel *Lehmann Timber* was attacked and seized by pirates while on a voyage from China to Europe, some 170 nautical miles offshore. The ship was carrying a cargo of steel ship hatches for a company in Warnemünde in Germany and rolls of steel for a Russian company in St. Petersburg. The ship was new and on its maiden voyage. The previous night a naval helicopter had circled the ship twice. In the afternoon the pirates armed with AK-47's attacked from two skiffs, and they opened fire on the ship. The ship transmitted a distress signal and then nine pirates boarded and took over the ship's bridge. Warships tailed the ship which was taken to Eyl for the ransom negotiations. The pirates demanded a sum of nearly $3 million dollars, the shipowner offered $200,000 and the pirates set a payment deadline after which they threatened to execute the crew, and the haggling continued. The ship ran out of food and water and the situation for the hostages became very dire. At one stage shots were heard being fired into the air on the ship and it was believed the pirates were doing so to intimidate and frighten the crew to pressure the ransom negotiation process. The ship and crew were released in July after 41 days in captivity and a payment of a ransom of $750,000 dollars which arrived on a Tanzanian tug. The pirates ransacked the ship and stole everything the crew possessed. The ransom was delivered in 18 bags distributed between 18 pirates and they took several hours to count and distribute the cash before the ship was released. Following their release, while headed for a safe port, the main engine broke down and the ship was adrift in Force 9 storm conditions. Fearful of another hijack and possibly sinking they transmitted a distress call. The US Navy responded with a Seahawk helicopter assigned to the Saberhawks Helicopter Anti-submarine Squadron Light (HSL) 47, who were based on the guided missile destroyer *USS Momsen*. The choppers took rice and water to the ships crew and stood by until a tug arrived. The ship was taken in tow by the tug *Dubai Moon* and slowly taken to the Oman port of Salalah. The crew was subsequently repatriated and the ship resumed its voyage but the story didn't end there. In July 2009 the ship was arrested and was under detention in the port of Dordrecht in the Netherlands. When the ship arrived in Europe it discharged the hatches in accordance with international insurance rules with respect to piracy cases. The Russian owner of the steel rolls however refused to pay their portion of the ransom and so the cargo was discharged and stored ashore in Finland. The case subsequently went to a London maritime court for resolution. The Russian owner of the cargo attempted on several occasions to detain the ship in Finland and Morocco and finally succeeded in the Netherlands.

On July 20, 2008, the Japanese-operated 52,500 dwt Supramax bulk carrier *Stella Maris* was attacked by an estimated 40 heavily armed pirates, and captured along with her Filipino crew. The ship was carrying a cargo of 50,000 tons of zinc concentrate and lead ingots. This ship was the largest to be captured to date. The ship was sailed to and anchored at Eyl. The initial ransom demand was $3.5 million dollars. The ship and crew were released 12 weeks later after payment of a ransom.

On August 18, 2008, the Thai cargo ship *Thor Star* was attacked and seized while on passage some 100 nautical miles out between Somalia and Yemen carrying plywood to Aden. The pirates contacted the owners and assured them that all crewmembers were safe and well. This was the second time the *Thor Star* had been attacked. In 2003 armed pirates boarded the ship in Indonesian waters near Bintan Island.

On August 21, the German ship *BBC Trinidad* was attacked and seized. Owned by Beluga Shipping GmbH, the ship was on a voyage carrying pipes and other oil industry equipment from Houston, Texas to Muscat in Oman. The ship started to make evasive maneuvers and when the pirates came in close, they fired warning shots into the air and demanded that the crew of the ship stop her main engines. The Slovakian captain had attended a class on dealing with such events and was prepared. When the ship was attacked the crew activated the automatic alarm that sends out the distress alert and exact position. The nine Somali pirates boarded, seven were armed with AK-47's and the other two with RPG's. The crew was forced to hand over all their personal effects, cell phones, money and provisions. The ship sailed to Eyl. The owners back in Germany immediately set up a crisis management team. A ship's officer was able to secretly transmit an email detailing the hijacking and reporting that the captain and the crewmembers were all in good health. It was four days before a satellite phone call was received in Bremen from the captain and then passed onto the Somali middleman who represented the hijackers. The Somalian made an initial ransom demand of $8 million dollars and added that if the ransom money was not paid the ship would be blown up.

The German chief negotiator offered $800,000 and stated

that the shipping company was new and didn't have that amount of money. The pirates responded very negatively and rejected the offer. The captain was able to tell the Bremen team how dangerous that he believed the situation was. He advised that the pirates were taking drugs, and they did not eat or drink anything, and that all they took were green leaves (khat). The pirate negotiator warned that Somali pirates had just seized several more ships and that some people had been murdered and that his group could kill the ship's crew. The Bremen negotiators said that they could get the money quickly as a means of moving things forward. On board the ship food was running short and the temperature were exceeding 40 degrees Celsius (104 degrees Fahrenheit). The Somali negotiator said he was getting impatient and intimated that his superiors may accept $2 million dollars. The pirates increased pressure by denying the crew food for a day. The haggling continued for two more weeks, with various threats to cancel all negotiations, bluffing and ever other device possible. On September 16 a ransom was agreed and paid and the pirates released the ship after a relatively short 21 days.

On August 19 the Malaysian 32,169 dwt chemical tanker *MT Bunga Melati Dua* was attacked and seized by pirates while on a voyage from Indonesia to Rotterdam. On August 29, the Malaysian palm oil tanker *MT Bunga Melati Lima* was also attacked and seized by pirates while on a voyage from Saudi Arabia to Singapore and the attack resulted in the death of one Filipino seafarer. Both ships are owned by Malaysian national carrier MISC. The pirates demanded a ransom of $4.7 million dollars and the ships were anchored at Eyl. As a direct response to the seizure of two vessels MISC immediately stopped all vessels from transiting through the Gulf of Aden. This would stay in force until MISC was able to strengthen security measures. In response to this crisis the Royal Malaysian Navy deployed three vessels, the offshore patrol vessel *KD Pahang*, the frigate *KD Lekui* and the support vessel *KD Sri In-*

derapura along with naval special forces. The ships were released in early October after a ransom was paid.

On August 21 the chemical tanker *MT Irene* operated by Japan's Koyo Company, and flagged in Panama, was hijacked with nineteen crewmen. The ship was on a voyage from India to France. They were freed in September after the payment of a $1.6 million ransom.

On September 15, the Japanese-owned, Indian-managed 25,500 dwt chemical tanker *Stolt Valor* was attacked and hijacked off the coast of Yemen with a crew of eighteen Indians, two Filipinos, one Bangladeshi and one Russian. The vessel was attacked and seized while sailing within the designated safety corridor. The ship was then sailed to Eyl and anchored. After seven days there was little progress on ransom and release negotiations. The Japanese ship management company in Hong Kong appointed a third party negotiator and the Indian authorities were reported as awaiting the ransom negotiation results. When negotiations started the pirates asked for $6 million dollars and this was reduced to $2.5 million dollars. The ship was eventually released after payment of a ransom on November 16.

On September 17 the French tuna fishing boat *Le Drennec* was attacked well out into the Indian Ocean close to the Seychelles. The pirates fired automatic weapons and two rocket propelled grenades but did not manage to seize the vessel. There was a heavy swell which also hampered the attack.

On September 18, the Greek-owned 19,556 dwt bulk carrier *Centauri* was attacked by pirates firing automatic weapons and three RPG's. They were hijacked 200 nautical miles off Mogadishu. The bulk carrier was using the designated security corridor in the Gulf of Aden that is patrolled by the international coalition of warships and aircraft. The ship was taken to Hobyo for ransom negotiations and released in November.

In September 2008 a Norwegian oil tanker *Front Voyager* owned by shipping tycoon John Fredriksen was attacked in the Gulf of Aden while on passage to Singapore. The crew observed a skiff closing fast on the ship, which then came up close alongside and attempted to board while firing automatic weapons. The Russian and Filipino crew of the ship initiated antipiracy measures and contacted the Danish naval vessel *Absalon*. The warship scrambled an armed helicopter to the tanker while the crew repelled the attack using water cannons to prevent them from getting onto the main deck. After the helicopter arrived, the pirates were captured and transferred to an American naval vessel.

In October 2008 the Greek-owned 9,000 dwt chemical tanker *Action* was attacked by pirates and three crewmembers were killed, although details of the killings are unknown. The ship was on a voyage from South East Asia to Suez when it was hijacked. The crew comprised 17 Georgians and three Pakistanis. The ship was released after a ransom payment on December 12.

On November 7, 2008, the Danish owned *CEC Future* was attacked by pirates who fired an RPG at the ship. The ship was sailed to Eyl for ransom negotiations and the initial demand was for $7 million dollars. The shipowner responded with an offer of $300,000. Eventually a deal was reached and the cash was dropped by parachute onto the vessel. There was a lot of confusion after the money arrived and many came aboard to claim their shares including a variety of creditors. There was evidently many arguments over the sharing of the money. Fights broke out and often involved shooting and knives. The two pirates who lead the hijacking were both killed. One was shot dead by members of his own gang on reaching the shore in a dispute over the ransom.

On November 10, the Philippines-flagged 33,209 dwt chemical tanker *Stolt Strength* was attacked while on a voyage from Senegal to India with a cargo of phosphoric acid. After its eventual release, the Chinese Navy frigate *Huangshan* was escorting the *Stolt Strength* and thwarted another attack by pirates to recapture the ship while it was on its way to safe waters after 162 days in captivity. A group of pirates on board two skiffs were able to close in on the *Stolt Strength*. The *Huangshan* came to the ship's aid and provided fuel, food, water and medicine until it reached a safe port of call in Yemen. The ship requested assistance from the NATO/EU fleet. A German naval vessel delivered supplies and a US Naval vessel also responded with food and water. A fuel bunker vessel was dispatched from the Kenyan port of Mombasa. The Philippine crew pleaded for help, protection, a military escort as they feared further pirate attacks. In a magnanimous gesture, the crew who had endured the long five months in captivity were advised that they were welcome to re-apply with the shipping company, Sagana Shipping Lines, once they returned home safely to Manila. This was of course farcical, as one of my Filipino seafarer friends said, since the long captivity was due to the fact that the company would not negotiate or the Philippine government wouldn't help.

On November 28, 2008, the 27,350 dwt chemical tanker *Biscaglia* was attacked and hijacked by armed pirates in two skiffs while transiting in the designated safety corridor. A distress message was transmitted and two coalition helicopters arrived at the scene and were unable to prevent the attack. This was another piracy maritime first. Three ex-British soldiers were hired to travel on, and help defend the vessel in the event of any pirate attack. These security men subsequently jumped overboard when their efforts to repel the attack failed. They were later rescued by a German naval helicopter and then transferred to a nearby French frigate. The director of the London-based company who had hired the unarmed guards later stated that the security team had come under heavy attack from pirates, and was unable to mount a sustained, non-lethal resistance. They claim that they denied the pirates' access to the ship long enough for the crew to seek safety below decks and to call for assistance from coalition warships, which means about two minutes! The ship and its Indian and Bangladeshi crewmembers were subsequently captured and held hostage. The security contractor spokesman also further stated that his team had reported that the level of violence was unprecedented and forced them to reluctantly leave the vessel after every effort was made to ensure the safety of the ship's crew. They therefore go into the piracy history books as the first to ever to cut and run and I am yet to meet a fellow seafarer who isn't quite appalled at their actions. The case against carrying unarmed security specialists is strengthened by this incident. The ship was finally released in late January 2009, after payment of a ransom.

2009 Incidents

Chapter 8 covers the numerous incidents in Somalia in the first six months of 2009. During June the following vessels were attacked and fired on and the pirates aborted after ships took evasive action and summoned coalition forces for assistance. The Liberian oil tanker *United Lady*. The Hong Kong-flagged bulk carrier *Cemtex Venture*. The Liberian oil tanker *Aisha*. The Turkish bulk carrier *Gokcan*. The Cypriot oil tanker *Hadi*. The Hong Kong-flagged bulk carrier *Kang Long*. The Singaporean oil tanker *Maersk Phoenix*. The Pakistani general cargo vessel *Bolan*. The chemical tanker *Gorgonilla*. The Bahamian-flagged tanker *Richmond Bridge*. The Panamanian-flagged oil tanker *Salalah*. The Yemeni product tanker *Al Masilah*. The Greek bulk carrier *Milos* and the Panamanian-flagged oil tanker *Tenjun*.

Piracy in the region is not restricted to offshore waters. Heavily armed pirates launched an attack on a UN convoy that was traveling up the Sobat River towards Akobo, where around 19,000 refugees were congregated. The UN vessels were carrying 735 tons of sorghum and various other food aid. During the attacks some 40 Southern Sudanese soldiers were killed and many more wounded. This attack left four of the five World Food Program (WFP) vessels sunk along with food aid being destroyed and this dealt a severe blow to local food aid operations.

The monsoon season is traditionally a period when no attacks take place due to adverse weather and rough sea conditions. It was a surprise to many when the Turkish cargo ship *Horizon 1* on a voyage from Saudi Arabia to Jordan with 33,000 cubic meters of sulphide and with twenty-three crew aboard was attacked and seized. The ship was attacked in the early morning by just three pirates, reportedly unarmed, in skiffs and in its fully loaded condition it was easy for pirates to get aboard. The ship was also passing through the recommended and warship patrolled transit corridor and soon after the hijacking was being shadowed by the Turkish frigate *Gediz* which forms part of the NATO naval force.

Pirates also unsuccessfully tried to capture another very large crude oil carrier (VLCC). The Singapore-owned and Liberia-flagged 265,000-ton tanker *A Elephant* was attacked by pirates firing automatic weapons in the Eastern area of the Gulf of Aden. The two pirate skiffs were operating from a dhow mother ship, believed to be an Indian owned and UAE registered dhow, the *MSV Nefya*, which had been hijacked outside the port of Boosaaso after discharging a cargo of sugar while heading back to Dubai along with eleven Indian crew. One crewmember was reported killed in that attack. The ship had sent out a distress call. The French EUNAVFO force *Aconit* responded and sent a helicopter to the scene. The attack was aborted. The *MSV Nefya* was subsequently released but not before the pirates looted equipment supplies and crew personal effects.

As the monsoon season started to wane it didn't take long for the pirates to launch an attack as the seas dropped off.

References

International Maritime Bureau. The world's principal maritime antipiracy organization. Piracy Reporting Center, Kuala Lumpur, Malaysia. E-mail: imbkl@icc-ccs.org; website: http://www.icc-ccs.org; telephone: + 60 3 2078 5763; fax: + 60 3 2078 5769.

Antipiracy HELPLINE (24-hour watch). Telephone: ++ 60 3 2031 0014.

International Maritime Organization. This is the United Nations agency for all things maritime, including the International Convention for Safety of life at Sea (SOLAS).
Website: www.imo.org/

Lloyd's List. The leading maritime incident and casualty information source. Website: http://www.lloydslist.com/

Garowe Online. Somali online news service, which provides a local perspective on piracy events.
Website: http://www.garoweonline.com

Mareeg Online. Somali news service.
Website: http://www.mareeg.com/

The East African Seafarers' Assistance Program, Mombasa, Kenya. Website: http://www.ecop.info

Baird Online. The Baird Maritime news.
Website: http://www.bairdmaritime.com/

Shiptalk. A maritime forum for merchant mariners.
Website: http://www.shiptalk.com/
ShipGaz. Maritime news website: http://www.shipgaz.com/
MarineLog. Leading U.S. magazine for mariners.
Website: http://www.marinelog.com/
Maritime Global Net. Website: http://www.mglobal.com/
Maritime News Clippings.
Website: www.maasmondmaritime.com
Hympendahl, Klaus. *Pirates Aboard! 40 Cases of Piracy Today and What Bluewater Cruisers Can Do About It*. Dobbs Ferry, New York: Sheridan House, 2003.
Sheridan House: www.sheridanhouse.com
For information regarding yachts and piracy, check out Klaus Hympendahl's website: http://www.yachtpiracy.org

Index

257

259

About the Author

John C. Payne is a professional mariner who has spent thirty-five years on merchant ships and offshore oil industry vessels. He has also been on ships that were attacked by pirates and robbers in his long career. He is a qualified Maritime Safety Auditor and Marine Surveyor as well as a cruising yachtsman. He has published more than a dozen marine books and numerous magazine articles. Currently, he works in Asia and the Middle East on various maritime and offshore projects.